Life Essence Awakening Process™

(L.E.A.P.)

An Energy Medicine Course & Holistic Reference Manual

- Kinesiology & Energy Analysis
- Holistic Methods for Achieving Well Being in Body, Mind & Spirit
- Vibrational Remedies such as Essential Oils, Flower Essences, Color, Sound & Gems
- Empowerment Through Energy Wellness Self-Care

JAYA SARADA

Divine Light Publishing

P.O. Box 1110

Gleneden Beach, Oregon 97388

1.855.505.3935

jayasarada@aol.com

Copyright 2017

All rights reserved.

Cover & Interior Design by: Dianne Rux- D'ziner Graphics

www.dzinergraphics.com

ISBN: 1-893037-05-3 - Vital Force, Self-Care, Energy Medicine, Emotional Healing,
Mental Healing, Spirtual Healing, Vibrational Remedies

DivineLightGifts.com

Life Essence Awakening Process™

Many words that appear in italics in this book are Sanskrit, translated informally.
See the glossary for meanings of these and any other unfamiliar words.

Dedication

"I dedicate this work to the unfolding love within all beings.
May this love create peace and harmony and serve to end the cause
of self-created suffereing. May this book offer a path of awakening for all
and lead us to our greatest potential as spiritual beings."

Jaya Sarada

"God is one life – eternal, immortal,
infinite, never beginning and never ending.
There is only one God, therefore, there is only one life."

– Practicing the Presence
Joel Goldsmith

Blessings,
I honor the place in you in which the entire universe dwells.
I honor the place in you which is of love, of truth, of light and of peace.
When you are in that place in you, and I am in that place in me...
We are One.

Gratitude is a way of being, a path that leads us to growth,
joy, abundance, love and resonance with the universe.

Gratitude is a prayer that is cultivated within our hearts, and inspires us to
give back to life, the many gifts that we receive. Gratitude, leads us to view life
as precious and understand how life has nurtured us to our fullest potential.
For this we give thanks by offering life our love, compassion, joy and service.

Whether you are a dear friend, a sacred sister, a family member,
a teacher or have been a team member in these book creations,
you have been a key part of the evolution of my life and work.
I want to express my deep gratitude to all who have crossed
my path and shared with me this sacred journey of life.

Jaya

Table of Contents

" In the beginning . . ."

In the beginning,
In the time before time begins,
In the rest before movement begins,
In the peace where nothing but
Elobim is, was and will be.

It all unfolds and moves like the wings of a bird taking
flight, like a spark turning to flame, spreading the fire in
all directions.

From this center everything travels towards its purpose,
somehow moving together and yet each with its own kernel
of destiny known only to the Holy one.

Gen, 1:1a B'reshrath
From Genesis Meditations
Neal Douglas Klotz

Praise for Jaya Sarada and
the Life Essence Awakening Process

Jaya is a masterful midwife for those of us searching for more. Her insights, clarity, and manner of *being* with you are all amazing gifts she gives freely. I am looking forward to seeing where the *Life Essence Awakening Process* will take us now!"
~*Andreanna Vaughan, Nurse Practitioner*

I have experienced the *Life Essence Awakening Process (LEAP)* and feel moved to share my experiences as a giver and as a receiver of this profound work. In both giving and receiving what emerged for me was a deepening into myself. To invite deep intimacy with self is the gift uncovered by this work. The process peels off the outer layers of the false self and, gently, the truer self arises from within. The practitioner becomes witness and guide as the receiver emerges. When a work reveals self to self, what more can we ask for? *LEAP* is like a map into the being and assists in discerning where to focus energy to heal our *self* whole. The map supplies the specific work that needs to be attended to. If you are interested in exploring the depths of yourself and want to share that process with others, *LEAP* is a wonderful tool to continue the excavation within. I liken it to fine tuning the soul!
~*Jeanne Lepisto, RN*

Jaya's wisdom, insight and depth of spiritual development is a gift to us all. She has the remarkable ability to translate the sublime into practical techniques that are easily accessible and invaluable in our daily lives.
~*Judyth Reichenberg-Ullman, ND. Co-author*
Mystics, Masters, Saints, and Sages:
Stories of Enlightenment.

Jaya's loving devotion to the spiritual path shines through her personhood, her healing work and her writing. Jaya's adept use of kinesiology leads her directly to the areas of the body and its energy field which are in need of clearing or support. She is always right on target. Having been both a client and a student of Jaya's has augmented my own practice immensely as I've combined her meticulous and comprehensive methods with sound healing.
~*Dr. Lotus Linton Howard*

It is a place of peace from which Jaya Sarada brings forth her soul essence as a healer. Her gentle, loving care provides a sanctuary in which one can easily and trustingly open to receive that which is desired for healing. In over 10 years of knowing and working with Jaya, she has remained heart-full with pure intent in all she does.
~Annapoorne Colangelo
Counselor, Intuitive Reader, Integral Yoga Instructor

Until one is committed there is hesitancy, the chance to draw back, always ineffectiveness. Concerning all acts of initiative (and creation), there is one elementary truth, the ignorance of which kills countless ideas and splendid plans; that the moment one definitely commits oneself, then Providence moves too. All sorts of things occur to help one that would never otherwise have occurred. A whole stream of events issues from the decision, raising in one's favor all manner of unforeseen incidents and meetings and material assistance, which no man could have dreamt would have come his way.

~William Hutchison Murray

Preface

Though the term *paradigm shift* may be overused or cliche, that is exactly what is taking place powerfully now in health care. Scientists have confirmed that we really are made up of vibrating interconnected energy fields. When one accepts this model of what we are, many previously misunderstood phenomena begin to make perfect sense.

Disease occurs when there is a disturbance in the energy movement in the field or system. All treatments are effective to the degree that they can stimulate movement and balancing of the energy fields.

Alternative and complementary therapies have been so successful that today people make more visits to these types of providers than they do to their primary care physicians. Most of these are based on facilitating movement of the energy field on some level. Even many conventional medical treatments can be understood in terms of energy and fields as well as through biochemistry and mechanics.

The ramifications of acceptance of this paradigm reach out to every level of existence. No longer are we talking just about the body or just about health care. Because all fields are interconnected to some extent, we can no longer completely separate fields of knowledge. Heath care is intimately related to physics, psychology, spirituality, astronomy, consciousness, biochemistry and even history. We are vibrational beings carrying patterns of energy. Call them memory, neurological pain loops, belief systems, etc. that have been formed either through our experiences in life, through our environmental exposures, through our relationships with others and ourselves, through our families and even through the beliefs and experiences of our ancestors. These patterns both define who we are and limit who we are.

Jaya Sarada has created an amazingly efficient and direct road map, a powerful tool to uncover where some of our patterning doesn't serve our greater health, passion and purpose. With this tool we can not only consciously release some of the conditioning that inhibits our full expression and vitality; but we can open the door to awareness of who we really are and how truly powerful and beautiful we are as we experience the gifts of divine grace, spiritual attunement or whatever one's sacred path calls *connection to God*.

Laurie Keith, B.A., L.M.P.
Langley, Washington

The root of the way of life, of birth and change is Chi (life energy); the myriad things of heaven and earth all obey this law. Thus Chi, in the periphery, envelops heaven and earth. Chi, in the interior, activates them. The source wherefrom the sun, moon, and stars derive their light, the thunder, rain, wind and clouds their being, the four seasons and the myriad things their birth, growth, gathering, storing – all this is brought about by Chi. Man's possession of life is completely dependent upon this Chi.

Nei Ching

Introduction

What can be done about the immense suffering of individuals and the collective suffering of the world? Is it possible to be of service in helping mankind rather than contributing to global sorrow?

Life in our world magnifies the importance of worldly values and temporary gain. In the pursuit of self-gratification at any cost, human society has become brutal. Our inner war to achieve our desires and self-satisfaction stops at nothing. Desires planted in the mind grow like weeds – uncontrollable, insidious, subtly affecting our entire life. We create a web of endless suffering, moving from satisfaction to dissatisfaction, pleasure to pain. A life spent searching outward for happiness robs our sacred self of all possible peace.

Looking carefully at the nature of desire, we find it to be a search for happiness. We have become confused as to what true happiness is and how it is attained. Each human has within their heart all the ingredients to be truly happy. But happiness is found only in the heart of those who see clearly that temporary gain almost always ends in an experience of pain. Our birthright is true happiness, found in the unconditional relationship with the essence of life. The sound of birds, a beautiful sky, the laughter of a child, the smell of a rose, the simple gifts of life bring great happiness, for happiness is a gift from life found through complete rest in the personal self. With *Life Essence Awakening*, I invite you to consider living as if there were a constant whisper guiding you, protecting you and revealing to you that which is for the highest good.

Life Essence Awakening

Our *life essence* is composed of energy fields that surround the physical body and extend outward portraying our luminous aura. This subtle, unseen energy that surrounds our being is an integral part of our existence. Each of the seven fields that make up our multidimensional energy system is a vehicle for our evolution to ever-greater creative expression as souls.

According to current scientific thought, there is a holographic energy template associated with the physical field. This holographic energy is characterized by a spectrum of energy bands radiating out from the physical. The first band of energy, the etheric field, is the cellular information that guides the cellular growth of the physical structure of the body.

The next plane, the emotional, is a higher frequency and is involved in the expression and repression of emotion. The third plane is the mental field, the field of concrete thoughts, mind mixed with emotions, conditioning and beliefs. The remaining three fields have to do with intuition and spirit and are composed of higher frequencies that provide healing and transformation on a soul level.

The Energy Fields and Their Functions

Physical – energy field that relates to the element earth and corresponds to the root chakra and the endocrine glands, and functions energetically to provide a ground for being.

Etheric – relates to the element water and corresponds to the navel chakra, the testes in males, and the ovaries in females and is the field of physical creativity.

Emotional – relates to the element fire and corresponds to the solar plexus chakra; externalizes as the pancreas and expresses personal power.

Mental – associated with the element air and corresponds to the heart chakra; externalizes as the thymus gland. Expresses divine power and guides us to surrender our personal will.

Causal – relates to the element of ether and corresponds to the throat chakra; externalizes as the thyroid gland and is the field of spiritual expression.

Monadic – relates to the sixth sense and corresponds to the third eye chakra. The monadic field develops a sense of knowing, intuition, and union of duality and externalizes as the pituitary gland.

Adi – pure consciousness, this field corresponds to the crown chakra. The Adi field functions to return our consciousness to oneness and integration. Externalizes as the pineal gland.

The *Life Essence Awakening Process (LEAP)* offers students and clients new avenues toward understanding the multidimensional energy fields and the pathways to optimal health and well-being. This powerful process teaches students kinesiology testing and pendulum work to determine the condition of each energy field. In holistic energy healing we take into account all energy fields when treating the affected element. Testing procedures analyze the subtle energy fields and determine the root cause of imbalances as well as the priority for healing. Sessions then are offered for healing and transformation and to increase the vital essence.

Energy Field Kinesiology

First Energy Field – The Etheric Field is the source of our life vitality and prana, or breath. Within this energy field we apply techniques to increase the life essence.

Second Energy Field – The Emotional Field is the seat of our desires and emotions. Within this field we apply techniques to balance and release emotional pain, increase positive energy through life affirming goals and build pathways to emotional well-being.

Third Energy Field – The Mental Field is the source of abstract thinking and the concrete mind. Here we apply techniques to balance and bring healing to the mental field by releasing patterns of negative belief and conditioning and offering new decision making techniques based on Conscious Choice Therapy.

Fourth Energy Field – The Intuitive Field is the source of our intuition and seeds of karma. Techniques such as Soul Dialogue are applied to this field to increase soul power and intuition, improve perception and strengthen the connection with guidance that can integrate the soul and the personality.

The strength of our *life essence* is determined by the energetic condition and integration of the energy fields. Through the study and application of the *Life Essence Awakening Process (LEAP)*, students learn kinesiology, or energy testing methods, to determine energetic imbalances in the etheric, emotional, mental and spiritual energy fields.

Our *life essence* is affected by many influences such as pollution, environmental stresses, the foods we eat, the things we watch, the thoughts we think and our feelings. Our relationship with others and ourselves, our self-esteem, our sense of happiness, our feelings of stress, our inherited weaknesses and strengths all play an important part in the vitality of our *life essence* and our health. Through energy testing we can identify areas that sustain our well-being as well as areas that are energetically incompatible.

Learning to test effectively guides students to discover the root causes of disturbed energy patterns in the aura and apply techniques to change these patterns. When testing energy we look for hidden causes of imbalances and learn to ask questions that lead to the source of healing. For example, energy imbalances may appear to be physical but often the origin can be found in emotional, mental or spiritual energy fields. Once the root cause is determined, testing processes further reveal which balancing procedures are most effective to assist the vital force to return to optimal function.

The Life Essence Awakening Process (LEAP) teaches the art of kinesiology to access all information from the higher energy fields that offers insights to profound, long-lasting healing. This work is based on research that has revealed the fact that each individual carries a soul purpose and divine gift. Many illnesses and energy imbalances have their root in the soul's inability to open to its full potential. After learning basic kinesiology methods, students will learn how to inquire about the effect of life scars, unrealized gifts and unrealized potential on present or past lives.

LEAP investigates how we can open the channel to our spirit and receive the wisdom to understand our life's challenges and tests. It reveals the tendencies and patterns that cause stress in our energy fields. It is a deep study of subtle energies and dialogue with the soul.

Enjoy your journey through the *Life Essence Awakening Process.*

Part One
You Are an Energy Being

Life essence is composed of energy fields that surround the physical body and extend outward portraying our luminous aura.

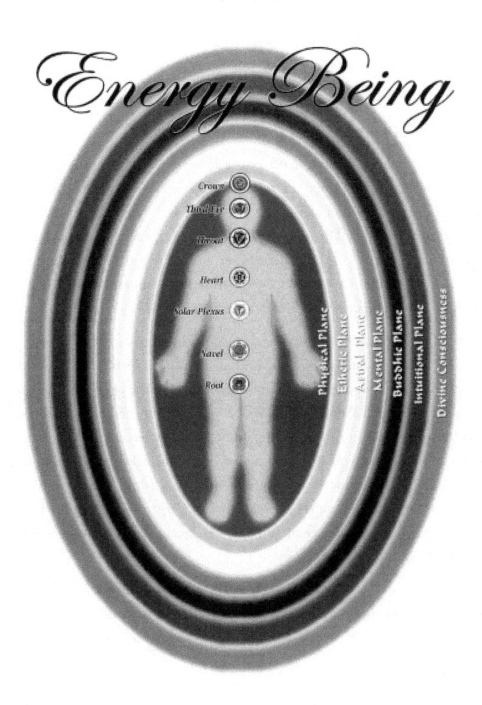

Your Luminous Essence

The Aura

The word aura comes from the Greek word *avra,* meaning breeze. The aura is the sum total of the seven fields of human and divine nature. The spheres of energy surrounding the physical body progressively spiral outward forming strong energy fields. There are seven fields in the solar system, which relate to the seven fields of the human being. Our journey begins in a physical body – the vehicle to fully realize that within us lives a divine and eternal soul. Our inner being uses this vehicle to explore not only what it is to be human, but also what it is to be divine. Our physical and personality expressions come from the first four fields of consciousness: the physical, etheric, astral and mental. As we ascend past the limitations of our personal identity, we open the door to our true nature.

The Energy Fields

The Etheric Field

Science has shown that everything in nature has an atmosphere or electromagnetic field surrounding it. This energy duplicates the physical and is called the etheric field. It is a fluid-like substance visible as a band of light around the physical, protecting and shielding it from outside negative influences. The etheric underlies and interpenetrates every atom, cell and molecule of the physical field. The etheric field is the framework on which the physical body is built and is the source of vital force. The etheric energies move in fine channels closely related to the nervous system, nourishing the entire field with *prana,* the life force.

The etheric field is also called the health aura because it emanates strong or weak streams of vital force according to the well-being of the individual. The electric energy of the health aura is seen as a luminous gray or violet mist that duplicates the physical field about a quarter of an inch from the skin. Another word for the health aura is ectoplasm, which is a term used to describe the etheric energy that constitutes the state between energy and matter. It determines our health as well as provides a protective force field which shields the field from negative influences. When the energy is strong the etheric field is smooth with streams of light emanating vertically from the physical field. When there is an imbalance in the system the rays will show signs of weakening and droop, reducing our ability to fight illness. The physical will then show signs of stress.

Unused etheric field energy is discharged from the pores and creates the luminous force field or health aura. Many alternative practitioners can detect imbalances through the condition of the health aura before they affect the physical. When imbalances are detected, holistic and preventative methods are applied to sustain, support and offer healing to strengthen the physical system.

The etheric field nurtures our blood, is the river of life, and is a transmitter of a vast aggregate of energies and forces. This vital force is responsible for the right functioning of our five senses and is a potent receiver of impressions, bringing the life force to all systems of the physical body.

The etheric field is an electromagnetic grid that weaves around the physical field. There are thousands of tiny nerves or nadis that cross each other throughout the field. These nadis are threads of life force that underlie every part of the body. Where they cross, especially along the spine, they form the chakras, which are energy gateways that can be described as wheels of light. The chakras are vital supports for the health of our multidimensional energy fields, affecting the way we feel physically, emotionally, mentally and spiritually.

The Emotional Field

Next, the emotional or astral field interpenetrates the etheric and is often seen as an aura of changing colors. As emotions, feelings and passions flow and change, so do the colors and shapes of the astral field. The emotional field can be viewed as the Sea of Emotions with water representing the uncontrollable nature of emotions. The biblical story of Jesus walking on the water (emotions) while rebuking the storm (mind) is an example of the kind of mastery he had over the aspects of emotions and mind that make up the lower self, the personality aspect of a human being. When we mistakenly identify the personality as our true self, we create a deep sense of separation from our source.

Between the etheric and the emotional field lies a protective sheath that prevents emotional energy from overwhelming the etheric. Injury to this sheath can be very dangerous and usually comes from emotional shock. Dark forces, which penetrate the etheric through violence, anger or fear, tear the sheath and open one to illness. Drugs and alcohol can tear the sheath and send poisons to the astral field. Since the etheric field is closely related to the emotional field, it is permeated at all times with emotions, which directly affect the physical state. When stress and emotional trauma enter our life, damage first appears in the etheric field, weakening the physical field and making it vulnerable to illness. The mental field, the next energy plane, has a strong impact on the emotional field. Negative thought patterns create corresponding patterns of negative emotional stress; positive thought patterns create positive feelings. Of course, positive energy greatly improves the state of energy health. It is important to identify negative mental and emotional habits, to resolve and release them.

After observing that we are truly multidimensional energy beings we can create health and wholeness through learning to detect imbalances in our energy fields and applying the corrections needed.

When the emotional field is in harmony with the soul and moral and mental development is of a high order, the aura, a visual expression of the emotional field, becomes bright and luminous and extends out to eighteen inches or more. When the emotional field expresses passions, emotions and desires that are out of harmony with the soul, the aura becomes dark and murky, contracting to ten to twelve inches around the physical body. Highly developed beings display large auras, showing the high degree of spiritual development that makes them candidates for initiation. Initiations in various spiritual traditions are the gateways to the next level of spiritual development.

The emotional matter is a grade finer than etheric matter. It surrounds the etheric field and shows areas of congestion that come from negative thinking and ill emotions. It also reveals the condition of the etheric field. The emotional field acts as a bridge between the mental field and the etheric field. The emotional field makes sensation possible and acts as an independent vehicle of consciousness.

The Kama-Manasic Web

Within the emotional and lower mental fields we become bound to earth by our desires. This Kama-Manasic state (mix of mind and emotion) sets the conditions for future incarnation. Many stay in this realm, not evolving past self-gratification into the light of the soul. The Kama-Manasic web, strengthened by the interplay of mind and emotions, creates veils that cloud our true nature.

Happiness is our deepest quest, but often we seek this happiness out of the temporary aspects of life, not realizing the impermanence of the search. The energy fields that surround us offer keys to the discovery of our true *life essence*. We search for temporary fulfillment of our bodies, which can never quench the thirst of our endless desires. We search for emotional fulfillment, not realizing that our emotions are constantly changing from pleasure to pain and then from pain to pleasure. Then there is a search for the true self in the realm of thought and mind, but again we find that everything changes in our mind. Our search for the long-lost sense of self takes us into the etheric field where we experience our vital force; to our emotional field where we experience our passions, power and desires; to the mental field where we experience the power of our mind and thoughts. Our desires are rooted in our emotional field and we often set out to obtain gratification at any cost. We are convinced that our desire and thought processes are the truth of truths and often will stop at nothing to obtain a particular desire. The desires obtained are temporary and the search for pleasure, that often results in pain, continues until we turn within to the real source of happiness. When the desire is fueled with thoughts from the mental field, an energetic web is created that becomes quite difficult to overcome. This is the Kama-Manasic web, the root of karma and reincarnation.

For most, the center of consciousness is located in the emotional field where the ordinary person is enslaved by thought tainted with emotions. Average humanity is submerged in the illusions of the emotional field. Emotions such as anger, worry, fear, etc. create a continuous irritation of the etheric field, which affects the physical. *The Life Essence Awakening Process (LEAP)* uses kinesiology, also known as energy testing, to analyze the emotional and mental fields and release the patterns of thought and desire that lead to disease and suffering. The *Awakening Process* gently guides you to realize your true nature, reaching beyond the energetic fields of the personality into the soul of love, light and wisdom.

The Mental Field

The mental field exists slightly beyond the emotional body. Mental energy comes through the crown center to let vibrations (impressions on the physical) of a higher nature pour through. The mental field provides a shield to protect the energy fields from imbalances and disease. This is the energy field where our affirmations, the spoken word, our choices, healing thoughts, and clear decisions play an important part in our healing and wellness process. When there are patterns of imbalance in the mental field stemming from negative thinking we are more susceptible to illness. When we strive for clear thoughts we transmit healing energy to the physical field via the spleen.

The energy of the mental field is constantly changing, moving rhythmically in response to thought. Good thoughts create an upward vibration and bad thoughts create a downward motion of the mental field. The mental field, when inspired from our higher or soul nature, expresses great beauty with moving iridescent light and color. Through the evolution of the intellect, the mental field becomes increasingly more radiant.

The mental field has two aspects, the higher mental and lower mental. This division is discussed in Sanskrit teachings, naming the lower mental *Rupa,* meaning having form. The lower mental field expresses through the personality in the form of concrete thoughts.

The higher aspect of the mental field, in Sanskrit, is called *Arupa,* meaning formlessness. This aspect of the mental field relates to intuition, perception and inspiration from our divine source. The higher mental is connected to the formless, eternal presence that resides within our soul and is not bound to a physical field for existence. We are simply sparks of this infinite life force and the higher mental is the field that carries us beyond time, thought, memory and form into our divine reality.

The lower mental expresses thoughts and emotions based on concrete knowledge of the personal self in relationship to the past. The lower mental is a vessel for the storage of memory, recording the sensations of pleasure or pain. The lower mind seeks to repeat the pleasurable or repel what is not pleasurable. Identifcation with our personality self is the aspect of our nature that is the greatest obstacle in our evolutionary path. Thoughts and emotions geared to self-importance and self-preservation obstruct the flow of our spiritual wisdom. The personality, or lower self, is attracted by the material world, perceiving it as true reality, perpetuating the wheel of cause and effect.

Truth that is accessed through the formless planes of the divine, the higher mental, is infused with the light of our true nature and it is here that the mind becomes an instrument of the soul. Our thoughts, actions and perceptions from the higher mental field access the love and wisdom of the heart and the knowledge of the higher world.

Deepening awareness shows us how emotions and thoughts play an integral part in understanding the key to good health and well-being. Reflecting on the causes of illness and suffering we must take into account the totality of our being and how all parts are interconnected. There are many ways to purify and enhance our body, emotions, mind and spirit. When these fields communicate, integrate and create an upward mobility of consciousness, we experience a great vitality.

Communication with the Soul

The Silver Cord (thread of life) – Infuses the physical body with the life force through the blood stream.

The Sacred Cord – Unifies the subtle bodies and is anchored in the heart center.

Creative Thread – Links up the center with the base of the spine, develops and expresses the personality through the throat center.

Consciousness Thread – Antahkarana, meaning bridge, inner organ or mind, is anchored in the pineal gland in the crown center.

The Causal Field - The Temple of Our Soul

The causal, celestial or intuitional field extends beyond the mental field about eighteen inches, in an ovoid shape that surrounds the physical field. The energy of this field is radiant and full of color according to our development. The more evolved we become, the more luminous the colors of this energy field. The causal field holds the essence of our higher intuition and is also known as the celestial field because it is composed of the vibrations of our soul's light and wisdom. This field is our Sacred Auric Egg, or the seed body, holding the blueprint of all future incarnations.

The causal field functions as a vehicle for the true self to express the divine law of love, wisdom and truth. The Akashic records, the records of nature and stories of our soul, are held within the causal field. These stories are strung like pearls along the sacred thread, or *Sutratma*, and bring forth the strengths and attributes the soul has acquired through all of life's experiences.

The causal field holds this thread, the records of our lifetimes, and determines the condition of future incarnations. This thread of our being weaves our stories and holds the essence of our evolving love, truth and goodness that is brought from each lifetime into our soul until we perfect ourselves as human beings. The true self uses the pearls of existence and seeks rebirth to further the evolution of God consciousness, each lifetime forming a new vehicle to refine or develop certain soul qualities and strengths. This intention, called Trishna in Sanskrit, is a thirst that attracts us to life experiences that provide soul strength on our homeward journey. Our soul's development is orchestrated by the great mystery of life, a continuous evolution into the consciousness of love and light.

Throughout all births the essence of our being remains whole and in truth, one with the source of pure consciousness. The *Antahkarana*, meaning bridge of light, connects our personality with our soul. Our inner development by way of this bridge channels the part of us that has been awakened into the part that needs to be awakened. The Antahkarana is constructed through the realization of our true nature. When we no longer identify with our temporary human nature of thoughts, emotions and sensations, as a separate sense of self, the bridge dissolves and we become one consciousness. The intuitive field not only holds the answers to our life's lessons and questions, it also opens the door to our inner guide or master teacher. This loving guide becomes ours when we turn our attention from the belief in our separate self to the eternal essence of our heart. Our inner guide offers assistance in the understanding and mastery of our personality nature.

There are four sheaths that clothe the soul and create the energy being that we are. The sheaths are veils that cover and connect the energy fields. The first sheath is the physical field and is called the food sheath. It is fed only by food. The second sheath is related to the etheric and is called the vitality sheath. It is fueled by prana. The third is related to our mind and emotions (the lower mental and emotional field together) and is called the feeling sheath. It is fed only by feelings. The fourth field is the causal, called the discriminating sheath because it has the function of pure intelligence based on intuition and soul wisdom. This level of intelligence is not affected by the senses, but operates according to divine will and creative power. The source of this intelligence is not the world or the senses, nor is it based on the knowledge of the personality but the pure wisdom of the divine source.

The causal field, also called intuitive field, is the temple of our true essence, where spirit and matter are unified, and is beyond the limitations of human consciousness. The pure consciousness of the soul is devoted to divine essence, whereas the lower mind is focused on details of the physical field. Thoughts generated from the higher mind are expressed in principles that have a powerful effect on life. These principles, perceived by the soul, reflect the divine wisdom found in the spiritual heart.

The sum total of all incarnations is stored in the causal body and the seeds lie dormant until we are reborn again. In each new physical manifestation these seeds have to be sown to bring to fruition the completion of past actions. These seeds, in Sanskrit called *Skandas,* are deep scars upon the soul that determine the conditions of the next incarnation. Skandas represent desires, impulses and obligations that cause a being to forever stay on the wheel of cause and effect.

The causal, or celestial, field is the temple of the divine spark and is called the *Monad.* Love is the force and the source of this spark. The Monad, the spark of divinity that awakens our heart, leads us beyond the limitations of birth to eternity. Our true essence is this divine spark – eternal, whole and untouched by disease and disharmony.

Life Essence Pathways

Through the etheric field we are an integral part of the entire kingdom of nature. A force of energy surrounds every living thing. Rays emanate from the aura's core just as solar rays emanate from the sun. The thousands of pathways of life forces, the nadis, keep energy flowing to the physical from the universal life force and the outer world: the sun, the energy fields and the seven cosmic rays. The soul uses these channels to pour life energy into the system.

Interlaced through the etheric field an energy stream, called the silver cord, links the physical and astral fields. An intricate weaving of subtle energies within the etheric, the silver cord connects all the vital centers, keeping us grounded through the many lessons and experiences of life.

The silver cord, or Sutratma, incarnates at the beginning of a lifetime and infuses the physical with the life force through the blood stream. This sacred cord unifies the energy bodies and is anchored in the heart center. The silver cord makes contact with the soul through evolution to the mental field. The pearls of human existence, containing the seeds for future births, are strung along this cord. The Sutratma is the central channel where the flow of life force travels on the energetic path of return connecting our personal self to our divine spirit.

A threefold thread runs along the spinal column: the Ida, Pingala and Sushumna, forming the path of life. The Sushumna is called the creative thread, a cord that links the center at the base of the spine and is anchored in the throat center. The Ida follows the left side of the spine and is the lunar channel, related to the love and wisdom aspect of our being. The Pingala is located on the right of the spine and is the solar nadi, related to matter and intelligence. The Sushumna is located within the spinal column and is related to the father or "will aspect" of love. The Sushumna is the most important nadi, the channel through which our soul energy travels. The creative thread is responsible for the development of the personality. As it gradually widens through evolution and through conscious awakening, the bridge of light, or Antahkarana, forms. This conscious awakening is the outcome of fusion between our personality and soul, opening a pathway to divine consciousness.

The pathways of the Ida, Pingala and Sushumna correspond to three centers: the solar plexus, which is related to the impulse of desire in life, creative urges and the physical sun; the heart center, which is related to the impulse of love and divine expression; and the head center, which is related to the will to live.

The Antahkarana, the consciousness thread, is the inner organ that connects the personality with the soul. Antahkarana means bridge. Anchored in the heart center and reaching to the crown center, this bridge of light is built as one awakens and evolves, until the entire being is linked in an integrated expression of divine consciousness. This process, called continuity of consciousness, is where the human soul awakens as an entity on the physical field, using the etheric, emotional and mental fields as vehicles of soul expression.

The life force begins in the etheric field, which represents a sense of being-ness, an acceptance of life and trust in its process. Holding this awareness in daily consciousness brings the etheric field into a healthy balance. The next field of consciousness, the emotional, is the plane of desires, emotions, feelings and sentience. Through life's journey we must learn to integrate the emotional field with the etheric field to create an unblocked flow of feelingsthroughout our heart and soul.

The mental field is the bridge between the emotions and the higher planes of spiritualconsciousness. The mind, when silent and receptive, takes in impressions and guidance fromthe soul and passes them on to the emotional and etheric fields and all are infused with theenergy of light, love and wisdom.

Kundalini Energy

A unique energy system that activates the energies of the chakrasand assists us in awakening to higher consciousness is calledKundalini energy. This powerful yet often dormant energy isstored in the root, or base chakra. The Kundalini energy canactivate and align all the major chakras with the higher centers,bringing illumination and spiritual enlightenment to our beings. Through the proper sequence of chakra transformation andrelease of energy over time, the Kundalini begins to awaken.When traumatic emotional events occur that hold back our growththere is a corresponding block in one of the chakras. Energyblocks impede the natural flow of the creative Kundalini energiesthat rise up the spinal cord to the higher chakras. Daily meditationraises the Kundalini, and imparts the emotional and spirituallessons related to particular chakras.We begin the path of awakening by learning to be a witness,turning within to listen to the voice of the heart, along with thewisdom of our inner being, and releasing the faulty perception ofthe self. The Kundalini energy is the aspect of us that awakens aswe become self-realized. This sacred energy can be viewed as thefire of our being. Everything in its path is purified.

Shakti

Kundalini is the rising or awakening of our inner Shakti (energy) from its latent state. Theroot word, Kundal, means to coil, depicting a snakelike energy, which lies dormant at the baseof the spine in the root chakra. Kundalini Shakti is the feminine energy of our innate power.A powerful electric current, Kundalini Shakti moves through the chakras along the spine. It isawakened through change in consciousness as well as through spiritual exercises, dance, yogaand music. Kundalini, although dormant in most people, has a surging force that propels usto awaken our being to merge with our source of pure consciousness.

Shiva

Our divine aspect, or Shiva energy, resides in the crown chakra and holds our spiritual nature. Shakti, residing in the root chakra, is the aspect of our being that relates to form and is our evolving nature. Shakti travels upward to merge with Shiva, in a marriage of spirit and matter. Through this union we touch unconditional love and joy. Our journey as souls leads us through the energy fields, opening the chakras and lifting the veil to our pure consciousness. The chakras open along the spine, one by one, through the transformation of our inner being. Our journey leads past the survival aspects of the first three centers of the personality into the doorway of the heart. The journey becomes lighter as the ascension process takes us into the throat chakra, where the rhythms of our true nature are expressed through sound.

When the energy opens along the passageway of the Sushumna it pulls and pushes, disentangling the knots of each chakra, bringing a profound life transformation. The journey continues to the third eye wisdom center where we awaken to our true nature. At this point, all duality ceases and we may experience a cosmic unity as the Kundalini Shakti, the matter aspect of energy, merges with Shiva, the energy of spirit. This awakening of true love, wisdom and will is fully realized in the crown chakra and rests in the temple of the heart. With all chakras open and fully energized the journey is complete and all our experiences are integrated, transcending time, space and form.

> *Wherever I shine the lamp light of Divine breath, there the difficulties of the whole world are resolved. The darkness, which the earthly sun did not remove, becomes through My Breath a bright morning.*
> *Rumi (1,1941)*

Pranayama – Breath of Our Life Essence

The breath is a powerful tool to realize our true nature and the divine in all of life. The word *Pranayama* is formed from three Sanskrit roots; pra – meaning first, na – meaning energy, ayama – meaning expansion. Seeing the illusory, temporary nature of life, we can just smile and breathe out. Through the realization of our eternal being we breathe in, affirming that awareness in all the moments of life. A slow steady breath of receiving and of letting go will guide us toward a life of peace and beauty.

Breathing in the essence of life, we learn about ourselves and listen to our body rhythm. Breathing opens our reflective consciousness and helps us to see past impressions that trap us. Exhalation can be used to let go of past psychological holding, renewing our vital force.

Improper breathing weakens the function of almost every organ in the physical body. When our breathing is shallow we become more susceptible to the full spectrum of illness: headaches, depression and constipation, emotional and mental disorders. Many researchers believe that bad breathing habits also contribute to life-threatening diseases such as cancer and heart disease. Poor breathing reduces the efficiency of the lungs, impeding oxygen flow to the cells and diminishes energy needed for normal functioning, healing and growth.

The breath is vital in supporting us in our daily challenges. Deep breathing increases our vital force; all of our senses come alive and are transformed. Our breathing gives us a spaciousness to observe where we feel heavy and where we can apply our healing light to release unwanted burdens. Breathing takes us back to our source and opens us to a sense of harmony with the universal rhythm. Proper breathing clears our energy channels and opens our system to a healing light that affects all aspects of our body, mind and emotions.

The Breath and the Vital Centers

The Ida, the Pingala and the Sushumna, the three main channels of life energy, carry the vital force to all areas of our body, mind and emotions. These channels depend on the life force breath to heal and balance the system. The Ida and Pingala, corresponding to the autonomic nervous system, are responsible for the maintenance of the vital essence throughout the body. The Sushumna is related to the central nervous system and is the channel for the Kundalini Shakti. The Pingala flows along the right side of the Sushumna and is related to the sun. It has the yang qualities of aggression, logic, analytical thinking, outer direction, rationality, objectivity, heat, masculinity, mathematics and verbal activities. The Ida flows along the left side of the Sushumna and is related to the moon. It has yin qualities such as calmness, intuition, holism, inner direction, emotional subjectivity, femininity and coolness. The energy channels of the Ida and Pingala flow from the base chakra, weave up the spine in a snakelike manner and unite in the third eye center. The Sushumna is the pathway of the breath, our divine force that runs along the spine.

The vital centers are located along the Sushumna channel and are energized by the prana they receive. Beginning in the base chakra the breath flows upward to the solar plexus and unites with the higher prana flowing downward from the crown chakra. These two forces, the Apana, meaning breath flowing upward and Prana, meaning breath flowing downward, form a duality of psychic energy creating a knot in the solar plexus chakra. This knot forms when we contract our breathing, holding on to a false identification that is rooted in suffering. Through the process of releasing our old identifications, we begin to open the sacred heart center and this knot becomes free. Breathing has a very important relationship to the opening of the heart center that serves our purpose of letting go of the past. Through our breathing we can practice this art of letting go; as we exhale we let go of the past and as we inhale we welcome the unknown mystery of life.

The Breath and Energy Field Healing

Breathing habits reflect the areas of our personal holdings and where we contract and identify with passing appearances. When we exhale we can learn to let go of all concerns and return to our natural state of contentment and stillness. When we inhale we can observe where we contract, identifying with the passing nature of life, e.g. our thoughts and emotions, and then we can return to the art of letting go through exhalation.

Within each chakra lay keys to our unfolding and our breath carries these keys. The lower back, lower abdomen and pelvic areas carry information about our roots, our family, our origin, our survival needs and our sense of grounding. Breathing deeply into the root chakra helps to keep us feeling grounded and balanced. The navel chakra holds information about our sense of self, our relationships, physical energy and creativity. Breathing deeply, along with deep exhalations, assists our second chakra to stay balanced as well as opens us to our vital force energy. Our solar plexus chakra holds information about how we use our sense of power and helps us unite our mind with our heart.

Breathing deeply relaxes our struggle for personal power. Our throat chakra opens as we breathe in and exhale. We feel the current of energy from the lower chakras and direct this energy upward and out the crown center. When this current is flowing freely we can feel confident to speak and walk our truth. Breathing deeply and exhaling fully allows our full energy to circulate up the chakras and through the crown. Then we feel we are in a circle of vibrant light. The third eye chakra softens and opens as the pranic energy moves up and bathes the inner eye in the warm wind of our breath. The third eye chakra tells the story of who we are and where we came from to help us meet our celestial nature. Holding the stories of all our births, the crown chakra creates a crown of glory as it opens and connects with our divine source. This is facilitated through conscious breathing.

Inharmonious emotions such as anger, fear, guilt and grief are poisons that enter our system if not released by the breath. Shallow breathing harbors these negative emotions in our energy field until there is a deep exhalation and affirmation of letting go. By observing any negative emotions or limiting thought that has entered our energy field, we can learn to seek the root cause and then release the disturbance through the breath.

Positive emotions and thoughts such as joy, peace and contentment sustain our health and well-being. Negative emotions and thoughts create disturbances that affect our energy field, eventually leading to disease. We can learn to exhale what is no longer serving us and inhale the qualities and principles of life we need. Breathing deeply creates strength in our energy field and shields us from negative thinking. Breathing with the energy of expanding corrects us with our intuitive field and allows us to meet our true nature. The art of breathing holds the key to all processes in healing the body, mind and spirit.

The *Life Essence Awakening Process (LEAP)* offers many ways of using the breath as a tool for empowerment. During emotional field release such as the Forgiveness Process and mental field release such as Conscious Choice Therapy, the breath is a powerful support.

Conscious breathing assists us on the path of mastery, teaching how to let go and receive our soul's wisdom. When our emotional or mental energy field is disturbed our breath can take us to a place of stillness where passing thoughts and emotions are dissolved.

When disturbed, our emotions or thoughts are like passing clouds in the sky. Breathing assists us in remaining centered and calm. Through the quiet mind we can choose peace, rather than problems or conflict, and release personal holdings. Our deep exhalation process provides the tools necessary to surrender the most difficult and challenging experiences. Remaining conscious of our true nature, remembering who we are – these are essential in working with the energy fields. We then can use all of life's experience as a gift to remain in peace and harmony, our intention to live free from personal suffering.

Meditation

The disciple said to Jesus, "Speak to us about our end;
how will it look? How will it happen?"
Jesus replied, "Have you found the beginning in
yourselves?
If not, why are you asking about the end?
For in the place in yourselves where you find the
beginning, you will also find the end. The blessed ones
will find their feet standing at the beginning. Then
they will know the end and not taste death."
Gospel of Thomas, Logion 18

Imagine You Are a Being of Light

Take a moment to relax, breathe, stretch. Prepare yourself for an inward journey of the soul. Breathe deeply. On each exhalation, let go of tensions, concerns, fatigue, thoughts.

Breathing in, allow the breath to fill any area that needs healing. Continue the slow, deep breathing. Your journey begins as a being of pure light, unconditioned by thought and emotion. The physical body is created as a vehicle of return. A divine child, you are Shakti, the evolving spirit surging through manifestation to find a way home to unconditional love, happiness, joy and peace. You discover a sense of self and personal power through the attainment of desires, cravings and attractions. The manifestation of your desires creates a search for something more, and the search for love continues. Deep inside your heart you hear a small voice saying, "Stop, stop seeking anything outside of yourself." You turn within and taste your eternal nature, the source of joy and peace. The path leads to the end of suffering, where you find a deepening presence awakening in your heart.

You hear the voice of the beloved within your heart and let go of personal burdens, preparing to enter the temple of light. You realize you are the witness of your life and see the miracle of perfection unfolding. Breathing in, you feel the grace that comes from entering life fully. Breathing out, empty and surrender, welcoming the beloved within. You affirm: I am not the body, or senses, nor mind. I am a divine being of pure energy. I Am that I am.

The journey leads you to deeper and deeper surrender, letting go of all obstacles that veil your true nature. The light of your soul awakens and becomes aware of a conscious presence that has been silently watching you throughout your life. This presence of being guides your soul to rest deeply in peace, the silence of the heart. Breathing in the love and wisdom of your heart, you rest in the presence of the beloved, sending this love into the world of all suffering beings. The love of the heart is the garden of your soul, where you and the beloved are one. In this oneness you take the path of Ahmisa, the gentleness of a deer, harmlessness.

With guidance, you open the Lotus of your soul, and awaken inner knowing, the point between opposites, beyond duality, into silence, wisdom and penetrating awareness.

THE CHAKRAS

The Chakras – Turning the Keys to Awakening

Chakra is Sanskrit for wheel of light. Each chakra is a whirling center of vital energy shaped like a cone. The chakras are found along the spinal cord or Sushumna, the energetic channel that runs along the spine from the root chakra, located at the base of the spine, to the crown chakra which is at the crown of the head. The chakras energize, control and maintain proper function of our body, mind and emotions.

Nadis are nerve-like channels that carry our spiritual and vital energies to the energy fields. Where they intersect, they form a lotus with unfolding petals: a chakra. The number of petals varies according to the number of nadis. When the chakra and the petals are facing downward, the energy is undergoing a transformation process. The transformation occurs when we learn the lessons of a particular chakra and receive the energy to proceed in the ascension process. The petals turn up as we ascend to the next level of consciousness.

The chakras below the heart move in a counterclockwise manner in response to the downward pull of earth's gravity. The purpose of the lower chakras is to turn clockwise in harmony with the upper chakras. Upon awakening to our true self, the light of our consciousness pierces the center of the chakra involved and opens it to the divine essence. Each chakra contains a lesson and has a deep and profound purpose – to assist us on our spiritual path.

These gateways to our soul are our centers of light and protection and allow accumulated energy to exist or enter the system under the direction of soul power. The chakras play an important role in the etheric, emotional, mental and spiritual fields of consciousness. They are the doors to understanding ourselves on all levels.

Chakras are the regulators of the life force, providing major points of contact with the outside world and reception of impressions from the higher realms. There are seven major chakras in the etheric field. Each plays a part in nourishing and sustaining the nervous system, organs and endocrine glands. The etheric chakras are different from the emotional and mental chakras. They keep the vital energy of the physical body balanced and healthy. These chakras are essential to the life of the etheric and radiate according to the development and health of the individual. The etheric chakras influence the vitality of the whole system. They distribute prana throughout the etheric field, which then brings the life force to the physical. The chakras also function as communicators or transmitters from one energy field to the other. For example; the etheric field to the emotional field, emotional field to the mental field, and the mental field to the spiritual field.

There are four main chakras in the body and three in the head. The root chakra is the seat of the physical body, the navel center the seat of the etheric field, the solar plexus chakra the seat of the emotional field, the heart chakra the seat of the lower mental field, the throat chakra the seat of the higher mental field, the third eye chakra the seat of the intuitive field and the crown center the seat of the spiritual field. The solar plexus, navel and root are related to our personality nature and function in relationship to our physical survival, needs and wants. They are also considered our power centers because they control the physical senses, express the tendencies of the personality and initiate the desires of clinging, craving, possessing, having and rejecting. The heart chakra is considered the bridge of light between the physical (those below the heart) and the spiritual (those above the heart). The heart, throat, third eye and crown are the transcendental chakras of the soul and higher mind and are related to our higher self. Their function is to help us express, expand and deepen ourselves, allowing us to become integrated beings of light.

The first three chakras — root, navel and solar plexus — are the testing zones of our spiritual being. The solar plexus chakra provides the key to transforming our personal will into divine will, for it is within that center that the battle between the personality and the divine self takes place. When we let go of the struggle to maintain our separate individual self we open the door to the heart chakra where we meet our true nature. The root chakra is our foundation or ground for being. When balanced it reflects the needed stability, security and energy for our life's journey. We welcome the assignment given by the universe and trust that our life is a gift and an opportunity to evolve in love. Through our relationship with our God or crown chakra, we infuse our being with trust and security from a long-lasting source.

After creating a strong foundation in the root chakra, we journey into the consciousness of the navel chakra. This is the chakra of our physical vitality and expression in the physical world and our feeling self. It opens and is balanced naturally through the throat chakra. The experience of the solar plexus chakra brings us lessons in personal power, judgments, opinions and self-mastery. The heart chakra assists us along our journey to transform our personal power, surrendering to our divine source, and teaches the art of surrender and the meaning of the affirmation, "Thy will be done."

Transcending the lower chakras opens the door to our spiritual nature. The throat center awakens as we begin to express our truth; divine miracles come from the spoken word. The heart chakra translates the message of compassion, surrender and letting go through evolving love. The wisdom of the third eye chakra shines with the light of cosmic consciousness.

When the chakras are blended and integrated they are instruments of divine power and glory. In a state of illumination the chakras are like jewels strung along the Sushumna, the life force that flows up the spine. Our chakras represent our state of consciousness and are indicators of the need to apply the healing attention of love. They are the tools for transformation, a map to our true self. We must carefully look at memories that we hold in the lower chakras. Once we release the past, the crown chakra can take its rightful place as the master of all the others, integrating and infusing us with divine light.

The Chakras

7 Keys to Awakening

Crown

Third Eye

Throat

Heart

Solar Plexus

Navel

Root

Journey through the Seven Chakras

The first three chakras make up the aspects of the personality. Related to earth, water and fire, they are associated with physical survival. The next three chakras relate to air, light and an integration of all elements, making up the spiritual aspect of our being.

The **root chakra**, located at the base of the spine, is called Muladhara, which means support at the root. With four petals of fiery red and orange tinged with gold and yellow, this chakra is a whirling vortex of energy flowing into the reproductive organs. Related to the earth element it energizes the sexual organs and externalizes as adrenal glands, governing the spine and kidneys. Kundalini, the serpent fire, resides here.

The **navel chakra**, called Svadhisthana, meaning sweetness, is located at the midpoint of the sacrum. Related to the etheric field, this chakra externalizes as the reproductive glands and governs the reproductive system. The navel chakra is related to the water element and has six vermilion petals. The life force circulates from this chakra with the purpose of nurturing the physical creative force. Energies come into the field through the spleen and then are distributed to the remaining chakras.

The **solar plexus chakra** - Manipura, meaning lustrous gem, is related to the emotional field and affects the digestive system. This third chakra corresponds to the liver, kidneys and large intestine and is associated with feelings and emotions. Because Manipura is the power center of the physical field, where instincts and survival play an important role, it is easily exhausted. Predominantly yellow, this lotus has ten petals. The solar plexus chakra is related to the element fire.

The **heart chakra** - Anahata, meaning pure or untouched, is located behind the heart in the dorsal spine. Its twelve petals are a golden green color for healing or a rose pink for divine love. It externalizes as the thymus and governs the heart, circulation and blood. The energy of the heart corresponds to the compassion and love of the Buddha or Christ. The heart chakra is related to the life prana and the element of air.

The **throat chakra** - Visuddha, meaning purification, has sixteen petals of whirling blue and other colored energies. Located at the base of the neck, Visuddha governs the vocal chords, bronchia, lungs and digestive tract and externalizes as the thyroid and parathyroid glands. It is called the chakra of miracles for its connection with the powers of life and its ability to express intelligence through the spoken word. The throat chakra is related to the element of sound.

The **third eye chakra** - or Ajna, meaning to know or perceive - is located between the eyebrows on the forehead. It governs the eyes, teeth, sinuses, lower brain and the brain stem. The ajna chakra has two main petals of intense white with hues of purplish blue and violet and is related to the pineal gland and etheric sight. When aligned with the soul it brings clear thinking and vision, intuition and truth. This chakra is related to the element of light, where visualization becomes the gift through manifestation. Opening this chakra merges our dual nature so life is unified and whole.

The **crown chakra** - or Sahashara, meaning thousand-petaled lotus - is located on the crown of the head. It governs the brain and nervous system and externalizes as the pineal gland. Through union and harmony of the heart and crown chakras love, will and intelligence are balanced, opening the channel for the soul.

Prayer by St. Francis of Assisi

Lord, make me an instrument of Thy peace.
Where there is hatred, let me sow love.
Where there is injury, pardon.
Where there is doubt, faith.
Where there is despair, hope.
Where there is darkness, light.
Where there is sadness, joy.
Oh, Divine Master, grant that I may not so much seek
To be consoled, as to console.
To be understood, as to understand.
To be loved, as to love.
For it is in giving, that we receive.
It is in pardoning, that we are pardoned.
It is in dying (to the false self), that we are born
To Eternal Life

The Root Chakra

Muladhara

Keeping of the Beginning

*The search for your inner, true nature
leads you to let go of all desires and
attachments that keep you from finding
freedom.
In reality your true nature is always free,
but the veil of the personal self is preventing you from fully experiencing the
vastness of your being.*

~Pg 41, Living Meditations

The Root Chakra – Our Ground of Being

With a strong foundation in our root chakra we become willing participants in physical existence, cooperating with the forces of mother earth. The root chakra - Muladhara, meaning support at the root - provides us with keys to our life purpose. In the root center we hold the information about our family of origin and ancestral memories. Any damage can be healed through affirming our purpose and value as an evolving self. The lessons of the root center teach us to release old programs and conditioning that retain our energy in an untransformed state. Reaffirming our sense of trust and safety with life's processes and lessons builds an inner foundation of strength and an unconditional relationship to life.

The home of our basic instincts, the root chakra drives us to find sexual unity, passion and the fire of life. This fire gives stability, power and the instinct to survive and deepens our relationship with joy and gratitude for being alive.

A vortex of primal force, this chakra can create or destroy. When our energies are positive, optimistic and life-affirming, the root center is balanced. When we feel disconnected, scattered and not present in life, we are not in balance. The root chakra strives for harmony with the spiritual centers by reaching for the divine while stabilizing and grounding on the earth. When this chakra is weak it manifests self-centeredness, anger, and fear rooted in the survival instinct. Worry is an expression of an unbalanced root chakra, feeling insecure in the world where everyday life tends to feel burdensome. When balanced we feel confident and safe in our lives.

In order to maintain balance, the root chakra must be in harmony with the third eye and crown chakras. Working with the higher centers in our transformation process we create a new sense of grounding. Integration of our lower three chakras with the chakras of our soul reconnects us with our divine purpose in life.

To remain as you are, without question
or doubt, is your natural state.
~Sri Ramana Maharshi

The Root Chakra Chart

Muladhara - Meaning support at the Root, the keeper of the beginning, the bearer of the foundation

- **Location -** Base of spine between anus and genitals
- **Physical Correspondence -** Bones, skeletal structure, spine
- **Physical Dysfunctions -** Sciatica pain, lower back pain
- **Subtle Body -** Physical/Etheric
- **Glandular Connection -** Adrenals - controls all solid parts, spinal column, bones, teeth, nails, anus, rectum, colon, prostate, glands, blood, building of cells
- **Emotional Plane -** Primary emotions: fear - released through a deep sense of security and trust. Other emotions - depression, confusion, feeling off-center, not belonging, obsessions released through a deep sense of stillness.
- **Mental Plane -** A strong sense of self, secure with little or no self-doubt; stillness
- **Color -** Fiery red
- **Petals -** 4
- **Element -** Earth
- **Symbol -** Elephant of earthly abundance and good fortune, four red petals around a square containing a downward pointing triangle that represents the relationship to earth energies and karma
- **Animal Correspondence -** Elephant
- **Sense -** Smell
- **Fragrance -** Cloves, cedar, patchouli, myrrh, musk
- **Ayurvedic oils -** Ginger, vetiver
- **Healing Stones -** Agate, hematite, blood jasper, garnet, ruby, tiger eye, bloodstone, smoky quartz, onyx
- **Sounds -** Vowel C spoken in lower c
- **Mantra -** LAM
- **Words to create healing affirmations -** Responsibility, nurturance, abundance, trust, security, safety, stability, oneness, unity, connection with source, empowerment (letting go of being a victim), boundaries, limitations
- **Verb -** To have
- **Yoga Postures -** Bridge Pose, Half Locust, Full Locust, Head to Knee pose
- **Balanced Chakra -** Deep trust in life, inner gratitude, life energy intact, connection with nature, trust in nature's laws, understanding life's changing ebb and flow
- **Unbalanced Chakra -** Self realization is a challenge as thoughts and emotions revolve around self interest and material possession, security, and survival issues. It is difficult to let go of our past experiences or integrate them and understand the lessons one has learned. There is often an experience of depression and a feeling of being out of touch with life.

The Navel Chakra

Svadhisthana

Where the Vital Force Resides

Living in gratitude is to experience the sacred in life, honoring and expressing it throughout all changes. Gratitude is seeing that we have been blessed with the time needed to realize the reason for this birth. Look within and discover the sacredness of being, seeing all as sacred, and walk in reverence of the divine force behind all manifestation.

~Pg 49 Living Meditations

The Navel Chakra – Journey through the Sea of Emotions

The navel chakra is called Svadhisthana in Sanskrit, meaning dwelling place of the self or sweetness. This chakra produces and assimilates internal energy received through air and food and distributes it from the spleen to the meridians and the vital force throughout all areas of the physical body.

Corresponding to water, the second chakra cleanses the body and mind of lower impulses and physical toxins. On the physical level the kidneys and bladder are strengthened and on an emotional level, emotions are centered and purified.

When in balance, the navel chakra creates a sense of abundance and appreciation for what life brings. This chakra is considered the seat of Shakti, where our physical, sexual and creative energy is expressed, the place of life, conception, change and movement. It can be visualized as a bright sphere of radiant orange light bringing forth creative energies and ideas. This chakra holds the magical wonder of our being and is related to the ages of eight to fourteen, when we most experience life's sweetness and unconditional joy.

The navel chakra represents change, duality, movement, flexibility and creative flow. When we energetically tune into this center we can observe that our lives are best served when we experience life in an unconditional manner. When balanced, this chakra represents a reservoir of fluid movement in all aspects of our lives, flowing with life's changes.

The navel chakra is depicted as a six-petal lotus that relates to the six passions of lust, anger, greed, deceit, pride and envy. The navel chakra can be damaged and blocked by misuse and misunderstanding of sexual energy resulting in weakened physical stamina that attracts illness. Through mastery we can overcome these qualities and open to our full potential as human beings. The transformation of these emotions assists us in the evolution to our heart.

The energy of the navel chakra works closely with the ajna, or third eye chakra. Awakening our inner eye to develop discernment assists us in mastering the challenges of the navel. Our inner eye creates a direct stream of consciousness to integrate emotions, desires, pleasures and feelings with our higher knowing and our intention for wholeness.

The Navel Chakra Chart

Svadhisthana - Meaning sweetness, self-abode, where the vital force resides

- **Location -** Lower lumbar area, lower abdomen, between navel and genitals
- **Physical Correspondence -** Sex organs, bladder, kidney, circulation system, vital force, sacral plexus, sacral vertebra, liquids of the body
- **Physical Dysfunctions -** Kidney, bladder problems, circulation and skin issues, lower back pain, sex organs, small intestine.
- **Subtle Body -** Etheric
- **Glandular Connection -** Ovaries, testicles, reproductive organs; controls pelvic area, sex organs, potency, fluid functions, kidneys and bladder.
- **Emotional Plane -** Desire, passion; ability to be comfortable with feelings, good self-esteem, healthy sexual attitude, physical creativity, emotional instability
- **Mental Plane -** Emotional principles (which work through the senses), understanding the duality of the world, working with opposites.
- **Color -** Orange
- **Petals -** 6
- **Element -** Water
- **Symbol -** White crescent moon and six orange petals containing a second lotus flower
- **Animal Correspondence -** Makara, a fish tailed alligator, fish and sea creatures
- **Sense -** Hearing
- **Fragrance -** Ylang ylang, sandalwood, jasmine and rose
- **Ayurvedic Oils -** Cedar, sage, patchouli
- **Healing Stones -** Carnelian, moonstone, citrine, topaz, coral, tourmaline
- **Sounds -** Sound and Vowels O sung in D
- **Mantra -** VAM
- **Words to create healing affirmations -** Happiness, fulfilled, acceptance of self and others, worthy, creative, expressive, honor, nurture, listen to feelings, working in harmony with truth and inner vision, vital energy intact, moving freely with ease through the world, acceptance of change
- **Verbs -** I feel, I open, I am
- **Yoga Postures -** Pelvic Rock, Leg Lifts, Hip Circles
- **Balanced Chakra -** Harmonious feelings, healthy sexual feelings, flowing with the creative energy of life; expressing physically, emotionally and mentally; physical action is creative. Second chakra opens when we have the ability to feel pleasure and pain, letting go of past fears, disillusion and disappointed memories. Unity with another, giving emotional support without condition. Happily connected with life.
- **Unbalanced Chakra -** Unhealthy relationship with our sexuality stemming from puberty, judgment regarding our sensuality, loss of innocence and wonder regarding the magic of life. Conscious mind is uncomfortable with painful or powerful feelings. We seek union at any cost, using lovers to fulfill our deep longing to unite with the other half of our soul.

The Solar Plexus Chakra

Manipura

Lustrous Gem

To live in a world where there is great suffering and negativity requires great courage. Living with courage is holding the intention to be free from endless personal sorrow and to no longer contribute to the suffering of humanity. Each moment is a new opportunity to reflect upon your life, accessing needed courage from your inner truth.

~Pg 25, Living Meditations

Solar Plexus Chakra – Journey to the Center of our Power

The solar plexus chakra receives and distributes energy throughout the physical form. This fire center - Manipura meaning lustrous gem, our emotional and power center - is also called the sea of turmoil because of the stormy seas we endure on life's journey.

Modern society works through the solar plexus chakra. People are conditioned to fulfill desires, seek personal power and build a false self. To calm this center affirm: "I have all I need and more, my power comes from the source."

Along with striving for personal power, the solar plexus chakra synthesizes and controls decision-making. Our transformation process makes us responsible for our true empowerment, which comes from listening to our intuition.

Under the influence of personal will and the personality, this chakra reflects a yellow color representing thought. When transcending the personal self and allowing true wisdom to come forth, this chakra reflects the gold of wisdom and abundance. The solar plexus is our guide to the world around us and provides an important protective force until our inner light becomes completely balanced. A balanced, open solar plexus chakra brings inner joy, surrender and lightness. Imbalance brings depression, hopelessness, separation and striving.

The solar plexus chakra governs impressions and discrimination. It repels, magnifies, and reflects the duality of thoughts and emotions. It is a connecting link to the mental and spiritual consciousness. The solar plexus receives information from the mental and higher mental and translates it through the chakras of the heart and throat. It also receives information from the physical and etheric fields and translates them through the root and navel chakras. This feeling center of the body picks up on the energy of others; it can be thought of as a transmitting tool, accessing information from all fields.

The energy of the solar plexus chakra is linked deeply with the heart. As we let go of our personal striving, the lotus of the solar plexus turns from pointing downward to pointing upward to the heart, forming a bridge of light that assists the lower chakras to unite with the higher. A journey into our heart chakra is an experience of peace and calmness.

The Solar Plexus Chakra Chart

Manipura - Meaning lustrous gem, city of gems

- **Location -** The well between shoulder blades (back side)/between navel and sternum (front)
- **Physical Correspondence -** Digestive system (particularly liver & small intestine), muscles, stomach, gall bladder, nervous system, pancreas, lower back, physical solar plexus, adrenals
- **Physical Dysfunctions -** Allergies, digestive problems, assimilation of energy, nervous disorders, fatigue, pain in middle and lower back
- **Subtle Body -** Astral and emotional
- **Glandular Connection -** Pancreas and adrenals - control liver, digestive system, stomach, spleen, gall bladder, autonomic nervous system, lower back, muscles
- **Emotional Plane -** Main emotion: fear - false sense of power through wrong identification, low sense of self, need to be in control, manipulation, insecurity
- **Mental Plane -** Letting go of unwanted thoughts and accumulation from the past, believing in your true nature, diving into the unknown essence of being, surrendering to the master in the heart. Relates to reasoning.
- **Color -** Golden or yellow
- **Petals -** 10
- **Element -** Fire
- **Symbol -** A ten-petaled lotus flower containing a downward-pointing triangle surrounded by three T-shaped swastikas, or Hindu symbol of fire.
- **Sense -** Sight, shaping of being
- **Fragrance -** Peppermint, lemon, rosemary, lavender, carnation, cinnamon, marigold, chamomile, thyme
- **Ayurvedic Oils -** Sandalwood, lavender and fennel
- **Healing Stones -** Citrine, turquoise, lapis, amber, tiger eye, topaz, aventurine, quartz
- **Sounds -** Vowel C spoken in lower c
- **Mantra -** RAM
- **Words to create healing affirmations -** Power, source, divine will, becoming, discernment, respect, receive, honor, surrender, let go, peace, wholeness, purpose, courage, inner strength
- **Verbs -** I can, I am
- **Yoga Postures -** Bow Pose, Belly Push, The Woodchopper, Sun Salutation
- **Balanced Center -** Feeling peace and harmony with inner self, actions are performed with a deep reverence for life; light and energy are your expressions. Living for the highest good for all concerned, wishes are fulfilled spontaneously because of the emission of light that you give. You live in a state of protection from negative vibrations with acceptance of others and yourself. Transforming personal power to divine power or will, you have the ability to make clear decisions. You have self-respect and trust in your intelligence.
- **Unbalanced Center -** There is a mistaken identification of the false nature of the self, driven by personal power. Power is used to manipulate life according to self-centeredness. There is a lack of genuine self-worth. Disturbance often due to emotions held deep within. Striving, positioning and aggression are expressions of a sense of low self-worth, as are fear of failure, unworthiness and using power for self-gain.

The Heart Chakra

Anahata

Unstruck - The Pure Essence of Love

*Forgiveness of yourself and others is
having the compassion to understand
that, from the illusionary sense of self,
mistakes are made and there is never any
harm meant.
All comes from ignorance when you walk
in the mistaken identity with the self. All
is forgiven when you turn to the light of
your true nature.*

~Pg 33, Living Meditations

The Heart Chakra – Journey to the Heart of our Wisdom

The fourth chakra, Anahata, is the source of all light and love. This is where the lower chakras and the higher chakras meet and become integrated, creating oneness of being. The heart center opening demonstrates the deepest action of love turned inward.

The heart is the meeting ground of the spiritual triad of love, will and wisdom. This meeting occurs when the head center becomes the point of contact for spiritual will, the heart center becomes the agent for spiritual love, and the throat center becomes the expression of the spiritual mind.

The heart chakra functions to protect, heal and bring balance to the body, mind and emotions. Because this chakra is closely associated with the thymus gland, which governs the immune system, it is quite vulnerable to our overall level of health.

The heart chakra awakens us to the qualities of love, forgiveness and compassion, helping to release the painful memories of the past. The heart chakra is a bridge of light between the lower centers and the higher. All must cross this bridge to move from the limited consciousness of personality to divine consciousness. The heart forgives, letting go of memories that bind us to the past. The forgiveness process opens the door to true compassion for our life and our relationships and creates the miracle of understanding, forgiving, and ending the habit of blaming others for our situation.

The heart chakra opens when the personal will is transformed to divine will and personal power evolves to an empowered heart devoted to peace, giving and receiving love, and the practice of discernment. Unconditional love and compassion towards others and ourselves replaces self-centered desire and want. Cherishing our sacred energy, we give from our overflow.

The heart center opens through surrender of our separate sense of self. The doorway leads us to meet our inner lord, our beloved guide. This sage within is with us through all life's experiences. Identification with our lower self obstructs our meeting with this inner teacher. Contact with our inner guide brings spiritual love, wisdom and will, in the rhythm of nature and according to divine law.

The Heart Chakra Chart

Anahata - Meaning un-struck, pure, unbroken; the love chakra

- **Location -** Heart, center of the chest
- **Physical Correspondence -** Thymus, blood, life force, vagus nerve, circulation
- **Physical Dysfunctions -** Heart disease, cancer, high blood pressure, breathing and circulation problems, immune system diseases, skin disorders
- **Subtle Body -** Mental and higher mental
- **Glandular Connection -** Thymus - controls heart, blood, circulation, immune system, lower lungs, rib cage, skin, upper back, and hands
- **Emotional Plane -** Love - co-dependency, melancholia, loneliness, betrayal, devotion
- **Mental Plane -** Love that is blocked by thought patterns and conditioning. Thoughts geared to conditional love based on ideas, things, bargains, comparison, the past.
- **Colors -** Green: healing; pink: divine love
- **Petals -** 12, inside of which are two overlapping triangles forming a six-pointed star, representing the ability of the individual to evolve upward or downward.
- **Element -** Air
- **Symbol -** Lotus of 12 petals, containing two intersecting circles that make up a six-pointed star descending toward matter & pointing upward, raising matter toward spirit. Small chakra below heart called Ananakanda Lotus is the celestial wishing tree holding deepest heart wishes
- **Animal Correspondence -** Deer, gazelle, antelope
- **Sense -** Touch
- **Fragrance -** Attar of roses, bergamot, clary sage, geranium, rose
- **Ayurvedic Oils -** Rose, lavender, sandalwood
- **Healing Stones -** Rose quartz, tourmaline, kunzite, emerald, jade, watermelon tourmaline, azurite, aventurine quartz, malachite, moonstone
- **Sounds -** Ay as in ray
- **Mantras -** YAM
- **Words to create healing affirmations -** Love, compassion, receive, accept, surrender, enjoy, unconditional, forgive, release, joy, peace, harmlessness, freedom, sacred, essence, honor, give
- **Verbs -** I love, I accept, I forgive, I release, I am
- **Yoga Postures -** Cobra, Fish, Windmill, Cow Head pose, Salutation to the Sun
- **Balanced Center -** When this center is balanced, all centers are in harmony creating a clear channel for Shakti energy. We become an open vessel for the divine and our personal will is deeply surrendered to divine will. When the heart center is open we radiate love, sincerity, happiness and warmth. Compassion becomes the foundation of our true nature, as we no longer feel the separation inherent in the world. We feel alive and joyful in the moment.
- **Unbalanced Center -** Love given from an unbalanced heart center has a conditional quality, expects something in return, or recognition. It is difficult to accept love & support from others; we are not open to receive. Being sensitive and gentle feels embarrassing and we build up a defensive mechanism. We can love too much and be co-dependent on love & care for others' needs before our own. We worry about rejection & have a tendency toward sadness and depression. We may experience coldheartedness or heartlessness.

Center of the Heart
"Anahata"

HEART OF LIGHT

THRONE OF WITNESS CONSCIOUSNESS

SEAT OF THE SOUL

TEMPLE OF THE SPIRIT

SOURCE OF DIVINE WISDOM

Services of the Heart

To give rebirth and resurrection in life

To raise vibrations of vehicles to become instruments of the soul

To act as a bridge of light between form and formlessness, becoming a
whole human being

To express divine love, peace, joy, service, courage, understanding

The Illuminated Heart

Through the opening of the heart chakra we become spiritual warriors, protecting our sacred energy from the pitfalls of illusion and cultivating harmlessness. The symbol for the heart chakra is the deer. The gentle deer finds Ahimsa, the path of peace in daily life. Like the deer, the aspirant places his complete trust in God.

The heart center opening can be painful. It is the cross that we must bear when leaving our identification with the temporary nature of life. The heart chakra masters the polarities of the emotional, mental and etheric fields. The lower impulses of the chakras of the personality are transformed to reflect our true essence of divinity. Initiation into the heart chakra develops the qualities of reverence, service, compassion and selfless love.

With the gateway of the heart open, we sense a deeper presence within our lives, giving us the protection, devotion and strength needed for our journey home. Our journey takes us into our luminous body of light where we begin a life of service and devotion to the divine.

The song of the heart brings great love, beauty and unbounded joy. Our divine call on the path of return, this song is heard in the silence of the heart, teaching us about deep compassion and forgiveness; the healing miracles.

The Flowering Lotus of the Heart

The lotus of the heart is connected to the world through compassion, remaining untouched by all worldly experiences. This most sacred lotus is always flowering in the rhythm of our inner life, releasing the divine nectar of pure love in support of our true nature. Within the depth of our divine heart is a sacred resting place where we can retreat in silence, a reservoir of love, pure wisdom and divine guidance. As each petal unfolds, the chalice of life is filled with sacred essence and we journey deeper into the silence of the heart through greater and greater levels of awareness. We no longer strive to be on the path of spiritual awakening – we are the path.

You will identify
with what you think will make you safe.
Whatever it may be,
you will believe that it is one with you.
Your safety lies in truth, and not in lies.
Love is your safety.
Fear does not exist.
Identify with love, and you are safe.
Identify with love, and you are home.
Identify with love, and find your Self.

Love is your power.

– A Course in Miracles

The Opening of the Lotus of the Heart

The **first** petal unfolds when we meet our innermost self within the heart sanctuary and awareness turns from identification with the body to knowing our true self.

The **second** petal opens through realization that we are neither our emotions nor our mind. Our true nature is an expression of divinity, found in the heart of goodness, in alignment with inner truth.

The **third** petal unfolds when thinking is used for higher aspiration and the mind becomes silent. The mind dissolves into the sacred heart, a silent observer. Thought transforms to intuition, perception and discernment.

The **fourth** petal opens when we release attachment to the things of this world. The knowledge obtained within our heart's unfolding lotus deepens our understanding of pure consciousness.

The **fifth** petal unfolds when we are firmly embedded in our true nature, demonstrating steadfastness, vigilance and uncompromising clarity.

The **sixth** petal unfolds when all that is not pure consciousness is burned in the sacred fire of our inner light.

The **seventh** petal opens when our inner being is adorned with all-inclusive love, harmlessness and devotion to the ever-present sacred self that resides in the spiritual heart.

The **eighth** petal opens as we directly perceive our true reality. The light of consciousness removes all doubt.

The **ninth** petal opens when there is deep and profound peace. The past is dissolved completely and true freedom has been realized.

The **tenth** petal opens when we fully live each sacred moment, awaiting life's call to service.

The **eleventh** petal opens when we experience the joy of our being and share it with others.

The **twelfth** petal opens when we walk the path of compassion.

The Throat Chakra

Visuddha

The Chakra of Miracles

*The art of letting go is seeing clearly that
your true nature is revealed only in
freedom where you no longer hold onto
the past.
In letting go and dying to the past, you
learn to truly live in the moment, giving
yourself to life instead of demanding
something of it.*

~Pg 55, Living Meditations

The Throat Chakra – Journey to the Chakra of Miracles

The journey of consciousness takes us through the limitations of the lower chakras into the higher centers of our true self. In the realm of the throat chakra, Visuddha, we have the opportunity to express the joy of pure *being-ness* through the voice. The throat center teaches us to use sound, prayer and affirmations for healing and balancing any discord of our body, mind and emotions. A beautiful blue light emanates from this center in various shades according to the vibration of our expression.

The lessons of the throat center teach the importance of honesty, discernment, listening and hearing, observing the voice of doubt, judgment, self-criticism and other untruths held deep within our conditioning. False perception of the self binds us to the conditioning of the past. The throat center is the bridge between the body and the mind, the connection between the feeling nature of our being and the higher wisdom of our sacred spirit.

As the throat chakra opens, we develop a clear expression of divine energies, creating a link between the lower chakras and the upper chakras, and ascend into the true essence, a new consciousness of willingness. Letting go of all habits, instincts and patterns of the ego that were based on preservation of the personality self, we now move into the expression of divine consciousness.

The highest expression of the Visuddha chakra is prayer – the deep communion between the true self and the higher omnipresent force of life. Prayer in this way is the process of ever-deepening devotion and surrender to the highest will of the divine. The throat center is where we take the path of surrender, turning our thoughts and attention inward to the silence of our true self.

When we are in touch with our true nature we receive the gift of manifestation, where our deepest wishes are expressed and affirmed and all self-doubt is removed. The throat chakra is the primary tool in healing and transformation, expressing the truth of our authentic self. In relationship to the health of an individual, it is connected to the thyroid and parathyroid glands, which metabolize the energy of the system. Expressing truth, we create an opening for the grace of healing to take place.

The Path of Silence

Silence is the unseen power of the throat center, the space in which the creative word is expressed. Silence heals all imbalances of the body, mind and spirit, realigning us with our inner truth. Silence is the avenue we must take in order to free ourselves from unwanted thought and disturbance that comes from identification with the changing nature of life. It is a great centering device, bringing coordination, order and calmness so that we may tap into our creative resources and co-create through our divine guidance. Through silence we build our vital force and keep it as a reservoir for our creative expression.

Silence stills our mind, emotions and bodily sensations allowing us to experience the peace of our heart and our witness consciousness. The voice of the silence within our heart is our divine guide and teacher, opening us to greater possibilities of self-understanding. Within silence and the intentional breath and the relaxation they bring, we enjoy a conscious communion with our source and keep the flame of our heart burning brightly.

The way to mastery is to turn within to the silence of the true self and live in stillness, unaffected by the changing appearances of manifestation in the eternal essence of life.

The Throat Chakra Chart

Visuddha - Meaning purification, simplified, sanctified, free from doubt. The chakra of miracles

- **Location -** Between collarbones, third cervical vertebrae, base of neck
- **Physical Correspondence -** Throat, neck, thyroid, parathyroid, ears, mouth, teeth
- **Physical Dysfunctions -** Sore throats, colds, swollen glands, neck pain, dental problems, thyroid problems, asthma, hearing or ear problems
- **Subtle Body -** Buddhic
- **Glandular Connection -** Thyroid and parathyroid - controls jaw, neck, throat, voice, airways, upper lungs, nape of neck, arms
- **Emotional Plane -** Inability to express emotions, blocked creativity, transformation of feelings and emotions, communication, reflections
- **Mental Plane -** Blocked flow of creative expression by thought and conditioning; the mind creates negativity about self and blocks ability to express emotions
- **Color -** Bright blue: expression; light blue: the quality of truth
- **Petals -** 16
- **Element -** Ether
- **Symbol -** Lotus with 16 petals, containing a downward pointing triangle within a circle representing the full moon
- **Animal Correspondence -** Elephant holding one of his seven trunks up victoriously
- **Sense -** Hearing
- **Fragrance -** Sage, eucalyptus, frankincense, lavender, sandalwood, chamomile, myrrh
- **Ayurvedic Oils -** Sandalwood, tea tree
- **Healing Stones -** Aquamarine, turquoise, chalcedony, lapis lazuli, agate, celestite, sodalite, sapphire
- **Sounds -** EEE
- **Mantra -** HAM
- **Words to create healing affirmations -** Express, self, listen, be truthful, voice, power, affirm, command, commune, allow, harmony in expression, harmlessness, wishes, invoke, prayer, communication, creative, ask, miracles, sanctify
- **Verbs -** I speak, I bring forth, I ask, I allow, I open
- **Yoga Postures -** Neck Rolls, Fish Pose, Shoulder Stand, Plough, Head Lift, Salutation to Sun
- **Balanced Chakra -** We express our thoughts, feelings & emotions with inner knowing, and without fear. We allow ourselves to be honest with others and ourselves. Speech is clear, & reflects inner truth. Silence is easily practiced from conviction in our truth. We remain true to ourselves and can say both yes & no to life, when we follow our heart. We are not swayed by opinions of others. We are in contact with our inner guide, giving spaciousness to our being.
- **Unbalanced Chakra -** Sometimes we will express ourselves in thoughtless actions or shut ourselves off from our feelings of truth. We sometimes carry a feeling of judgment of others and ourselves. When unbalanced, our voice is comparatively loud and our words lack inner meaning. Through being unbalanced in this center we can act defensively and use words harshly to hurt others. Sometimes there is a tendency to manipulate others. Insufficient energy in the throat chakra can express itself in shyness, being overly quiet and getting a lump in the throat when needing to speak.

Notes

The Third Eye Chakra

Visuddha

Ocean of Nectar

The mastery process requires an inner strength that is generated by your truth. You learn the art of looking inward, gradually increasing steadfastness in observation, until there is no more looking or observing, there is just being. This is when the observer and the observed becomes a unified whole. When the light of the soul is awakened there is no longer thought of self as a separate individual. The self is neither free nor bound, neither separate nor whole, and you live in absolute stillness as an open channel to the Light of the Soul.

~Pg 61, Living Mediations

The Third Eye Chakra – Journey into Clear Perception

The Third Eye Chakra is Ajna – Sanskrit for "to perceive the eye of wisdom" – the center of higher intuition. Our sixth sense, clairvoyance, is developed in the Third Eye Chakra. The related endocrine gland is the pituitary gland, which is said to be the seat of the soul.

This sixth chakra gives will and the power of visualization. The master for all the other chakras, the opening of the Ajna is vitally important to achieving full potential in our lifetime. Quieting the mind, deep contemplation and inquiry into the nature of the true self are the paths to accomplishing this opening. This center, when fully awakened, has the power to transform all conditions of our life, releasing karmic patterns from the past and healing body, mind and emotions.

The Third Eye center, when awakened, illuminates our path with the radiant light of spirit and takes us to deeper levels of perception and balance where the energy of matter and spirit become one. Closing our outer eyes, we find a deep peace within our inner eye. Meditation becomes a vehicle to rest in the light of our pure consciousness.

The saying, "Be in the world but not of it," is appropriate for the development of the Ajna center as we learn to shift our attention from the world of change to the changeless essence of the divine.

The question, "Who am I?" leads us safely to the essence of our true self. The wisdom eye is the window to our radiant true nature and, when opened, give us insight to our divine purpose. This window reflects the light of the soul, the realm of our higher knowledge, and frees us to discover the eternal presence within our hearts.

If you are born only of flesh, you identify with the stuff of you, which is limited to a particular form, name and appearance in the moment you view it. What about the One who gives it energy and whose purpose it serves?

If you were born of the breath, you identify with something much closer to Sacred Unity; your breath is part of Holy Spirit and it changes every moment, as does the One.

Without this kind of birth, you will always be puzzled when I say things like, "Be born from the First Beginning!"

John 3:7, Aramaic Peshitta Version
The Genesis Meditations – Neil Douglas - Klotz

The Third Eye Chakra Chart

Ajna - Meaning servant, or ordered from above, not ignorant, ocean of nectar

- **Location -** First cervical vertebra, center of the head at the eye level or slightly above.
- **Physical Correspondence -** Pituitary, left lower brain, left eye, nose, nervous system, ears
- **Physical Dysfunctions -** Headaches, poor vision, eye problems, nightmares
- **Subtle Body -** Intuitive
- **Glandular Connection -** Pituitary, controls endocrine system
- **Emotional Plane -** Lack of ability to integrate feelings with wisdom, learning difficulties, hallucinations; how we see determines our experience.
- **Mental Plane -** Thoughts and conditioning; mind blocks clear perception
- **Spiritual Plane -** Extrasensory perception, knowledge of being
- **Color -** Indigo
- **Petals -** 2; hemispheres: left (analytical, logical, & linear), right (spatial, artistic, & intuitive)
- **Element -** Ether, light and telepathic energy
- **Symbol -** Lotus with two large petals on either side, resembling wings, around a circle containing a downward pointing triangle.
- **Sense -** Sixth sense, light
- **Fragrance -** Mint, jasmine, violet, rose, lotus, geranium, rosemary, basil
- **Ayurvedic Oils -** Sandalwood, basil, lavender, jasmine, eucalyptus
- **Healing Stones -** Lapis lazuli, blue sapphire, sodalite, quartz, opal
- **Sounds -** Vowels, sound therapy vowel sound E sung in A
- **Mantra -** KSHAM
- **Words to create healing affirmations -** Understanding, harmony, oneness, knowing, trust, intuition, light, seeing, awareness, vision, recognition, inner truth, divine plan, imagination, visualization, clarity, purpose, willingness, servant
- **Verbs -** I see, I am, I create, I ask, I command
- **Yoga Posture -** Palming the eyes
- **Balanced Chakra -** Means living in harmony with divine law, no longer manipulating life with self-interest. Celestial perception becomes second nature, using thought from the intellect as tools to employ a divine life-style. There is no longer a sense of duality as this center, when fully awakened, expresses the middle path of equilibrium and inherent unity of life. We attain the gift of visualization and the ability to comprehend life intuitively. We are open to cosmic truths and see the world of appearances as temporary illusions and do not get caught up in them. Our thoughts are vehicles of reality and are used for the purpose of divine order and work. We learn to perceive the world in a different way, noticing the grace of life with ever deepening awareness. We become intuitive, ever opening and unfolding to the divine aspects of reality. Joyous communication, untouched by fear, self-preserved and protected.
- **Unbalanced Chakra -** Overly intellectual, overly rational, lacking a holistic way of thinking, an inability to integrate. We block the light of our vision with our conditioned thought. We sometimes are not able to integrate the experience that we have had in our changing life and lose perception of reality. Our ideas are based on concrete thinking and we have not developed the ability to move beyond rational thought into perception. We have suppressed our feelings and live in dependency on the will of others.

The Crown Chakra

Sahasrara

Possessing The Thousand-Petaled Lotus

Real happiness is found by turning within to your timeless nature. Happiness is found when there is a complete letting go to the timeless flow of life, where you are not bound by any conditions at all.
When you surrender to the timeless flow of life, energy is used on behalf of the eternal presence, and life is lived in devotion to everlasting divinity.

~Pg 103, Living Meditations

The Crown Chakra – Journey into Unity Consciousness

The crown chakra or Sahasrara, the thousandfold lotus, is located on the top of the head at the baby's soft spot. This exquisite white thousand-petaled lotus forms a most beautiful crown on the head with the stem, or Antahkarana (the bridge of light between personality and soul) reaching upward as a channel for divine energies. It is the soul's point of entry and exit as well as a receiving and distributing station for our life force. It is most activated through yearning to unite with our inner true nature as well as the inquiry into the sacred nature of life.

Opening the crown chakra allows the divine to clear past impressions and to create an unconditional relationship to life based on the present. Jesus said, "Empty thyself and I shall fill thee," which implies a divine energy entering through the crown. When we empty ourselves of the scars and conditioning of the past we are born anew into the light.

The crown chakra is a center for universal consciousness with the duty of integrating and synthesizing all energies into one unified whole. The seventh chakra connects us with divine energy that purifies and unifies us with our life's purpose. The channel widens as our consciousness expands, taking us deeper into our unknown mysterious nature.

Related to the pineal gland, the crown chakra holds the thread of consciousness that connects us with our soul. The seventh chakra is an organ of synthesis where the will, creativity and consciousness are integrated. It unifies the beauty of the heart center, the truth of the throat center and the goodness of the third eye center.

We develop a closer connection with our true self with each step of our ascension process. Opened through silence, purity and meditative prayer, energy of center moves down through the spinal column unifying, healing and balancing our body, mind and spirit. The centers along the spine come into full expression when all negative conditions are released.

The Crown Chakra Chart

Sahasrara - Meaning granting victory, possessing one thousand-petaled lotus, or immortal self.

- **Location -** Top and center of the head, the baby's soft spot
- **Soul Lesson -** Unity, integration
- **Physical Correspondence -** Pituitary, pineal, upper brain, right eye, central nervous system
- **Physical Dysfunctions -** Immune system, circulation, endocrine disorders
- **Subtle Body -** Divine
- **Glandular Connection -** Pineal, controls cerebrum, right eye and brain hemisphere, central nervous system
- **Emotional Plane -** Depression, obsession, confusion, hopelessness, disassociation, ungroundedness. When the seventh chakra is closed the accumulated wisdom and lessons of the soul remain unconscious. The open seventh chakra becomes the channel of communication to the higher self.
- **Mental Plane -** The chatter of the mind becomes unbearable, psychotic – thoughts that create anxiety, frustration, and fear.
- **Colors -** Gold, white or violet
- **Petals -** 1000
- **Element -** All elements, thought, cosmic energy
- **Symbol -** A 1000-petaled lotus flower
- **Sense -** Beyond self, thought
- **Fragrance -** Lavender, frankincense, lotus, rosewood, spruce, olibanum
- **Ayurvedic Oils -** Sandalwood, frankincense, myrrh
- **Healing stones -** Amethyst, clear quartz, diamond, crystal, topaz, alexandrite, sapphire, selenite
- **Sound or Mantra -** Om
- **Words to create healing affirmations -** I am, universe, connections, spirit, channel, open, radiant, choose, transformed, release, surrender, open, contentment
- **Verb -** I know, I am, I realize
- **Yoga postures -** Half lotus, head stand, meditation
- **Balanced Center -** We have journeyed from our expression as separate individuals and have integrated all our experiences and gifts. Now we experience life as a divine inner child and remember the magical journey of our childlike nature. We can see that we are the same energy that flows in all aspects of life; we are the wind and the sea. Through the development of this center we are balanced with our earth energies & can access our subconscious feelings.
- **Unbalanced Center -** Our thoughts and emotions are still holding onto identification with our lower self. We feel frustrated at our inability to let go. Our power is suppressed in the lower self, holding onto time, memory and the past. We often experience depression and feel out of touch with life.

The Art of Meditation

Meditation is a state of communion with the divine – the pure essence of God within our heart. True meditation begins when we know ourselves as a spark of the divine source. The knowledge of our true self gives us the inner strength and courage to live in a way that honors our purpose in life.

As the mind dissolves into the heart of stillness, the divine in all of creation becomes visible. No longer a separate self, believing in our thoughts as essential truth, we experience a unity in life. All is laid to rest in the peace of the sacred quiet mind. This force will guide, inspire, encourage and bring a positive energy to whatever we need. We cherish this light, this precious force, quietly abiding in its presence, ever faithful to the holy energy encountered.

The Living Meditations section of this text provides many meditations for daily practice and spiritual self-care.

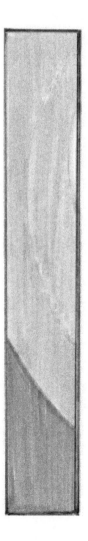

SHEN REVITALIZATION

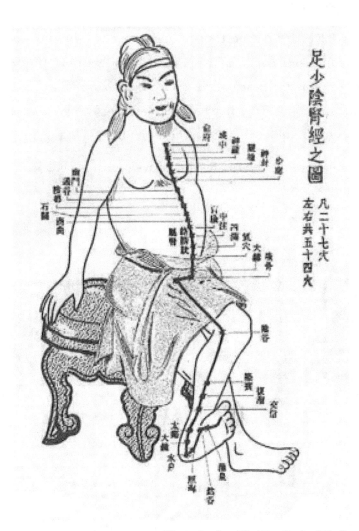

Illustration from The First Book of Do-In

Meridian Charts

Yin & Yang

Yin	Yang	Yin	Yang
In Nature		**Energetic Functions**	
material	immaterial	calming	energizing
substantial	non-substantial	inhibiting	stimulating
matter	energy	cooling	warming
condensation	expansion	absorbing	transforming
descending	ascending	storing	transporting
darkness	light	generating	eliminating
coldness	warmth	moistening	protecting
moisture	dryness		
space	time	**Psychological Aspects**	
		feeling	thinking
In the Body		impression	analysis
structure	function	sensation	idea
inferior	superior	intuition	inspiration
exterior	posterior	receptive	expressive
medial	lateral	observant	articulate
anterior	exterior	implicit	explicit
		yielding	assertive
		adaptable	single-minded
		spontaneous	structured
		serenity	excitement
		inward security	outward confidence

Shen and the Meridians – Channels of Spirit

The Chinese word for spirit is *shen,* meaning the vitality of an individual, which is the very life force of the personality. The spirit of a person is connected to the overall health of the body, mind and emotions.

Chinese medicine views the human being as a microcosm operating on the same principles which govern the flow of energy throughout the universal macrocosm. Energy, *shen,* flows from the environment, through the etheric field, to portals of entry at acupuncture points along specific meridian systems through which the *shen* flows to sustain our body, mind and spirit.

Western medicine rarely addresses the relationship of soul or spirit to health. Energy medicine and other holistic healing modalities are trying to bridge Western medicine with Eastern medicine. The *Life Essence Awakening Process (LEAP)* demonstrates that it is possible to assist the health of the body, mind and spirit through the application of simple self-care energy healing techniques.

Shen Revitalization and Reconnection Therapy offers the student tools for balancing the energy of the meridians through meridian massage, regulating over- or under-energized meridians, and manipulating specific points to revitalize the body, mind and spirit. These simple techniques will greatly assist the student or practitioner in the effort to improve overall health.

Shen Vitality

The *shen* runs through the meridians, the body's energy channels, to the major organs of the body. The meridians, either yin (passive) or yang (aggressive), circulate up and down the body according to the direction of flow.

Each of the twelve paired meridians is either yin or yang and is named for the major organ it associates with. In addition to the twelve meridians there are two additional meridians that run up the front and down the back. These are called the Central and Governing meridians. There are an additional eight meridians, The Strange Flows, which will be presented in more advanced material.

The yin meridians flow generally on the inside area of the body – inner legs, inner arms – and relate to the organs that are always working, such as the lungs, spleen, heart, kidney, pericardium and liver. The yang meridians are the energy flows that run on the outside of the body – outsides of the legs, arms and trunk. They correspond to the organs that rest and work according to their functions such as large intestine, stomach, small intestine, bladder, triple warmer and gall bladder. Charts of these meridians appear in the next section.

According to meridian therapy a perfect balance between the forces of yin and yang will result in perfect health of body, mind and spirit. Excessive energy or insufficient energy leads to imbalance. When the energy is deficient there is a tendency to exhaustion, lethargy and lack of will. Excessive energy produces a tendency to feel pain along the path of the affected meridian. The meridians distribute the subtle magnetic energies of *shen* necessary to provide correction in the energetic flow, thereby allowing sustenance and organization of the physical cellular structure of each organ system.

The meridians can also be viewed as electrical currents connecting the superficial acupuncture points with the deeper organ structures. Acupuncture and acupressure therapies use specific points to either increase or decrease energy in the meridian flow.

Analysis of the meridian energetic system can enable the increase of the overall life force of a body-mind system. By measuring the energy system and noting if a meridian is too active or deficient, then applying pressure or moving energy out of specific meridian flows, the disorder can be corrected.

In the *LEAP* process we check each meridian to find out if it is over- or under-energized and then apply therapies such as Meridian Massage, Meridian Tapping, Pain Chasing and Shen Revitalization and Reconnection.

Rise up nimbly and go on your strange
journey to the ocean of meanings. The stream
knows it can't stay on the mountain. Leave
and don't look away from the sun as you go,
in whose light you are sometimes crescent,
sometimes full.

~ Rumi

Central Conception Meridian

Location: Begins at the perineum between the anal orifice and genitals, rises up the midline in the front to a point at the tip of the tongue. Channel of Bliss, the central channel.

Alarm Point: At the center of the chin, below the lower lip.

Healing Energy: Helps create protection from negative energies. Use zip-up procedure to increase energy, centeredness and protection.

Chakras: Root, Navel, Solar Plexus, Throat.

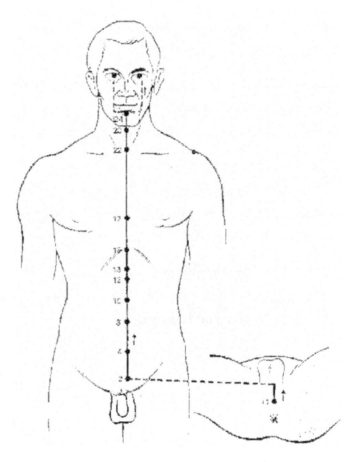

Illnesses and Effects: Conception, sexual organs, circulation, menstruation, male and female hormones, chest, hernia, circulatory system and breathing, sexual dysfunction, reproductive problems, chest pain, problems of expression, esophagus problems, and bronchitis.

Healing Colors: All.

Healing Smells: Most flower essences.

Lesson: Creative expression.

Affirmation Words: Centered, blissful, protection, circle, light, complete, whole, creative expression, fertile, and nurturing.

Meridian Massage: Start at the pubic bone, up the midline to the lower lip.

Governing Meridian

Location: Starts at the sacrum, travels up the spine, neck and over the head, down the face and nose to the end of the upper lip with an internal point just behind the upper front teeth.

Alarm Point: Tip of nose or just above upper lip.

Chakras: All Chakras

Illnesses and Effects: Spine, nervous system, skeletal system, anus, sexual organs, brain, and face. Fever, shock, mental illness, ability to govern life, coma, nervous disorders, paralysis, sexual dysfunction, headaches, back pain, fever, mental disease, shock, and coma.

Lesson: Ability to govern areas of life.

Affirmation Words: Govern, protect, shield, connect.

Meridian Massage: Start at the tailbone, go up the spine, over the top of the head, over the nose to the upper lip.

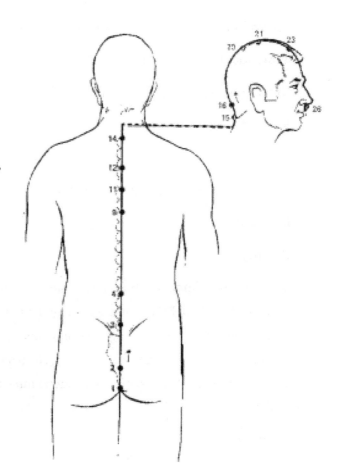

Stomach Meridian

Location: Below the eye to the jaw line, around the back and down the neck, traversing the rib cage, down through the abdomen, along the anterior aspect of the leg and foot, ending at the second toe.

Alarm Point: Central 12, halfway between the xiphoid process and umbilicus.

Time most active: 8 a.m.

Related Muscle: Pectoralis Major Clavicular.

Related Gland: Pancreas.

Chakra: Solar Plexus.

Emotions: Sympathy, empowerment, and anxiety.

Element: Earth.

Polarity: Yin.

Illnesses and Effects: Abdominal distention, headache, sinus, stiff neck, tightness of chest, thigh pain, pelvic pain, skin problems, fevers, gurgling, groaning, knee pain, lip and mouth sores, vomiting, nose bleeds, stomach aches. Worry, fairness, balance, digestion, general intestinal health.

Healing Colors: Orange.

Healing Smells: Sweetmint.

Affirmation Words: Sympathy, reflection, tranquility, contentment.

Meridian Massage: Start under the pupil of the eye, straight down to the jaw, circle up around the face to the frontal eminences, drop straight down over the eye to the clavicle, go out to the side directly over the nipple, straight down over the chest, jog in at the stomach and out at the hips, down the leg (outside knee) and out the second toe.

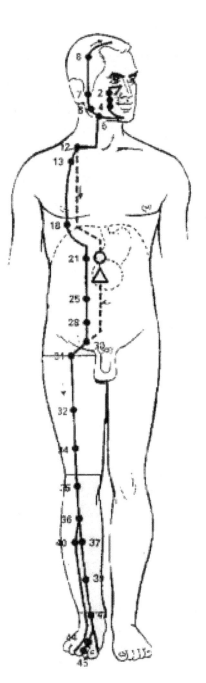

Spleen Meridian

Location: Begins on the middle border of the big toe, ascends through the leg, thigh, abdomen, and lateral border of the axilla (inner legs, groin, and ribs).

Alarm Point: Liver 13, just anterior to tip of 11th rib (the first floating rib).

Time most active: 10 am

Related Muscle: Latissimus Dorsi.

Related Glands: Pancreas.

Chakra: Spleen, navel.

Emotion: Feeling inadequate.

Element: Earth.

Polarity: Yin.

Illnesses and Effects: Appetite imbalances, belching, weight problems, diarrhea, lymphatic congestion, abdominal pain, dysentery, menstrual difficulties, nausea. Leg, knee and thigh pain, palpitations, adrenals, groin area, organs, menstruation, pancreas.

Lesson: Sympathy, reflection.

Healing Color: Orange, yellow.

Healing Smells: Mint or sweet.

Affirmation Words: Faith, confidence.

Meridian Massage: Start on the outside tip of the big toe (medial side) go up the inside of the leg, veering to the outside of the chest and up to the arm crease.

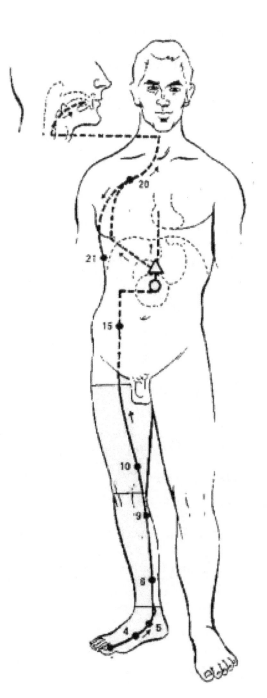

Heart Meridian

Location: Starts at the arm pit and descends down the middle border of the arm, ending at the little finger of the hand.

Alarm Point: Central 14, level with the nipples.

Time most active: 11 am - 1 pm

Related Muscle: Subscapularis.

Related Gland: Thymus.

Chakra: Heart.

Emotion: Joy.

Element: Fire (acute).

Polarity: Yin.

Illnesses and Effects: Chest pains, palpitations, insomnia, hysteria, pain, sweating, heart, impatience, cruelty, inner joy, speech, shoulder, circulation, tongue.

Lessons: Release sadness, calling in joy.

Healing Colors: Pink, rose, green.

Healing Smells: Rose, attar of roses.

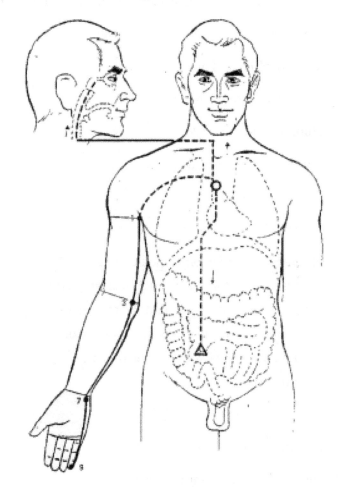

Affirmation words: Forgiveness, compassion, receive.

Meridian Massage: Start at the armpit, go straight down the inside of the arm, over the palm and out to the inside of the little finger.

Small Intestine Meridian

Location: From the little finger of the hand, up the outer border of the arm, with a zigzag across the shoulders, neck and up the face.

Alarm Point: Central 4 - divide distance between Central 3 and umbilicus with two equidistant points. Central 4 is the first point above Central 3.

Time most active: 2 pm

Related Muscle: Quadriceps.

Related Glands: Adrenals.

Chakra: Root.

Emotion: Loneliness.

Element: Fire.

Polarity: Yin.

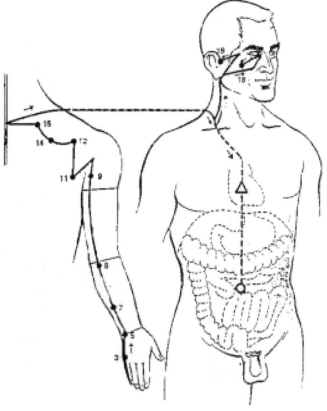

Illnesses and Effects: Intestines, ear problems, digestive difficulties, Crohns disease, arm pain shoulders, speech, diarrhea, hearing difficulties, ear aches, tinnitus, tonsillitis, deafness, sore throat.

Lesson: Release.

Healing Colors: Red & blue.

Healing Smells: Bitter fragrances.

Affirmation Words: Joy, assimilation, honor, boundaries.

Meridian Massage: Start at the outside tip of the little finger, go up the back side of the arm to the back, trace the edge of the shoulder blade, then go up the side of the neck to the earlobe, over the cheek and then back to the ear.

Bladder Meridian

Location: Begins in the middle of the eye, rises over the head and descends vertically down the back to the coccyx, then down from the scapula to the buttocks, continuing down the thighs and ending at the little toe.

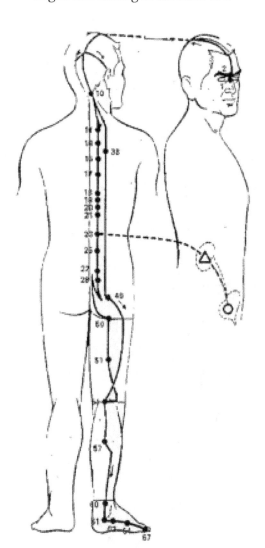

Alarm Point: Central 3 - just above the pubic bone.

Time most active: 4 pm

Related Muscle: Peronus

Related Glands: Adrenals

Chakra: Root

Emotion: Shame

Element: Water

Polarity: Yang

Illnesses and Effects: Spasms, headache, muscle problems, neck pain, sciatica. Bladder infections, hearing, eyesight, neck, back of legs, buttocks, painful urination, kidney, spinal, low back pain, foot and leg pain

Lessons: Fear, anger

Healing Colors: Earth tones

Healing Smells: Lavender.

Affirmation words: Harmony, peace, flowing, release fear, anger.

Meridian Massage: Start at the inner corner of the eyes. Move up, over the head, down the back alongside the spine and around the curve of the gluteus maximums. Start again at the neck, go out to mid-shoulder, down the back and back of leg, behind the ankle bone and out to the little toe.

Kidney Meridian

Location: Starts from the sole of the foot and ascends along the lateral aspect of the leg, through the thigh, to the abdomen, then to the sternum, and ends at the clavicle area.

Alarm Point: Gall bladder 24, just below the joining of the 9th rib and coastal border.

Time most active: 6 pm.

Related Muscle: Psoas.

Related Gland: Adrenals.

Chakra: Navel.

Emotion: Fear (fear of feeling).

Element: Water.

Polarity: Yin.

Illnesses and Effects: Cold, hypersensitivity, ear problems, neck pain, headaches, soles of feet pain, menstrual problems. Gentleness, bones, feet, inner legs, groin, diaphragm.

Lesson: Release of fear issues, will to live.

Healing Colors: Blue, orange.

Healing Smells: Mint, orange.

Affirmation Words: Energy, vibrant, free will, release fear, gentleness.

Meridian Massage: Start on the ball of the foot, go up the arch and just back of the ankle bone, loop back on the inside of the heel, continue straight up the inside of the leg, up the chest right next to the midline, to the inner end of the collarbone.

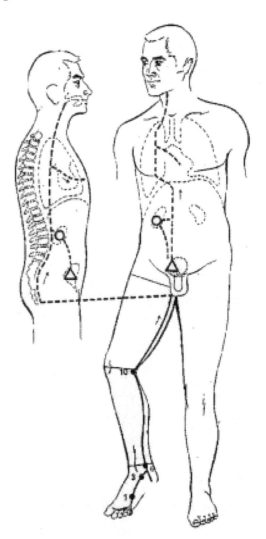

Circulation Sex Meridian

Location: Starts near the axilla, descends to the anterior aspect of the arm, and ends at the tip of the middle finger.

Alarm Point: Central 17, the tip of the xiphoid process below the sternum.

Time most active: 8 pm.

Related Muscle: Gluteus Mediums.

Related Gland: Thymus.

Chakra: Heart.

Emotions: Trust and hope. Protects the heart.

Element: Fire (acute).

Polarity: Yin.

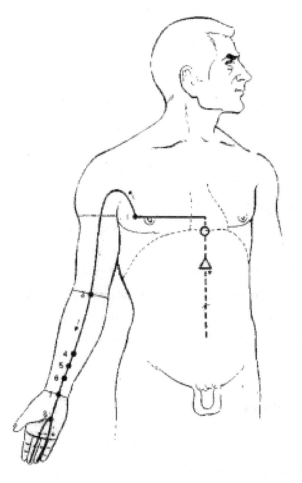

Illnesses and Effects: Arm and elbow stiffness, chest distended, eyes dull, heart discomfort, chest, dry mouth, lung congestion, lower back, hip pain, incontinence, knee and ankle pain, foot pain, hemorrhoids, hernia growth, angina, drowsiness, coughing, tremors.

Lessons: Integration.

Meridian Massage: Start just outside the nipples and go up around the arm crease, down the middle of the inside of the arm and out to the middle finger.

Triple Warmer Meridian

Location: Starts at the ring finger, ascends along the outer surface of the arm to the lateral border of the neck, around the ears and ends at the edge of the eyebrow.

Alarm Point: Central 5, the next point from central 4.

Time most active: 10 pm.

Related Muscle: Teres Minor.

Related Glands: Thyroid.

Chakra: Heart.

Emotions: Joy.

Element: Fire.

Polarity: Yang.

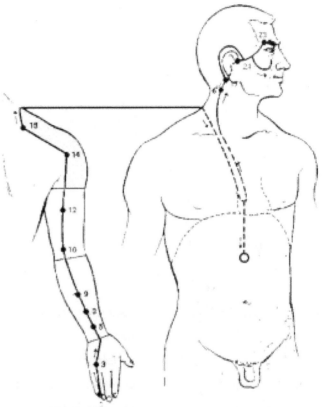

Illnesses and Effects: Colds and fevers, ear problems, pain behind eye, mental confusion, perspiration for no reason, lack of energy. Circulation problems, ears, cold hands and feet, jaw pain, shoulder, arm, chronic fatigue, immune deficiency, menstrual irregularities, eye problems, temples, face and head.

Lesson: Utilization, transformation.

Healing Color: Orange-red.

Affirmation Words: Circulate, communication, clarity, energetic.

Meridian Massage: Start at the ring finger, ascend along the outer surface of the arm to the lateral border of the neck, around the ears and end at the edge of the eyebrow.

Gall Bladder Meridian

Location: Starts at the lateral border of the eye, travels the parietal and temporal region of the head, descends along the side of the chest, loin and thigh to the foot, ending near the fourth toe.

Alarm Point: Gall bladder 24, just below the joining of the 9th rib and coastal border

Time most active: Midnight.

Related Muscle: Anterior deltoid.

Related Gland: Pancreas.

Chakra: Solar Plexus.

Emotion: Resentment.

Element: Wood.

Polarity: Yang.

Illnesses and Effects: Gall bladder, brain, sight, organs, body parts on side of body, gallstones, hearing difficulties, eye problems, joint pain. Stagnation of food, headaches, hepatitis, common cold, infection, vision, colds. Transports pure liquid exclusively and then stores it until it becomes bile. Weakness results in intolerance of fatty foods which require bile for digestion, causing lower leg, ankle, hip and joint pain.

Lesson: Anger, decisions, proper expression of will.

Healing Color: Green.

Healing Smells: Sour fragrances.

Affirmation Words: Choices, clarity, empowerment, will.

Meridian Massage: Start at the outer corner of the eye, to the ear, then loop up and forward, coming down and back behind the ear. Return to the frontal eminences, then go down the back of the head, behind the shoulder, forward on the ribs, half-circle backwards to the waist, forward on the hip, then down the side of the leg and out the fourth toe.

Liver Meridian

Location: Begins with the big toe, ascend through the foot and inner side of the leg and abdomen, ending in the mid-thorax at the beginning point of the lung meridian.

Alarm Point: Liver 14, where the plumb line from the nipple crosses the coastal border of the rib cage.

Time most active: 1-3 am.

Related Muscle: Pectoralis Major Sternal.

Related Gland: Pancreas.

Chakra: Solar Plexus.

Emotion: Depression and anger, willpower.

Element: Wood (letting go).

Polarity: Yin.

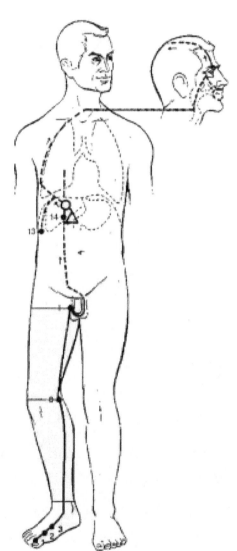

Illnesses and Effects: Allergies, bruising easily, dizziness, eye problems, indigestion, gas, premenstrual tension. Liver problems, anger, kindness, proper expression of willpower, abdominal pain, irregular menstruation, lump in throat, back and rib pain, knee problems, skin problems, arthritis.

Lesson: Letting go of anger.

Healing Color: Green, blue-green.

Healing Smells: Sage, carnation.

Affirmation Words: Anger, acceptance, happy, cheerful, abundance.

Meridian Massage: Start on the inside (lateral side) of the big toe next to the second toe. Forward on the edge of the ribs about halfway to the center.

Lung Meridian

Location: Anterior aspect of the arm and forearm, ending near the thumbs (chest, inner arm and thumb tip).

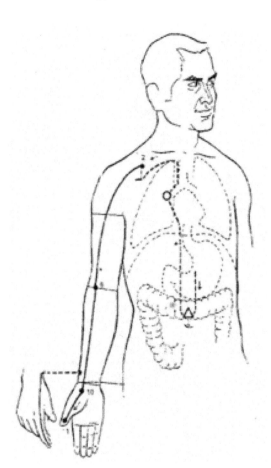

Alarm Point: Lung 1, the beginning of the Lung Meridian.

Time most active: 9 am

Related Muscle: Anterior Serratus.

Related Gland: Thyroid.

Chakra: Throat.

Emotion: Grief.

Element: Metal (insight).

Polarity: Yin.

Illnesses and Effects: Sweating, diarrhea, constipation, colitis, shoulder, elbow pain, chronic cough, chest, breathing, sore throat, asthma, bronchitis.

Lesson: Letting go.

Healing Colors: White and blue.

Healing Smells: Pungent smells.

Affirmation Words: Humble, tolerant, modest, release grief, breath, open, expand, accept, receive, letting go.

Meridian Massage: Start on the upper chest just outside the shoulders, down the inside of the top of the arm, through the palm to the thumb.

Large Intestine Meridian

Location: From the index finger, along the outer arm to the shoulder, the lateral border of the neck, and up to the bottom corner of the nose (outer arms, teeth, sinuses).

Alarm Point: Stomach 25, on the stomach meridian, level with the umbilicus.

Time most active: 6 am

Related Muscle: Fascia Lata.

Related Glands: Testes and ovaries.

Emotion: Over-critical, letting go.

Element: Metal.

Polarity: Yang.

Illnesses and Effects: Irritable bowel, intestines, sinuses, teeth, digestion, sense of smell, nose, arm, shoulder pain, neck swelling, nose bleed, throat sore, toothache, constipation, diarrhea.

Lessons: Letting go, accepting, assimilation.

Healing Colors: White and yellow.

Healing Smells: Clove.

Affirmation Words: Worthy, release, letting go, accepting.

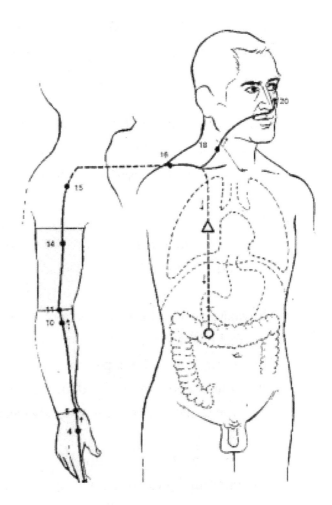

Meridian Massage: From the top of the index finger go up the outside top of the arm, over the shoulder, to the front of the neck. Continue up to the corner of the mouth, under the base of the nose and end at the crease next to the flare of the nose.

Parashakti

Para means divine, Shakti means energy. Parashakti is the study of accessing divine energy for the healing and alignment of the body, mind and spirit.

The vital energy resides deep within each of us, in our heart center, and nourishes our physical, emotional, mental and spiritual aspects. Experiences both good and bad have an effect on all these parts of us and, over the years, can wear down the source of vital force.

Periodic renewal is essential to well-being and the maintenance of health. When the vital force flows through the energetic channels without hindrance, the body, mind and spirit enjoy balance and health.

Revitalization begins when we look honestly and deeply at what the stress we feel might teach us. Learning to avail ourselves of the lessons that life brings can loosen the grip of unresolved memory and enable the energy to flow unimpeded. In the freedom that follows, the unified body-mind can face the challenges of life without dwelling on the encumbrances of the past.

Surrender to the divine nature in quiet moments of observation and accept the opportunity to understand the meaning of all challenges. The healing process begins in this stillness within. Listening, we meet our Innermost Self in its perfection.

Study Questions

1. Describe the function of the Etheric, Emotional, Mental and Intuitive Fields.

2. What is the Kama-Manasic Web (mind and emotions) and how does it affect our overall well-being?

3. Describe the energy pathways of the body and their functions.

4. What is the Antahkarana or Bridge of Light?

5. Explain the term Kundalini Shakti and its relationship to awakening consciousness.

6. Discuss the chakras and why they are the keys to awakening.

7. Explain the significance of the heart chakra awakening.

8. Summarize why meridian health is essential to maintaining a strong life essence.

9. Write your understanding of the significance of the life breath in relationship to health on all levels.

Playfully, you hid from me
All day I looked,
Then I discovered
I was Joy,
and the celebration of That
began

   Lalla - Naked Song
   By Coleman Barks

Part Two
Energy Field Awakening

"Lost in the wilderness
between true awareness and the senses
I suddenly woke inside myself,
like a lotus opening in waterweeds."

Lalla — Naked Song
By Coleman Barks

In the Light of calm
and steady self-awareness
inner energies wake up and work miracles
without any effort on your part.
~Sri Nisargadatte Maharshi

The Background of Kinesiology

The word Kinesiology comes from the Greek word kinesis, which means movement. Applied Kinesiology was developed by a chiropractor, Dr. George Goodheart, in 1964. His discovery was based on the premise that body language never lies. Muscles in the body can be used as indicators of body language, a diagnostic art to inquire about the state of health chemically, structurally, etherically, emotionally, mentally or spiritually. This assessment procedure was christened Applied Kinesiology, commonly called muscle testing. There are several branches of Applied Kinesiology; the *Life Essence Awakening Process, (LEAP)* focuses on one that has impacted many lay people and professional healers, Touch for Health.

Dr. John Thie, president of the International College of Applied Kinesiology, founded by Dr. George Goodheart, began giving his patients self-care work to do at home. This work made such an impact on people's health that Dr. Thie wrote a book for lay people and health practitioners to use with their clients. That book, *Touch for Health*, has gained worldwide recognition and become a health care practice that offers preventative health maintenance and in-depth balancing procedures for optimal well being.

Life Essence Analysis

Life Essence Analysis is a process that uses muscle testing and/or pendulums to dialogue with the soul, or higher self, about the condition of the energy system, subtle bodies and planes of consciousness. This energetic assessment reveals the priority healing pathways that support the whole system: the physical, etheric, emotional, mental, and spiritual fields. The process also identifies what the soul requires for resolution and a return to optimal health.

The Emotional, Mental or Spiritual Causes of Imbalances

Many kinds of imbalances can occur in the energy fields. The energy balancing procedure offered in the *Life Essence Awakening Process (LEAP)* is not a substitute for proper medical care. The purpose of this work is to free blocked energy in the fields so that it is possible to reach a higher level of functioning. When the energy fields are all working in harmony the vital force is strong. When, on the other hand, one of the fields such as the emotional field or mental field is not in agreement with the intention for healing and wholeness, it hampers the achievement of long lasting results and optimal health.

LEAP is founded on the premise that all beings have a life intention, purpose or soul's goal. During a session spiritual guidance assists in discovering the soul's goal. We use testing methods that access information from the chakras, the files that hold information about our soul's lessons. As we journey through the lessons of the chakras we can uncover our spiritual gifts and life goals.

Through kinesiology testing we can determine what part of the being is blocked and unable to receive the gift of fulfillment of the soul's goal. Once this is clear a sacred dialogue occurs between the part of us that is opposed to the fulfillment of our life purpose, and the part that is reaching for the highest potential. The aspect of our nature that is resistant to attainment of the life purpose could be called the *Energy Culprit*. This deviation of the energy field wants to spiral down to lower vibrations and feed off the sorrow created from emotional pain and suffering.

The etheric field functions to protect us from toxic debris of a physical, emotional or mental origin. To prevent imbalances from entering the system, this web around the physical must remain intact, strong and impenetrable. If weakened by toxins or emotional or mental stress, it allows a vulnerability to negative energy that often results in a breakdown of our system. Keeping our energy strong requires developing an awareness of our spirit nature and listening to its guidance. Our lives can be very fragile; at times we weaken under outside stresses and are damaged by memories of the past. As we identify with life's passing sorrows, our soul light withdraws and we lose vitality and optimism. This drains emotional energy, leaving the physical body susceptible to illness and creating confusion in our mental field. To effectively regain and maintain health we must learn to revitalize our soul force and call our fragmented selves back to the present moment. This requires breathing in vital energy, surrendering our hold on the past (good or bad) and reenergizing our life goals. The physical body guides us to listen to warning signs such as fatigue or pain, the emotional body asks us to transform and release unresolved emotions, and the mental body calls us to renew our sense of self through the release of our conditioning and self-limiting belief systems. Healing the vital force requires that all aspects of our energy being be in alignment with the light of our soul.

Learning to be responsible for our energy field health, we can understand the cause of energy imbalance and apply the appropriate technique for healing and alignment. When looking for the cause of an imbalance we must look to all areas of the body/mind. For example, when our physical body is experiencing symptoms we must not only observe our physical condition but look to the emotional and mental component to discover the causative factors. The art of observing our whole being is the key to long lasting healing.

Most imbalances stem from carrying frozen traumatic memories in our energy fields. Through developing awareness we learn to observe how our wounded past is repeated in our lives. We often attract relationships that have the same factors as those that originally damaged us. These repetitions have much to teach us. It is also possible to see our life patterns manifesting through our children, our work and all aspects of life. Our patterns can often be traced back into the roots of our existence creating a map by which we can transform our lives. These roots are tied to the conditioning of our ancestors. It is possible to heal all patterns of illness and conditioning by seeing the original error in misidentification. Awareness can lead us to freedom of being and return us to the wholeness of our authentic self. When we deepen our heart's compassion and begin the healing process in our life, it will radiate light to our relationships and our family and will act as preventative medicine for our future. The miracle of life is that we have the ability to instantly transform unresolved emotions from the past by seeing their core cause. Although the past may hold stories of untold suffering, we can bring these stories into a new light and reframe them by learning what gifts they have brought to us. Like the fertile ground of our gardens, the events of our past experiences can be used beautifully to prepare our life for new and positive growth.

Intentional Evolution

LEAP offers assistance in finding the life aspiration inherent in our human nature. Our goals are simply a search for happiness, a search that ends with the connection to the soul's purpose and discovery of the path of joy.

When you set out to follow your joy, you tap into the secret chamber of the heart, the Anakanda Lotus, the celestial wishing tree that holds the deepest desires of the heart. The heart's aspiration is the guiding light of your path. The saying "follow your heart" is so very true when it comes to being healthy, happy and holy on all levels. Physical, mental and emotional health are all linked to this path and many times it is not until this heart's path and desire is revealed that one is finally able to achieve health and well-being. This is demonstrated in an accelerated manner when a person hits bottom and then makes a breakthrough that shifts their identity, their mode of life and even their spiritual attunement, allowing them to make a miraculous recovery.

Our life force moves through phases of soul lessons that offer the opportunity to open to receive and deepen our wisdom. Each chakra that opens and is transformed brings more soul energy and a greater possibility of a vital life. Becoming aware of unhealthy and healthy patterns, we observe the part of ourselves that wants to move ahead or rise upward, saying "yes" to life. At the same time we also see the part that does not move, or says "no" to life. Often a crisis develops because of these opposing forces and within this crisis, illness can take root. Some aspects of our being are magnetically attracted to the downward spiral of life. Fortunately these aspects can be trained to move upward with the aspect of our being that yearns to evolve in consciousness.

LEAP healing discovers the root cause of an imbalance by using kinesiology to evaluate the etheric, emotional, mental and spiritual energy fields. Learning to tap the source of all healing and direct it to the energy field requires attention. If we need to forgive something in our past, we can access the healing light for assistance in the forgiveness process. If we need to change a certain belief or mental conditioning, we can create a new life affirmation or living prayer and energize it with our healing light. Understanding the healing process is simple but requires receptivity to the healing force. The healing light is supported by prayer, humility and a willingness to receive.

We are Vibrational Beings

Everything is energy. We are energy beings that bring in and discharge energy in the great recycling system called Life. Our energy flows as part of the natural process of life, from observing nature and learning from her rhythms. Nature teaches us how to release, how to die, how to be reborn, how to blossom in beauty and how to let go again. It teaches us about stillness, movement, energy, light, dark, cold and hot. It teaches us about fire, wind, earth and water. These elements all reside in our body and express themselves energetically. Nature always leads us back to a feeling of equilibrium and calm. Because we are energy beings, we have the opportunity to see with our sixth sense and trust that inner vision. We can also learn to see where we need energy protection and to ward off negative forces.

Our delicate etheric energies need protection from illness-producing forces. Though in time we are all subject to the simple processes of life, we can become the caretaker of our souls and work with our energy fields to create harmony, peace, good will and service in this lifetime. Saying yes to life means saying yes to good health, to positive thoughts and positive emotions. Saying yes means eliminating fear and negative thinking from our energy fields. We all have access to a great method to attain energy wellness, the source of all healing. The source is accessed through our willingness to receive our prayers, our breath, and great humility. Breathing healing light into our energy fields opens the path to the miracle of life itself. This source, when consciously applied to any area of imbalance, brings us the miracle of healing.

To spirit, getting is meaningless and giving is all.
- A Course in Miracles, T,67

The Art of Energy Balancing

A current of electromagnetic energy travels through our body, mind and spirit, giving us our life direction, life essence and life vitality. When energy is in balance there is a free flow of our *life essence*. Each energy field functions optimally at a balanced frequency, an energy equilibrium. With energy balanced in the etheric, emotional, mental and spiritual energy fields, health follows.

The frequency at which we resonate depends upon how we function on the etheric, emotional, mental and spiritual fields. The *LEAP* testing process measures each energy field and if any is deficient or over-energized the appropriate treatment can be applied. The balancing procedure literally frees up blocked energy, enabling the system to use all available energy.

Awakening the Vital Force

The Etheric Energy Field

The etheric blueprint duplicates the physical body and when weakened shows signs of stress. Etheric energy imbalances are a result of stress on some level, of ignoring warning signs such as fatigue, loss of energy, depression and pain. When we listen to the body we can detect imbalances before they manifest as illness. We can learn to sense our internal messages and follow what the body is requiring for its sustenance. When the body speaks to us in the form of pain or discomfort, we become its most cherished caretaker. Honoring its messages and yielding to its direction brings balance to all aspects of our being. Through this listening we learn to apply the healing force of love to our life, observing the root cause of the imbalance. For this we must be honest about our thinking habits, our emotional expressions and our connection with nature and the divine in life. If we are diligent we can usually trace a physical symptom back to an emotional experience or a time of negative thinking. We can also observe when life is calling for communion with nature and the silence of our divine self.

Our life essence enters through the chakras, and then flows into the nadis and meridians, nourishing the energy fields. Since the etheric energy is the blueprint of the physical it is important to keep it strong and free from disturbances and energy blocks.

LEAP uses kinesiology to locate energy blocks in the etheric field. This is accomplished through testing the overall life force of the etheric field by measuring the frequency of the meridians, chakras, aura, and endocrine glands. After the frequency is determined, specific energetic revitalization treatments are offered to bring the energy up to optimal levels. It is important to understand the messages of the body/mind system and make needed adjustments. The etheric field is a bridge that relays information from the emotional and mental fields to the physical. Any emotional disturbance is very likely to impose some level of stress or pain on the body. If there is continual unresolved emotional or mental field disturbance it can eventually create disease in the physical body. The universal energy, functioning as life breath, or Prana, is received and distributed throughout the entire body. When Prana is distributed freely throughout the etheric and released freely, the energy fields stay in harmony and balance.

LEAP offers balancing procedures, breathing techniques and a complete guide to Vibrational Medicine and Energy Field Self Care. Learn the kinesiology procedures offered in this book and use them to become more empowered in your health care of body, mind and spirit.

Awakening Mind and Emotions

The Emotional Field

In the emotional field, imbalances usually begin during periods of emotional stress when we are not allowing emotions to flow through and out of the body. When anger, for example, is suppressed time and time again, it often turns into depression, which can lead to a weakened system. On the other hand, continuous expression of strong anger can break down the internal organs and open the body to disease and disharmony. Healthy anger is merely a call to speak our truth at the appropriate moment with ease and honesty, but anger that is rooted in fear is a reflection of our disharmony with divine energies. Transcend this kind of anger by increasing the vibration of love.

Emotions are a gift to understand others and ourselves. From them we learn the art of listening to the voice of the heart. This requires energy and freedom from past emotions that color our experience of life in the *now*. When emotions accumulate from the past they become lodged in the aura, waiting for new experiences to assist in their release. Because of these past emotions it becomes difficult to live in the *now*. To be well emotionally we must learn to let go, die to the past and release all past trauma. This means we must consciously surrender our attachment to memory, give all to the sacred fire of life and begin to fully live in the present.

The Mental Field

In the mental field, imbalances begin when the mind is not used constructively. The mind is like a piece of clay and needs to be molded and refined to become the most useful tool. When the mind is not directed properly, it is open to negative thinking habits that can result in illness and disharmony. The mind, when quiet, can be an instrument of beauty, perceiving spiritual truths of the universe. Through the quiet mind we have access to our higher nature which holds the healing light of love, wisdom and compassion. The mind, when allowed to run unguided, expresses thoughts of a lower nature, directing the emotional level to anger, greed, desire, attachment, fear, envy and so forth. When the mind is used as a witnessing tool, it is of great service on our journey, assisting us to stay centered, still and well-balanced through life's changes. When the mind is mastered, unwanted thoughts no longer dictate our actions and the attention turns from outward things back to the silence of the heart.

The Kama-Manasic Web

LEAP for the emotional and mental fields offers a method for uncovering blocks that impede energy flow.

The inner energy fields of the etheric, emotional, mental and spiritual bodies radiate out in the aura like a spectrum of rainbow light. When the energy is free from disturbances, the aura is luminous with light, beauty and aspiration.

The school of life brings many tests and lessons so you can grow into your full potential as a *Light Being*. Awakening to your true potential invites you to let go of areas in your life that hold a false sense of self through misidentification. You realize that you are not just your body, mind and emotions, and begin the search for deeper answers as to the nature of your true self.

Your emotions and thoughts influence your energy frequency. When you feel and think in ways that support your health and well-being, your energy frequency vibrates at a higher level. When you feel and think in ways that are not supportive to your health and well being, your frequency is at a lower level. The conscious raising of your vibration serves to maintain your health on all levels.

In Eastern teachings, Kama-Manasic is the word used to describe the web of mind and emotions. When there are unresolved emotional and mental patterns, it becomes frozen energy in the field, creating a web that is often difficult to overcome. This frozen energy produces a deficiency in the flow of your life force and eventually could affect your health.

LEAP is a kinesiology testing method that helps you to identify disturbed patterns in the energy fields and offers techniques for releasing them as well as guidance on the path of true healing and transformation. Now we begin the journey of unraveling the false energy structures in our life through accessing the hidden files of our shadow self.

Unveiling What You Are Not – Recovering What You Are

Wouldn't it be refreshing to just feel brand new, unburdened by impressions and memories of the past? Your life is a flower; and your true essence is within the core of your flower. Each petal represents your experience in life. The true essence of you is found in the core.

Life can be understood as a long journey in which you start out with an empty suitcase and, through time, the suitcase becomes full of the content of your experiences. These experiences form your identity as a personality but deep inside there is something alive that is not affected or changed through your experiences. This first step in awakening is to realize you cannot be defined through the accumulation of your experiences, your image, or through any means found in the outer world.

Throughout your life there are many tests and lessons, or cause and effect, which are your karmic condition. The condition of your karma directly relates to your actions from the past; each action plants a seed of a new life possibility. That is why it is most important to see your life as a karma bank account, where you invest the right energy for the right results. Each lesson of your karmic condition offers you the choice to let go of aspects of your being that are no longer functioning for your higher good. Each lesson holds a hidden gift in the transformation process that aligns you with your higher purpose such as living in truth, compassion, awareness. Your path of awakening guides you to release obstacles to your inner gifts and reclaim your birthright of freedom.

Looking inward leads you to the realization that your sense of self is not confined or defined by your identification with body, mind or emotions. The deeper you inquire about what you are not the closer you come to meeting your authentic self. As you surrender to what is no longer true, you embark upon the mysterious, sacred path of life. Your precious life is an opportunity to live in awakening communion with the source of your life, opening, flowering and meeting the truth of your being. Realizing that you can no longer define who you are through any conditioning, you seek to open the door to the eternal mysterious flow of life.

Your path leads you to the inner chamber of your heart, where you hold the compassion and forgiveness for your errors that were born in ignorance. Your scripts, your story and the stories of others, and all your relationships around the stories, are released and you take a deep breath of freedom and well-being.

In this very moment you can see that the story cannot thrive without the belief in it and all of its contents. So, you begin the process of embracing the truth of yourself now, releasing your past and truly loving the freshness and newness of your most precious life. Your true joy comes through the simple path of letting go, welcoming the flowering of your soul. This miraculous opening occurs when you journey to the unknown places of your being, the spaces that are free from the content of the past and the accumulated identification with false images of the self.

Transformation of Spiritual Fear into Spiritual Love

Your life intentions and goals create a path of ascension or upward striving through seeing and knowing your true purpose in life. Your true purpose is to evolve in love. Through working with a life goal or healing intention the focus is on co-creating with life the true desires of your heart. To begin the healing process there must be a calming of thoughts that project into the future, and an establishment of faith in divine grace. The action of trusting in divine grace makes it possible to eliminate fear from the body.

Fear is twofold. One aspect comes from imminent danger, a natural warning to yield, or make the changes necessary for survival or protection. The second aspect, spiritual fear, stems from feeling separate from the source of love, a feeling of going against the stream of life. The emotion of fear is held in the body in the form of memories, shocks, losses, suffering and personal tragedy. Life is full of painful memories, a sense of victim consciousness and endless searching for the reasons things have happened the way they have.

Buddha suggests that the first premise of the four noble truths, the first step to becoming awakened, is the importance of seeing that suffering exists. From this premise you can see that within your life and the lives of your loved ones, your children, your ancestors and the whole world, suffering exists. Life is a school of deep soul lessons, a school of hard knocks.

The third premise is that, after understanding the cause, you can do something about it and the guidelines are found in the Eight-Fold Path of Right Seeing, Right Intention, Right Speech, Right Action, Right Livelihood, Right Effort, Right Mindfulness, and Right Attention. (See the Self-care Manual for more information on the Eight-Fold Path.)

Through *LEAP* we gently lead participants to uncover the seeds of suffering and take responsibility for becoming a Light Being. It takes courage and strength to look within, discern the origin of fear and trace it back to its source. When you become a Light Being, you align your energies with the light and live according to its guidance.

Facing the Shadow Self

The shadow aspect of our energy field, also called the *Energy Culprit*, often expresses through resisting right or corrective action of the moment. This is the part of us that holds back in subtle disagreement with our intention for healing and wholeness. The deeper the conflict between that part of us that is unaware and drawn to perpetuating suffering, and the part of us that has the intention to evolve, the more spiritual crisis we might experience. The ascension toward the light requires that we let go of our baggage so we can travel freely without heavy burdens. The ascension process takes us deep into the heart where our sacred presence heals all sense of separation. The shadow part of us creates suffering from holding onto a separate sense of self that has its roots in the past. When we begin to take responsibility for the light of our being, we simply bring the shadow into the light. With great compassion, the negative and self-limiting aspects of the shadow are infused with this great healing light.

In the *Life Essence Awakening Process,* the chakras are investigated deeply. You learn to analyze which chakra holds unresolved emotions or belief systems that prevent you from realizing your true nature. Each chakra holds the potential of divine flowering and the seeds of suffering that keep you from this flowering.

The **Root Chakra** holds the shadow aspect of our being that relates to unresolved fears, family, ancestral karma and security issues.

The **Navel Chakra** holds the shadow aspect of our being that relates to our sense of self, our feelings of shame, relationships, finances and physical creativity.

The **Solar Plexus Chakra** holds the shadow aspect of ourself regarding our power issues, our judgment and opinions, our self-esteem and taking responsibility for ourself.

The **Heart Chakra** holds the shadow aspect of us regarding overconcern for others, codependency, lack of self-love and compassion and deep feelings of loneliness.

The **Throat Chakra** holds the shadow aspect of self regarding our inability to tell the truth, our lack of silence, and how we express truth and the right use of will.

The **Third Eye Chakra** holds the essence of the shadow in our inability to perceive things, thinking in terms of duality and our lack of inner vision and trusting in our intuition.

The **Crown Chakra** holds the shadow aspect in our inability to integrate life experiences and bring the energy from each chakra up to a higher vibration. The crown chakra also reflects our ability to receive divine grace, release our inner obstacles and open to our God-Self.

LEAP assists you in identifying areas of the shadow self. The work uncovers hidden patterns in the emotional and mental fields and, with the intention of freedom and well-being, they are released. As you bring forth new intentions, the universe supports and co-creates with you to bring about radical change and the evolution of love.

Conscious Choices and Healing Intentions

The Life Essence Awakening Process sees that energy follows thought; our clear intentions and conscious choices pave the way of our life. Through realizing the deepest desire of our heart, the energy of the universe supports our endeavor with mind and heart in agreement.

The foundation in which we dream, live our life and believe in our life comes from our inner sense of self. We have the choice in the essence of life to dream consciously, creating dreams that offer the most happiness and peace to our world. Our self-esteem is perhaps the most important area of our life to nurture and protect as it is the ground of being from which all acts spring. We have the choice to return to our original authentic self and discover what life means to us, without the conditioning of the past. The core conditioning and programming that creates self-limiting beliefs and emotional responses stem from our sense of unworthiness that is rooted in our past conditioning. This core programming is released through conscious choice and healing intentions.

To begin our life healing and transformation process, we must reconstruct the ground of our being. Breathing in, we reaffirm that life is safe, abundant, and secure and all our needs are met. We teach our inner precious being to believe and trust in the goodness of life, the flowering of life. We see that our inner garden of spiritual gifts is full of living potentials and we become a willing participant in letting go of ideas, concepts, beliefs, and conditioning that are not in harmony with our inner flowering.

The path of life teaches us how to trust in ourself. We learn from the ascending path that life brings many lessons. This inner classroom teaches us to witness the roots of our sorrow, see the lessons, receive the gifts and release the energy of the lesson for the higher good. The *Energy Culprit*, as discussed previously, is the part of us that is not in agreement with the power we have to create our own reality of positive energy and abundance.

When we pay attention to the *Energy Culprit*, the self-defeating part of our life, we increase its power. We learn to create the life we want from believing in the fullness of life, not the lack. Each moment is an opportunity to live responsibly toward our soul and learn to respond to the teachings of the moment, living according to its divine messages. Daily we are given the opportunity to meet the challenges of our self-limiting belief systems and open ourselves to our endless opportunity to co-create with this most blessed universe.

Our life path offers glimpses of our joy, what truly brings happiness and peace. Opening, surrendering and reaching for our potential, we may find our greatest joy in service to others who are suffering. Being true to our inner self is perhaps the most important part of service, for it helps others in finding and being true to their path. This truth is the raising of consciousness into the light, for the good of all concerned and the fruits are unconditional joy.

Living with clear intentions and healing aspirations allows the energy to focus in a channel of ascension, a path in which to travel through all the obstacles to reach our full potential. When the mind and emotions are in harmony and reaching for a higher good or our soul's purpose, the universe supports this evolution of love. When self-limiting thoughts, fear and self-centered desires are at the root of our life intention, the universe vibrates at a much lower frequency. This creates a display of self-limiting experiences in our life that reflect our fear based thinking. Thoughts and emotions directed toward upholding and striving for goodness, beauty and light create higher frequencies that allow for divine action in our life.

The soul holds the truest and deepest desires of our heart. These are usually spiritual aspirations that reflect the light of our soul, and are the foundation in which life manifests. Creating a life goal comes from the foundation that you believe you can reach and attain your full potential, a positive attitude being the first building block.

Through seeing that the highest good is always manifesting in our life, we can reconnect with our sense of trust and affirm that there has always been a presence operating and witnessing our life. Paying attention to our inner being is most essential, seeing the pure witness consciousness that has been present throughout all our life changes. Deep inside we embrace and commune with the eternal unchanging aspect of our being. We connect the threads of our life and see a most beautiful tapestry of love and protection, affirming there is a reason for everything.

The mind of light generates thoughts that support the upward movement of the soul evolving in love. All thoughts bear seeds that burrow into our energy fields and are fed by emotions and the belief in them, and then are reinforced by further thinking. Most self-defeating thoughts have their roots in fear and need to be infused with the light of spiritual energy. We must re-establish our faith in our life purpose, a soul goal, healing intention, or conscious choice. Then we embrace the *Energy Culprit*, the part of us that is in a state of fear, and release it to the greater light of our true nature.

The creative force of our evolving soul is empowered through willingness to let it go and let it flow in our lives. We must not be afraid of our inner power to create and manifest life in our fullest visions. We must take the steps needed to let go of self-limiting beliefs that stem from conditioning and embedded patterns. Belief in the unlimited possibilities of being is vital to the path of true empowerment.

The core ingredient for manifesting a life of joy, light, and abundance is clear intention and the ability to release obstacles to this intention. In the *Life Essence Awakening Process*™, kinesiology is used to determine the core emotion, intention, or conscious choice that will bring about true healing and transformation. Testing methods further reveal any obstacles held within the energy fields that prevent you from reaching your goal.

What is not love is always fear, and nothing else.
A Course in Miracles T,302

Awakening Intuition

The Light of the Soul

Soul Kinesiology offers ways to discover the emotional and mental blocks that prevent us from accessing the plane of our soul, the home of our true nature. Through sacred dialogue we communicate with our soul, reaching for what brings us joy and long lasting happiness. Blockages between us and our soul, or intuitive energy field, form in the emotional and mental fields due to negative emotions and belief systems such as fear, anger, doubt, hatred and judgment.

Our highest potential can be discovered in the intuitive plane as we reach beyond the confines of our rational mind into the unknown, mysterious aspects of our being. The Ajna or *Third Eye Chakra* - the center of perception - opens through the evolution of the intuitive plane. An awakened intuitive field gives clear, perceptive thinking that stems from our soul energy. Personality linked with soul expresses true unity and harmony. This integration uses personality as a vehicle for our soul to follow the will of the higher good.

As discussed previously, the Kama-Manasic personality is a web of mind and desire, which brings many challenges to our life. When our desires and thoughts are stilled, we hear the voice of our soul and can surrender to its sacred guidance.

The causal field holds the essence of our true nature and endures all we experience along our path of evolution. This celestial energy field is also known as the Karana Sharia, meaning plane of cause and effect or karma. This plane holds the essence of the seeds of goodness that are extracted from life experiences, our karmic bank account. This plane of consciousness or seed body holds the energy for manifesting our deepest soul desires, aligned for the higher good of all concerned. The focus of thought or idea with attention manifests the secret of our soul power. On this plane the higher mental is expressed through blending mind and love, as wisdom.

Beauty
Let Beauty be your constant ideal.
The beauty of the soul
The beauty of sentiments
The beauty of thoughts
The beauty of the action
The beauty in the work
so that nothing comes out of your hands
which is not an expression of pure and
harmonious beauty.
And the Divine Help shall always be with
you.
                    - The Mother

Life Essence Awakening for the intuitive and spiritual energy fields assists our evolutionary path by opening the channel of our intuition. The spiritual energy fields hold the essence of our soul's evolution in love. Uniting the energy of spirit and matter enhances the power of our soul.

The evolving energy of our personality travels through the tests of the chakras, passing through initiations into higher levels of consciousness. The correct use of will develops the solar plexus chakra and the surrender of our personal power. This surrender opens the gateway of our heart where the power of presence awakens to become our inner guide, leading us to purity of mind and the ability to truly love. This guide teaches us to discern unreal or false aspects of life and to know the real and true aspects. We are lead to the realization that we truly are a light being.

The heart center is related to either the higher or lower mental energy field. When it is related to our lower mental energy field, it functions through self-centered love that is limited and geared toward selfishness. Our higher mental energy field expresses impersonal love that acts unselfishly and unconditionally. The heart chakra, when awakened, transcends the personal seeds of suffering and lives in harmlessness of body, mind and soul. The sacred presence within our heart asks us to release the past and be reborn into the light of our true reality. This inner chamber purifies, awakens and brings peace to our new life. Harmlessness in word, deed and action are the qualities of our new found being where we no longer can live in the consciousness of personality self. We return the mind to the silence of our heart and dissolve all sense of separation. Our hearts beat to a new rhythm, one that is in harmony with our higher calling, the inner beat of the master.

The Heart Initiation is the first initiation of the disciple of truth and it is at this time in the evolution of our soul that we take the *Path of the Lighted Way*. The opening of the heart center awakens the sacred presence within that holds our hand on the journey of ascension. Life changes deeply from living of the world with worldly pursuits to living in the world but not of it, knowing it is a temporary stopover for our traveling souls. Our awakening is supported through our practice of meditation, contemplation, spiritual study and right perception. The foundation of our evolving soul enriches us with the divine qualities of love, wisdom and spiritual will.

The lower vehicles of our personality have been of great service, bringing us to the clear reality of our soul's purpose. We embrace our body, mind and emotions by infusing them with the light of our soul. Our mental body expresses the light through intelligence; our emotional body expresses the light through love and compassion. The spiritual will is the highest aspect of the soul and is the force that guides the lower vehicles in the unification process.

The light of our soul removes the false layers of the personality aspect of our being. This light must be cherished as a sacred possession. We learn to sustain our light by keeping it burning bright through the trials of worldly life. This luminous light is the conscious building block of our inner temple and must be held as a most precious jewel. The light of our soul makes contact through a silent mind and energizes our spiritual will to evolve in consciousness. When our mind, emotions, and soul are in harmony they unite in service to the Brotherhood of Light. This is the collective consciousness that holds the positive intention for unity, harmony and peace for all of mankind.

Opening the Lotus of Our Soul

Within our sacred heart is an ever unfolding divine lotus. Each petal of the lotus represents a moral development that allows the inner nectar to flow. These petals are expressions of our unfolding soul, the eternal timeless blossoming of life. Through the process of birth and death our evolution gradually unfolds along the many stages of individualization or initiation. Meeting our true nature, turning the attention inward to the ever present love within, we can stop the wheel of cause and effect of suffering. In this turning, we must remain devoted to our innermost source of power, the very center of our being.

We have within our reach a current of consciousness that flows from our soul down through the various subtle bodies into our personality consciousness. It is through the strengthening of our soul, our alignment with God and devotion to freedom, that the bridge of light - Antahkarana - to our higher nature is built.

The personality has within its nature desires that are not in harmony with self-realization or God Consciousness. The channel between the personality and the higher consciousness of man must be purified to allow the continuous inflow of divine energy, which brings the gifts of wisdom, power and love. We must recognize that our lower vehicles, which are based on survival, reproduction, desires, self-importance, fear, anger and greed, have directed our way of thinking in an uncontrolled and chaotic manner. Samskaras are scars from our previous lives, creating negative patterns within our subconscious that often dictate the way we feel and think in our present day life. Through realignment with our inner god force, we begin the mastery process of our lower bodies.

To begin this most sacred process of meeting our true nature we must learn the art of looking inward, gradually increasing our divine power and self-control. Meditation, the art of quieting the mind and emotions, can assist in this effort, opening a channel for our soul to pour forth its essence and the personality becomes absorbed in divine consciousness.

Purification of our lower nature opens the channel so that divine energy and soul essence can travel freely through the crown chakra, permeating all aspects of our being. The energy fields of the physical, the emotional and the mental must become willing instruments of the higher self.

One way of becoming an instrument of the higher self is to observe when tendencies are not conducive to this state. Developing our inner consciousness and connection with our divine truth decreases the impact of the emotional and mental bodies. Through deeper awareness of our true nature we begin to discern between that which is temporary and pleasing to the personal self, and that which is pleasing to the higher self, which brings more permanent joy and deepening awareness of our true nature.

When this process begins, it stimulates the Dhyanic consciousness (a state of meditation) on the higher centers in the spiritual plane. The pure consciousness of the divine is, in reality, the consciousness of all beings veiled by the workings of the personal self. The more we realize our true essence, the less we are bound to the aspects of the personal self. When full realization and unity occur, we become whole and radiant beings.

The Path of Initiation

The soul is the developing spark of God, our true essence. It is the immortal spark that is in each one of us, with the attributes of Divine Light, Love and Will. As the soul opens it radiates more and more love energy, developing vehicles of expression to act, feel, think and change into its true nature. Progress of the soul can be achieved through study, meditation, service, actualization, transmutation, transfiguration, and transformation. The Heart Initiation is the first step on the spiritual path where we are no longer subservient to our ego self. The initiation process begins as we let go of the ego and the content of identification that is held in memory. Through this letting go, the opening to our sacred heart occurs and our lives are changed forever.

Immense suffering leads many beings to the point of soul exhaustion and begins the inquiry process into their true nature. Questions appear to these beings such as: Who am I? Why am I here? What is the point? Through questioning, life becomes a daily contemplation as outward life and the ongoing experiences of pain and pleasure lose their appeal.

> *The one wholly true thought*
> *one can hold about the past*
> *is that it is not here.*
> *A Course in Miracles - W,13*

We know intuitively that we are missing something; something is lost or forgotten so we begin the search for the lost sense of self. Through questioning our realities, we see that our life is spent believing in changing appearances, knowing that they are all subject to death. We yearn for something more permanent and long lasting, not knowing that the nature of the true self is the answer to our search. We begin to pursue our inner truth as if we have lost a child along the way. The passion and yearning to meet our true self grows deeper and deeper.

Observation of our inner life is the first step in liberation and enhancing control of the body, emotions and mind. When there is a distinction between the divine self and the ego self, observation occurs to refine our discernment. Through embracing our divine nature within our Sacred Heart, observation is no longer needed. For the nature of the true self is pure awareness, not obtained by any effort. Your pure awareness is found when all seeking stops and you simply turn your outward vision to look within the Sacred Heart for your answers.

Each incarnation begins a new level of consciousness development, as we move through awareness of our physical, emotional and mental natures, to eventually reside in the spiritual plane of our soul. We have had many experiences within our being carrying the seeds from previous lifetimes within each birth, beginning where we left off in our previous learning pattern. These experiences are stored from one life to another in the records of the soul, also called records of nature, or *the Akashic records*.

Our ever-evolving soul has within its essence a spark of the divine that is transmitted into the personality or mental body where it finds its anchor in our sacred heart. The more evolved we are through knowing our true nature, the more divine energy we can transmit from the higher planes of consciousness into the personality. As we remove the sheaths to our true self through surrendering our ego identification to the supreme force of our being, we tap into the plane of our spiritual energy. Awareness of our true nature stops the wheel of suffering, allowing us to return to our home of pure consciousness.

Soul Initiations

In our evolution as souls, we embark upon many tests and initiations on our journey. According to ancient teachings, these initiations come at certain times in our spiritual growth. At the time of the first initiation, the heart center opens, transcending the lower aspects of the self. This transcendence brings a greater light of love and service to our life and we begin to assist the suffering of humanity. Through the first initiation into the Sacred Heart, the love we once had for personal gratification turns in toward the presence of God.

The path unfolds as the yearning to be at peace and rest with our true nature deepens and we begin the unification process with our soul and the personality. This process can bring a major conflict of spiritual forces within when the soul begins to gain control of the personality. The personality, at this point, fights to hold on to its identity, causing an inner battle between these forces. It is through mastery of the personality by the soul that one enters into the first initiation, when the mind is infused with the love of the Sacred Heart.

This **first initiation** is considered the probationary path where we are tested daily regarding our relationship to our spiritual consciousness. The awakening path guides us to turn our mind into our heart of silence.

Some of the experiences one may have during the first initiation are: a great loneliness which leads to facing the test of being alone, detachment from all outer form, discrimination from the real and the unreal and a deep emptiness, which is then filled with white light. As the heart opens, the experience changes to an awakening of soul vitality and a deep feeling of dying to the old and being reborn in our true nature.

The **second initiation** comes when there is a surrender of the emotional body. When we see that the emotional body is no longer in control of our responses, we respond clearly to each situation without our emotions ruling the response. This initiation brings the heart and head centers into balance, allowing the heart center to respond with love and the head center to respond with wisdom. Through this process we can obey the voice of our soul and the emotional nature no longer dominates our inner light. The second initiation is when the soul and personality are one.

The **third initiation** is related to the life of the soul and its alignment with the spiritual triad of love, wisdom and divine will. We know clearly that the temporary nature of the physical, emotional, and mental bodies is subject to birth and death, but our true nature is eternal and unbounded. When there is complete oneness with our true nature we become a disciple of the path of truth. Upon entering the path of the third initiate the memory of our entire history as an incarnated self disappears and we come into direct contact with the divine source of life.

The **fourth initiation** is consummated by the release of the soul vehicle. This is when the Antahkarana (Bridge of Light) is completed, allowing the being to travel upward through the spiritual triad of love, wisdom and divine will. The fourth initiation is symbolic of the end of the cycle of incarnation. When one passes through this gateway there is no need to return to the physical body.

The **fifth initiation**, also called the "Summit of the High Mountain," occurs when all space and time are negated. It is the time of the third death when relationship to the physical plane dies, leaving no possible way to return.

The Akashic Records – The Book of Lipaka

Akasha means ether. The Akashic Records are our Book of Life or nature's records. Our soul's records can be thought of as a pearl necklace on a sacred cord, each pearl holding the essence of each lifetime. Each record reveals the dormant potential of our being and holds the key to unlock our potential. *Trishna,* meaning thirst or deep yearning for God, is our innate quest to continue evolving in love, returning to our divine source.

The Akashic records are the sacred files that hold information regarding the evolution, tests and initiations of our soul. Each record of our soul holds the qualities of goodness that have been developed throughout our lifetimes.

Through our evolution into the causal field, we carry forth the soul qualities of peace, contentment, harmony, joy, and unconditional love. We no longer see the illusory life as problematic, for there is nothing to fix in the changing world. Our realization is that we are a drop of light in the eternal manifestation of life, timeless, with no beginning and no end.

Only you can deprive yourself of
anything.
Do not oppose this realization
for it is truly the beginning
of the dawn of light.
- A Course in Miracles, T,186

The *Life Essence Awakening Process* past life research program is investigating ways to untie karmic knots, the repeated discordant energy patterns, with the intention of freedom. Patterns in the emotional and mental fields that need healing can be difficult to identify and can create a continuous deficit in the life force. The weakening of the life force is often the root cause of illness. The Akashic Records reveal rebirth patterns and offer insights into deep soul healing. To access the records it is important to develop the intuitive field of consciousness and hold a high level of purity of heart, mind, speech and intention for freedom.

The Akashic Records hold the memories of karma and our present and past lives and information about them is accessed through the chakras. Through energy testing we can dialogue with these memories and release them. Memories are the part of us that functions in time and often lives, blindly, under the influence of ancestral conditioning and worldly consciousness. We often fall into the trap of time, losing our sacred souls in the sorrows of life. Through identification with the changing appearances in life – our losses, failures and broken dreams – our vital force is greatly diminished. We then become prisoners of past memories and captives of worry about the future. As this painful habit of identification continues through the passing years of life, our vital force is chipped away leaving little or no energy to be in the moment. A deep questioning begins to occur when we turn inward to discover our true self.

Transitions

Transitions are experienced throughout physical existence in the form of change, such as letting go of loved ones and material possessions, or losing physical ability. These transitions teach us about the impermanence of life, that life itself is change. In the process of releasing and letting go of relationships, situations and circumstance, we learn the lessons of attachment. Attachment can hold us in the grip of the emotional level, the plane of the personality, where we are bound through time and illusions.

Within the Akashic Records of the soul are the seeds of all future incarnations and the results of past lives. Genes are considered a permanent living record that determines the development and the characteristic of the physical body. We also have determining factors of our emotional and mental states. There are six permanent atoms that hold the records of manifestation. The physical permanent atom records all physical level experiences and impressions. This record shows all that has been done physically. When it is time for the next incarnation, the etheric body is built according to the physical permanent atom. The emotional record (emotional permanent atom) contains the emotional state which includes reactions and impressions both conscious and unconscious. The emotional body operates in a state of reaction to sensation. It is continually reacting to the state of desires and feelings, attracting attention to the lower self's needs. During this time it is difficult for the mental body to remain pure, as lower emotions contaminate the thought processes. Observing how attachment leads to bondage in our life and the suffering it can bring, we begin to practice detachment from outer forms, thus awaking to a life of freedom.

What does physical attachment teach? Our inquiries lead us to the universal truth that we are not just a physical body, and therefore anything on a physical level is a dream, an illusion. For example, is it possible to love another fully without attachment? If we can learn to love this way, we create a new kind of love which allows ourselves and others to be free souls and assist in each other's soul growth. The essence of death has the lesson of life within it: as each moment dies, a new opportunity is born to live fully in the moment.

When our understanding of love is limited to self-gratification and what we can get from another, the result is attachment and neediness. Pure love develops through compassion, understanding and interest in setting others free from suffering. As we progress in perceiving our real essence, we can quietly observe the workings of our separate sense of self and begin the healing process. In this very seeing, transformation occurs, leading us to true freedom of being as we develop the ability to recognize self-centeredness and awareness of ego patterns.

If we remain in the unobservant condition, we are trapped by our physical, emotional or mental needs. As awareness develops, an inner eye begins to see the web created in us by the strong identification with the needs of the self. The quiet state of observation allows the letting go of all things not in harmony with our true self. The art of releasing and the art of living are wonderful gifts to practice in daily life; dying to the old and allowing a new day to be born without memory of the past. Each moment lived anew is alive with vitality. The beauty and wonder of life lies in the fact that each new moment allows for renewal and rebirth. With each new breath healing occurs and life opens to our greater purpose, spiritually transforming toward the beautiful soul within. The art of dying to the past is critical to the growing soul as it develops trust, surrender, divine will, and renunciation in daily spiritual practice.

All your past except its beauty
is gone and nothing is left
but a blessing.
A Course In Miracles - T, 76

The Great Invocation

From the point of Light within the Mind of God
Let light stream forth into the minds of men.
Let Light descend on Earth.
From the point of Love within the Heart of God
Let Love stream forth into the hearts of men.
May Christ return to Earth.
From the centre where the Will of God is known
Let purpose guide the little wills of men —
The purpose which the Masters know and serve.
From the center which we call the race of men
Let the Plan of Love and Light work out
And may it seal the door where evil dwells.
Let Light and Love and Power restore the Plan on Earth.

Study Questions

1. Considering the influence of each of the subtle bodies, write your understanding of the cause of energy imbalances and how to identify them using Energy Field Kinesiology.

2. Explain the concept of Intentional Evolution and its importance in the *Life Essence Awakening Process*.

3. As vibrational beings, how can we protect our life force?

4. Write your understanding of the awakening process for the etheric, emotional, mental and spiritual energy fields.

5. The Kama-Manasic web creates deep challenges in our lives. Explain.

6. Write your understanding of the unveiling process and facing the shadow self.

7. How does conscious choice play a significant part in our path of healing and transformation?

8. Write a small essay on The Light of the Soul and the Paths of Initiation.

9. What are the Akashic Records?

10. How do transitions and attachments throughout life impact one's health?

Notes

The Opening Soul's Goal
The Soul's Goal & Living Prayer

When the soul or higher self is aware of its purpose in life, it naturally gravitates towards a way out of suffering through the use of life affirmations, prayer, invocations and re-framing the purpose of life. This is called the soul's goal, the gateway to enter the system and begin to remove all obstacles to alignment and harmony with divine consciousness.

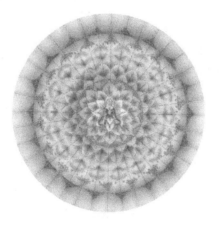

Come, come whoever you are!
Wanderer, worshipper, lover of learning.
It doesn't matter if you've broken your vow a thousand times,
Still and yet come, come again.

—Rumi

Part Three

LEAP Energy Field Kinesiology

To the most high:
We raise our consciousness here and now and expand our auras with the
unconditional divine light and love. We join in the circle of spirit, asking
guidance to become whole, asking nature to fill us with thy essence, fill
us with divine life so we may radiate the life force. Lord of the universe,
enrich our lives with thy love and guard the treasure of our innermost
souls. Om

Om Namah Shivaya

The Art of Kinesiolgy

About Energy Testing

Energy Testing is a valuable biofeedback tool that offers insights into etheric, emotional, mental and spiritual questions. Energy Testing asks questions in which the body's response indicates a *yes* or *no* answer. The test offers a way to dialogue with the patterns of the energy fields and change the frequency of the patterns to raise the *Life Essence*. If the muscle tested is strong the energy test is saying, "I am doing fine, thank you." If it is weak it says so or, in effect, gives permission to analyze a certain area. When the correction or balance is offered and the muscle tests strong, then the body is answering, "This is what I needed." A muscle that is still weak is saying, "Let's investigate further." Energy Testing is a key giving us a way in which to find out information, and also ways to dialogue with the intuitive part of us. Follow the guidelines for Energy Testing until you feel confident about testing muscles. Then move on to learn *Life Essence* analysis for the etheric, emotional, mental and spiritual energy fields. Follow by learning the *Life Essence* balancing procedures. The entire process is known as *LEAP,* an acronym for *Life Essence Awakening Process*, a method to awaken dormant energy in the subtle bodies to bring greater vitality, joy and spiritual well-being.

Note: This method is offered only as a tool for research toward self-awareness and to explore the possibility of enhanced energetic well-being. *LEAP* makes no claims as to its effect or outcome in any individual case.

Attunement: Opening Procedures for All Levels of LEAP

It is very important at the beginning of each session to take the time to slow down, breathe consciously together and call in assistance from our higher guidance. Ask that all the information received, and progress made in the session, be for the highest good. You can invite your own and the client's spirit guides by name, as well as God, Great Spirit, The Mother, or any name by which you or the client wishes to address the higher power. Create your own spontaneous prayer, or invocation, or use something like the following:

"Together we breathe in the oneness and allow the light, sound and vibration of this divine presence to protect us and assist us in bringing through the highest good and the highest possible healing here and now."

Hydration

The electromagnetic system is very sensitive and requires sufficient hydration for effective function. Before testing, have the subject drink a small glass of water. Test for hydration using the Pinch Test. Hold a small piece of hair at the nape of the neck and at the same time test the arm muscle as described in the following paragraphs. If the test is weak, water is needed. Offer water, and then test again. If the test is strong, then water is not needed.

Setup

Have the client either sit or lie on a treatment table. Make sure they are comfortable and check on any neck, shoulder or arm injuries, or pain that might have an effect on testing of their arm. Remove watches, rings, and other metal or electronic things from pockets, etc.

Indicator Muscles

Begin by choosing a muscle to test. For simplicity, we will use the deltoid or pectoralis muscle.

Pectoralis Major Clavicular

Place one hand on the subject's shoulder while lifting the arm into position. Put arm out at a 90 degree angle at chest level. Then pause; wait about six seconds before pressing the arm down. Look for a yes or no answer. Use a steady, light pressure (no more than the tester can exert with two fingers). Feel for the muscle lock using strength designed for the person being tested. The message is in the lock and within two seconds. Remember to test lightly, gently, slowly. Apply enough slow, gentle pressure so that you can feel whether the response holds firm or weakens in response to your question.

Deltoid Muscle Test

To test the body using the deltoid muscle the subject holds their arm out to the side with the palm facing the floor. The tester pushes straight down on the forearm, near the wrist, with a smooth, light pressure. Be sure that the pressure is applied above the wrist, toward the elbow, so that there is no tendency to bend the wrist. Two inches of movement are all that is necessary to indicate a weak muscle. Do not push the arm all the way down. Apply light pressure downward and out to the side.

Establish a *Yes* or *No* Answer

When the muscle is strong it locks in within two seconds and two inches. This indicates a *yes* answer. When the muscle is weak it does not lock in within two inches or two seconds; this indicates a *no* answer.

Hints for Success

Lightness is the Key to Accuracy!

Use light pressure. Using two fingers above the wrist, test until the muscle locks in, generally within two seconds. Apply gradual pressure even when testing lightly. Do not overpower the subject. This is not a test of muscle strength or a competition of forces. A muscle is locked if it does not move when tested within the two second, two inch rule. The subject remains in a relaxed posture. Both subject and tester breathe consciously.

Fine-tuning Your Muscle Testing – The Rule of Two

Two fingers – this means the pressure is light enough to do a muscle test with two fingers and you feel it lock in or remain strong.

Two inches – If your arm moves more than about two inches we say that it is switched off, or weak. Eventually, you will be able to feel a switched-off muscle with less movement.

Two seconds – This is long enough to apply the gradual increase in pressure and to feel for the switched-on locking-in effect.

Check for Permission

Important: At the beginning of any muscle testing session always ask your client for permission to test. Ask for a verbal answer and muscle test for that as well.

Muscle Strength Clarification Sample Tests

"My name is _____." (correct name, test) (incorrect name, test).

"I am 100% well on all levels." When the body goes weak in response to this statement, it is indicating that the statement is not true for the subject. In most cases this is a confirmation that the testing is working, as so few people are 100% well on all levels.

"The sky is purple," "My name is Sigmund Freud," "I am a bird," etc. When these test negative, again it is a confirmation that testing is working.

Test for Clarity and Switching

Sometimes the bioelectric or neurological circuits in the body become reversed, or switched. One can test for this situation in the following two ways:

a. State: "This system is clear for testing." Check *yes/no*. When the answer is *no* it means the energy system is switched off and needs to be cleared.

b. Bridge test: Place your fingertip between the client's eyebrows. Muscle test the arm. Then place the same finger, with the nail against the skin, at the same location. Muscle test again. If results are the same, either both strong or both weak, then the energy system is switched and needs to be cleared. If one test is strong, the other weak, they are not crossed and you are ready to proceed.

1. **General clearing/circuit balancing**

   Use any or all of the following clearing techniques until a recheck tests clear.

   a. Rub K-27 (on the chest, two inches below the collar bone, the area that is tender to the touch), and the navel. Do these one at a time initially until you become more practiced, then rub both spots simultaneously.

   b. Rub upper and lower lips simultaneously.

   c. Do sweeping figure eight motions around the body as shown below.

   d. Follow an imaginary circle with the eyes. Think of a clock and follow the numbers clockwise.

   e. Tap Thymus points (2 inches below clavical and 2 inches from the sternum) about ten times. Good for cleaning switched electromagnetic energy.

   f. Float your hand up the central meridian from pubic bone to lower lip.

   g. Perform Cross Crawl Exercises (see diagram, next page).

Figure Eight Energy Flow   **Switching Points**

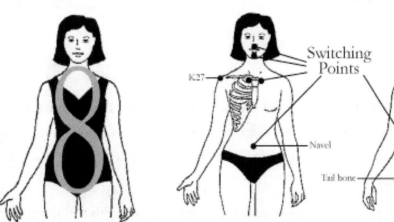

2. **Special Clearing Techniques for both strong and weak responses.**

   If all tests are positive or all negative, proceed to balance as follows:

   a. If all tests are positive: Energy is focused too much in upper body.
      Do CV/Hara balance beginning with CV point and stimulating both points with clockwise balance beginning with Hara and stimulating both points with counter-clockwise pressure.

   b. If all tests are negative: Energy is focused too much in the lower body.
      Do CV/Hara balance beginning with Hara and stimulating both points with counter-clockwise pressure.

Cross Crawl

This brain-eye exercise can easily be done standing, sitting, or lying down with legs straight and arms down at the sides.

Breathe in and raise the right arm above the head while bending the left knee to raise leg.

Re-pattern by turning the head towards the raised arm. Then exhale and straighten the head as the arm and left leg come down.

Repeat with left arm and right leg, turning head toward the raised left arm.

Do 12 right and 12 left for a total of 24 movements.   Visualize marching.

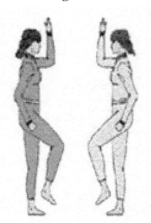 May be done 50 to 100 times daily as a discipline practice.

Cross Crawl activates the brain for:

Improved binocular (both eyes together) vision.
Improved left/right coordination.
Enhanced breathing and stamina.
Greater coordination and spatial awareness.
Enhanced hearing and vision.
This is an ideal warm-up for all skills, especially academic skills and comprehension.

No Contest

Both client and tester should remain relaxed and open to any result. The muscle test is a search for information. It is not a contest of strength. Stand erect with your best posture. Do not contract or recruit muscles other than the muscle being tested. Subject should look straight ahead, eyes open.

a.   Use a steady, light pressure (no more than the tester can exert with two fingers). Feel for the muscle lock using strength designed for the person being tested.

b.   Do not overpower a muscle.

c.   Range of motion is firm but gentle, telling the subject to resist. Give the subject a moment to resist your pressure.

d.   Lightness is the key to accuracy.

e.   Keep the subject's hands from contact with their body and keep their legs uncrossed.

f.   Breathe continuously. Do not hold your breath.

Other Methods of Testing

Surrogate Testing

Surrogate testing is performed when it is difficult or impossible for a person to test for themselves. This could happen for a variety of reasons. The subject may be elderly or too young to follow directions or there may be medical reasons, illness, sensitivity issues or injuries that would preclude this type of testing. Follow the opening procedures of the LEAP manual and then proceed with the surrogate method. The surrogate should be balanced before testing for another person. Alternatively, you can ask the question. "Is the surrogate for _____ (subject's name) clear for testing?" "Do we have permission to test using a surrogate?" Have the person being tested touch the surrogate, then have the surrogate perform the desired kinesiology procedure.

As the spark
That shall give warmth
Is hid in the gray ashes,
So, O friend,
The Light
Which shall guide thee
Under the dust
Of thine experience
　　From Darkness to Light
　　　J Krishnamurti

Energy evaluation using the pendulum

You may find that you prefer to use a pendulum for energy testing instead of muscle testing. One advantage of this method is that you can perform it without the use of your client's arm.

Guidelines for Pendulum Use

Accurate pendulum use requires that the practitioner stay alert and attentive while also being relaxed and tension free. Yoga breathing and prayer can help deepen intuition and a sense of selfless service. The pendulum is influenced by the attitudes held in the mind of the practitioner, so make every effort to maintain a detached frame of mind, remaining neutral and open to any answer.

Hold the pendulum between the first finger and thumb and establish your *yes* or *no* answer. The pendulum will move on one of two axes as shown. Usually, movement along the vertical axis (up and down) is *yes* and horizontal movement (back and forth) is *no*. It may also move in a clockwise circle for *yes* or counter-clockwise for *no*.

Pendulum Swing

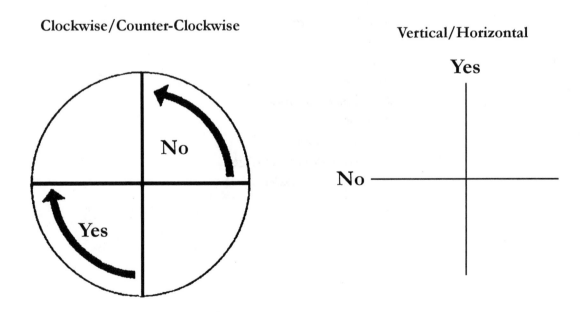

Clockwise/Counter-Clockwise

Vertical/Horizontal

Pendulum use for chakra evalution

1. When working with the chakras and a pendulum, place the pendulum over or in front of the chakra and observe the way it spins.

2. If pendulum doesn't spin, then the chakra could be inactive or under-energized. It may also spin in a counter-clockwise manner, which indicates that the energy is unbalanced. A clockwise manner should indicate the chakra is fully functioning. You can determine the differences between chakras and notice some are spinning more rapidly than others. These may require some balancing. Through breathing and affirmations you can often bring a particular chakra back into balance.

3. You can also use the pendulum to discover the condition of a chakra by holding it over your palm chakra and asking about each of your chakras in turn.

Opening Procedures for all Levels
of the Life Essence Awakening Process
Energy Field Analysis and Kinesiology Testing.

Kinesiology Testing Review

1.   Have client fill out forms that apply to your practice, such as health questionnaire, client release, healing intention, etc.

2.   Offer water at the beginning and at the end of each session.

3.   Have client remove watches, jewelry, etc., then lie or sit on table.

4.   Always begin a session with the attunement process. This brings forth the spiritual guidance needed for a LEAP session and offers protection and clear intention, as well as creating a sacred environment for the work.

5.   Discuss the art of muscle testing, showing examples if necessary. See section on *The Art of Kinesiology* (page 124).

6.   Before testing, ask permission of your client.

7.   Ask for the healing intention or soul's goal for the session. Check in, with dialogue and careful listening, regarding what has been occurring in your client's life. Write down the opening soul's goal on the form provided in the Sacred Appointment section of the book (pages 201-202).

8.   Perform rechecks, switching, etc. (for review see *The Art of Kinesiology* page 124).

LEAP Energy Analysis Procedures for All Levels.

1.   Rate overall *life essence* at the beginning of the session and remember to re-check at the end to note changes.

2.   Using an indicator muscle, say to your client, "We are now going to rate your system, regarding your overall life essence, using a percentage scale." Example: Is the overall Life Vitality or Essence of the system at 50%, 60%, 70%, 80%, 90% or more?

- 60% indicates there is a lack of overall energy and that there could be a crisis or shock occurring on some level - physical, etheric, emotional, mental or spiritual.
- 70% indicates there is a deep exhaustion. There could also be a crisis or shock but not as severe as at 60%.
- 80% low energy is indicated.
- 90% a slight energy deficiency of 10%.
- 100% *life essence* is at optimal energy.

3. After determining the rate of *life essence*, next ask which field is the priority energy field needing attention. Check each field until you get a *yes* answer.

    *   Is it the etheric field?
    *   Is it the emotional field?
    *   Is it the mental field?
    *   Is it the spiritual field?
    *   When the answer is *yes* with a strong indicator muscle, confirm the *life essence* rate for that energy field. Example: The priority energy field tests strong (*yes*) for the emotional field. Next, ask if the *life essence* of the emotional field is greater than 50%. If *yes*, then ask if it is greater than 60%.
        If *no*, then the answer is 55%.
    *   You have now determined that the *life essence* rate of the emotional field is 55%.

4. Note your findings on the forms provided, or on any piece of paper, and remember to rate the energy again after the session.

5. Next, ask your client to rate the overall level of discomfort, pain or disturbance.

    *   Example: "Please tell me, on a scale between 1-10, how you would rate the discomfort you are feeling (physical pain, emotional pain, mental disturbance, spiritual imbalance)?"

    One - Absence of stress.

    Two - Slight discomfort, mild irritation.

    Three -Unpleasant feelings.

    Four -Tolerant of stress, but uncomfortable.

    Five - Very uncomfortable, but not completely out of control.

    Six - Very uncomfortable, life is altered.

    Seven -Severe pain on some level.

    Eight - Very disturbed, crisis is imminent.

    Nine - Disturbance is becoming intolerable.

    Ten - Extreme crisis.

    *   Note the level of discomfort and whether it is physical, emotional, mental or spiritual.
    *   After determining the level of pain, disturbance or discomfort, and which energy field is the priority, next investigate whether the system is grounded.

6.   **Life Force Grounding Analysis Test**

Life force grounding is a centering process. The body can be compared to a battery. The head and pelvis are the opposite poles, with electromagnetic energy flowing between them. Vibrant health is a result of the unimpeded flow of that energy and when the life force grounding points are out of balance one may feel disconnected, experience depression, become teary-eyed, spacey or weak. Any one of these symptoms may combine or be accompanied by a lack of energy. The chakras are greatly affected by the condition of the life force grounding points.

Perform the Following Tests

•   Have the person being tested lie on their back and raise their right leg and left arm, straight up into the air, perpendicular to the body. Test the arm and leg by asking the client to hold them up while you press (light muscle testing here) the raised leg down toward the other leg and, at the same time, press the arm toward the head. Make a note if test is strong or weak. Then take the opposite side and test in the same way, again make notations.

•   Simultaneously press the right leg down and the left arm back toward the head.

•   Repeat with the left leg down and the right arm back toward the head.

•   Press down on both the right leg and right arm, simultaneously.

•   Repeat this procedure with the left leg and left arm.

•   Make a note as to which tests are out of balance.

7.   **Chakra Analysis**

Please review the chapter on the chakras or refer to the chakra charts for more information. When a muscle test for a chakra appears weak, it could be that the chakra has too much or too little energy. Note which chakra is out of balance and if it is over-energized or under-energized. Then test to see which chakra is the priority for healing. Also check to see in which energy field (the etheric, emotional, mental or spiritual) the chakra is out of balance.

Seven Chakra Analysis

Place one hand over the chakra to be tested, while testing on the client's arm with your other hand. Test each one of the seven chakras in turn. Alternatively, the client can place their hand over the chakra, while you perform the muscle test.

- Test chakra.
- Note if it is over-or under-energized.
- Note in which energy field the chakra is out of balance.
- Note which chakra is the priority chakra.

Chakra Chart	Unbalanced	Over Energy	Under Energy
Root			
Navel			
Solar Plexus			
Heart			
Throat			
Third Eye			
Crown			

Review of Chakra Meanings and Locations

For a detailed explanation, see *Turning the Keys to Awakening* (page 34).

1. Root Chakra Location: in the area of the pubic bone, hold hand above pubic area and test with other arm. Qualities of a balanced chakra: groundedness, security, trust.

2. Navel Chakra Location: below the belly button. Qualities of a balanced navel chakra: healthy relationships, good self-esteem, and creative expression in the outer world.

3. Solar Plexus Chakra Location: just below the rib cage in the abdomen area, above the navel. Qualities of a balanced chakra: healthy emotional nature, non-judgmental, unopinionated, healthy self-worth, receptive to abundance and balanced power.

4. Heart Chakra Location: between the breast bone. Qualities of a balanced chakra: self-love and self-care, integration of wisdom and feelings, ability to receive, as well as give, unconditional love.

5. Throat Chakra Location: center of throat area. Qualities of a balanced chakra: expression of truth, responsibility, power of prayer, ability to *be* in silence.

6. Third Eye Chakra Location: between eyebrows. Qualities of a balanced chakra: clear perception, centered in truth, in balance between life's changing dualities, right understanding.

7. Crown Chakra Location: top of the head at the baby's soft spot. Balanced chakra: openness, connected, integration of life's experiences and lessons.

The Chakras

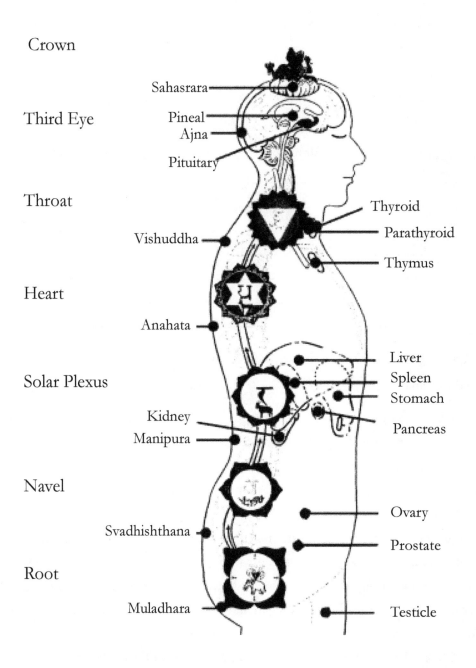

Crown

Sahasrara

Third Eye

Pineal
Ajna
Pituitary

Throat

Thyroid
Parathyroid

Vishuddha

Thymus

Heart

Anahata

Solar Plexus

Liver
Spleen
Stomach

Kidney
Manipura

Pancreas

Navel

Ovary

Svadhishthana

Prostate

Root

Muladhara

Testicle

Alarm Point Analysis

The alarm points are specific acupuncture points along the meridian flows that determine whether the chi or life force is running freely within the meridian. Alarm points are usually tender to the touch and it is possible to determine if the meridian is balanced through kinesiology testing. These points will appear weak if they have too much energy or too little energy running through the associated meridian. They will also reveal emotional stress held in the body.

To test, you touch the alarm point with the index and middle finger of one hand, while testing an indicator muscle with the other hand. When the arm goes weak while testing, there is most likely an imbalance of energy in the meridian. The next test is to ask if the meridian is over or under energy.

The alarm points are either bilateral or run down the front of the body along the Central Meridian. There are eight alarm points that run down the Central Meridian and six alarm points that run on each side of the body. The eight alarm points that run down the center of the body are: Central, Governing, Circulation Sex, Heart, Stomach, Triple Warmer, Small Intestine, and Bladder. The remaining six alarm points that are bilateral, that are found on the sides of the body are, Lung, Liver, Gall Bladder, Large Intestine, Spleen, and Kidney.

When the indicator muscle goes weak while touching a meridian, it indicates that there is a deficiency or excess in the meridian. There are several ways to balance the meridian flow. After noting which alarm points are weak, go back while touching the alarm points and ask while testing the muscle, "Is this alarm point over or under energy?" Note your results from all the alarm points on the forms provided in the LEAP manual. After completing the alarm point kinesiology test you can correct the imbalance in the meridian through several ways. To increase the energy in an under energy meridian, trace the meridian along the direction of the meridian flow (see diagram, pg. 142). You can also apply strong pressure to the alarm point; simply use your index and middle finger and massage in clockwise movements.

To remove energy from an over energized meridian, trace the meridian backward one time, always remembering to trace it forward three times. This creates a cleansing and energizing effect on the meridian. Other means of sedating excess energy is to lightly flutter the alarm point by flicking or scrambling the energy just above the alarm point. This will assist in removing excess energy of the meridian. Another method is to take your hand and make counter clockwise circles around the areas of the point. Always make sure to test, to see if the energy is completely balanced after working with the alarm points.

Additional pointers and cautions: Do not sedate the heart meridian. Use the suggested healing affirmation words, color, sound and smells that are related to the meridian. Also, affirmations that balance the associated meridian are also helpful.

Test each alarm point in turn. If weak, retest to see if it is over- or under-energized. Energy in the meridian can be deficient or excessive. Below are instructions for locating the points.

Review of Testing Points (see diagram, pg. 142, and Meridian charts, pages 78-91)

Governing – Tip of nose or just above upper lip.

Central – At the center of the chin below lower lip.

Lung – Testing Point Lung 1 - Beginning point of the Lung Meridian. The Lung Meridian indicates an imbalance of the physical system or it can indicate an emotional/mental field imbalance. Test the point. If imbalanced, ask if it is related to the physical system or emotional/mental field. Related emotional/mental field issues: grief and thought forms around grief.

Circulation Sex – Testing Point Central 17 - Along the midline of the chest, on the ribcage between the nipples. Related emotional/mental field issues: trust, hope and protection.

Heart – Testing point Central 14 - Along the midline of the chest just above the tip of the ziphoid process and below the sternum. Related emotional/mental field issues: sadness and joy.

Stomach – Testing Point Central 12 - Located halfway between the ziphoid process and the umbilicus. Related emotional/mental field issues: sympathy, empowerment and anxiety.

Liver – Testing Point Liver 14 - Where the plumb-line between the nipples crosses the coastal border of the rib cage. Related emotional/mental field issues: anger and willpower.

Gall Bladder – Testing Point Gall Bladder 24 - Just below the joining of the 9th rib and coastal border. Related emotional/mental field issue: resentment.

Spleen – Testing Point Liver 13 - Just anterior of the tip of 11th rib. Related emotional/mental field issues: feelings of inadequacy.

Kidney – Testing Point Gall Bladder 25 - Along the stomach meridian, level with, and about 2 inches out from, the umbilicus. Related emotional/mental field issue: fear.

Large Intestine – Testing Point Stomach 25 - On the stomach meridian, level with the umbilicus. Related emotional/mental field issues: holding and resistance.

Triple Warmer – Testing Point Central 5 - The next point from center 4. Related emotional/mental field issue: joy.

Small Intestine –Testing Point Central 5 - Divide into two equal segments the distance between central 3 and the umbilicus. Central 4 is the first point above central 3. Related emotional/mental field issues: vulnerability and loneliness.

These are the opening procedures for the analysis of the etheric, emotional, mental and spiritual energy fields. Now, continue with the specific energy field that you are working with.

LEAP
Etheric Field Analysis

- **Shen Alarm Point Test**
- **Aura Scan Test**
- **Endocrine Gland Test**

Notes

_____

_____

_____

_____

_____

_____

_____

_____

_____

_____

_____

_____

_____

_____

_____

_____

_____

_____

Etheric Field Analysis Background

The etheric field is the first band of energy that radiates from the physical body. This energy field extends out about one quarter inch from the skin and reflects the state of health in the body, mind and emotions. The functions of the etheric field are to receive, assimilate, transmit and discharge prana. The field has the important role of providing protection for the vital force. Energy that is discharged from the pores forms around the physical and creates the etheric field. We can understand a great deal about our overall health and vitality from learning about the etheric field and ways to keep its vital force strong.

Begin etheric analysis with opening procedures for all levels then proceed with the Shen Alarm Point Test.

Shen Alarm Point Test

Check Alarm Points (see pages 137-138 for review..)

Lung - Lung 1. The beginning point of the Lung Meridian. Related emotion: grief.

Circulation Sex - Central 17. Level with the nipples. Related emotions: trust and hope. Protects the heart.

Heart - Central 14. The tip of the xiphoid process below the sternum. Related emotions: sadness and joy.

Liver - Liver 14. Where a plumb-line between the nipples crosses the coastal border of the rib cage. Related emotions: anger and will power.

Gall Bladder - Gall Bladder 24. Just below the joining of the 9th rib and coastal border. Related emotion: resentment.

Stomach - Central 12. Halfway between the xiphoid process and umbilicus. Related emotions: sympathy, empowerment and anxiety.

Kidney - Gall Bladder 25. Just anterior to the top of the 12th rib. Related emotion - fear.

Spleen - Liver 13. Just anterior to tip of 11th rib (the first floating rib). Related emotion: inadequacy.

Large Intestine - Stomach 25. On the stomach meridian, level with umbilicus. Related emotions: holding and resistance.

Triple Warmer - Central 5. The next point from central. Related emotion: joy.

Small Intestine - Central 4. Divide the distance between Central 3 and the umbilicus into two equivalent segments. Central 4 is the first point above Central 3. Related emotions: vulnerability and loneliness.

Bladder - Central 3. Just above the pubic bone. Related emotions: irritation and shame.

See the Meridians and the Five Elements for extensive lists of related emotions.

Alarm Point	Over	Under	Alarm Point	Over	Under	Alarm Point	Over	Under
Lung			Stomach			Sm. Intestine		
Circ. Sex			Kidney			Bladder		
Heart			Spleen					
Liver			Lg. Intestine			Conception		
Gall Bladder			Triple Warmer			Governing		

Use chart above to note condition of alarm point. Check the alarm point that is not balanced and then determine if the energy is over/excess (+) or under/deficient (-). Put the plus or minus in the chart.

Alarm Points

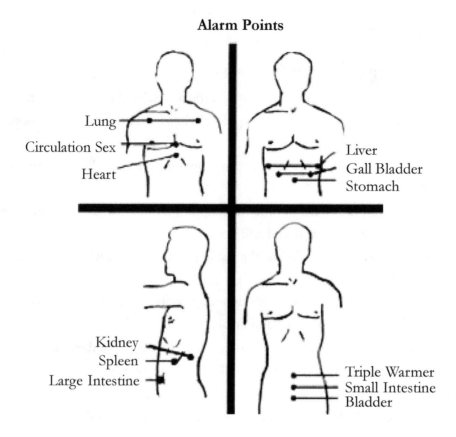

Lung
Circulation Sex
Heart

Liver
Gall Bladder
Stomach

Kidney
Spleen
Large Intestine

Triple Warmer
Small Intestine
Bladder

Aura Scan Test

In LEAP we have discovered that the life essence of the aura can be uneven in one or more of the four energy quadrants listed below. For example, not enough energy circulating the pelvic area or leg might be the cause of congestion in the upper part of the energy field with a variety of symptoms. After checking the flow of energy in the aura, you can use the method called AuraTouch to balance and distribute energy where it is needed. (See Etheric Treatments section) Once you work with this Aura Scan analysis you will find many ways to balance the energy according to your own healing preferences.

To do an Aura Scan test, hold one hand over the area of the aura being tested, muscle test (if weak, there is congestion in the area) and note if the energy is over- or under-supplied. You can also ask questions about the aura such as: are there cords, tears, congestion, etc. Note your findings in the table below and use them when checking the four aura quadrants that are listed.

	Over+/Under –	Cords	Tears	Congestion
Head/Neck				
Chest				
Pelvis/Abdomen				
Legs				

Aura Scan Radiance Touch

The aura is composed of collective bands of luminous energy: the etheric, emotional, mental and spiritual fields. The amount of radiance from the aura is determined by the health of the energy fields and the release of energetic toxins. The etheric field is the duplicate of the physical body and radiates out about an inch. When there is a healthy release of energy toxins from the etheric field, this band of energy will be strong and vibrant. The next band of energy is the emotional or astral field and is shaped around the body in an oval, egg-shaped form. Seen as an aura of moving colors, this energy band projects about 18 to 48 inches into the aura. When the emotional aura is contracted to 10 or 12 inches, it usually indicates disharmony in the individual emotions. The mental field radiates out another few inches from the emotional field. The mental and emotional field are often viewed as one energy body.

To review, when the mental field is deeply interwoven with the emotional field, it creates an energetic web called the Kama-Manasic Web. The mental field surrounds the physical in a heart shaped vortex and is opened at the top of the crown chakra to let the vibrations of a higher nature pour through. The mental field reflects the qualitiy of our thoughts and emotions; thoughts of a positive nature that are founded in love, wisdom and truth are expressed in our aura as a great radiance of beauty and light. The mental field protects the subtle bodies from imbalances and diseases through clear intentions, affirmations, and the spoken word. The higher mental or spiritual energy field, the home of our soul, is the next band of energy from the mental field.

Learn how to meaure the aura with Kinesiology testing

To measure the etheric field, scan about one inch away from the body with one hand; test an indicator muscle with the other hand. Move from the head down the front of the body and test in sections. For example, move hand about one inch away from the body from the head to the abdominal area and test. Where the arm goes weak will show signs of stress in the field. Continue on in this way, measuring the etheric field from the head to the feet. In a healthy field the aura should radiate out past the fingers when the arm is extended outward with fingers stretched.

To measure the emotional field, the person can be either lying down or standing. Place the client's arms straight out from the body. While touching the elbow area of the body, test an indicator muscle. If the arm goes weak when holding the arm straight out and touching the elbow of the client, it may indicate that there are discordant thoughts and emotions held in the emotional field. If strong, move your hand out to the tips of your client's fingers and test while touching the tips of the fingers. If the muscle is strong while testing as far out as the tips of the fingers, it indicates a healthy emotional field and mental field.

To measure the spiritual field, move your hand out from the tips of the finger about another 18 inches. Test the indicator muscle. If strong, the energy of the aura is balanced.

If any areas of the aura appear to be weak, there are many suggestions in the book for energy field well being. Test to see which method will increase the energy of the aura by using the priority testing methods in the book. After working to increase the auric energy, retest to see if the aura is strong again.

Testing the Endocrine Glands

Check the level of life energy of the endocrine glands for more information on etheric level health, in general, and the chakra centers in particular.

Reproductive – Includes ovaries and testes. Externalized as the Root Chakra.
Testing point: Hold a hand over the reproductive gland, then test.

Adrenals – Situated on both sides of the abdomen, behind the kidneys. Related to growth of brain cells. Externalizes as the Navel Chakra. Controls the balance of salt in bodily fluids, secretes adrenaline during emergencies. The adrenals are glands of combat, offering an immediate response to danger, anger and stress. As they are blood sugar regulators, and inflammatory responders, adrenals are vital to many life processes including regulating the immune response system.
Testing point: 2-3 inches above navel.

Pancreas – Controls liver, digestion, stomach, spleen, gall bladder, and autonomic nervous system. Externalized as the Solar Plexus Chakra. Lies in the abdomen near the solar plexus. The brain of instinctual nature. Governs metabolism and the secretion of insulin.
Testing point: 2-3 inches left of the adrenal point.

Thymus – Controls heart, blood, circulation, immune system, and skin. Externalized as the Heart Chakra. In the chest, covers the upper area of the heart. Related to nutrition and growth. Part of the immune system, controls immunological defense system and production of white blood cells and "T" lymphocytes. Affected by thoughts and attitudes.
Testing point: 2 1/2 inches below thyroid point.

Hypothalamus – Controls the pituitary gland and is the chief of information from all body states. Coordinates the nervous and endocrine systems. Externalized as the Third Eye Chakra.
Testing point: Center of forehead.

Thyroid – Controls jaw, neck, throat, voice, airways and metabolism. Externalized as the Throat Chakra. Above the larynx, a large gland connected to the sex glands. Controller of metabolism and energy, lubricates energy transformation and brings energy to the body. Keystone of endocrine system, regulates metabolism and is indispensable to life. The thyroid has a direct relationship to learning, education, and response to situations. Close connection to memory.
Testing point: 2 inches below Adam's apple.

Pituitary – Controls endocrine system. Externalized as the Third Eye Chakra. The size of a pea, the pituitary lies at the base of the brain, a short distance behind the root of the nose. Related to the formation of the personality, moral and intellect development, self-control, emotional and mental fields and has a great impact on memory. Master gland of all other glands.

Testing point: Above nose at the third eye point.

Pineal – Controls cerebrum, right brain and central nervous system. Externalized as the Crown Chakra. The pineal controls skin, mental state, sanity and helps the pituitary gland. Related to light and brain growth, it is considered the seat of the soul. The pineal gland secretes the hormone melatonin. When daylight turns to darkness, the pineal gland is the body clock that keeps the rhythm of day and night and the passing seasons.

Testing point: Entrance point of crown chakra.

Test the area of the gland, the related chakra, and ask if the gland is in balance, *yes* or *no*.

You can also check for the percentage of vitality in that gland.

	Strong %	Weak %
Reproductive		
Adrenals		
Pancreas		
Thymus		
Thyroid		
Pituitary		
Pineal		

Endocrine Glands and Corresponding Chakras

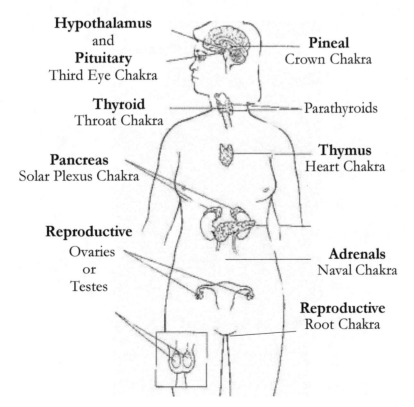

Precious Guide,

One with all Awakened Ones throughout time and space,
Blissful presence and source of all spiritual accomplishments,
Fierce destroyer of illusion who dispels every obstruction,
We pray to you for blessing and inspiration:
Please remove all outer, inner and secret obstacles,
And spontaneously fulfill our aspirations.

Author Unknown

L.E.A.P.
Emotional & Mental Field Analysis

By steady and continuous investigation into the nature of the mind,
the mind is transformed to that which the "I" refers, and that is, in fact the Self.
I am the Heart.
– Sri Ramana Maharshi

*As river have their
source in some far-off
fountain, so the human
spirit has its source.
To find this fountain of
spirit is to learn the
secret of heaven and earth*

– Lao Tsu

The *Life Essence Awakening Process* for the emotional and mental fields requires a solid foundation in Kinesiology as well as a good understanding of the energy healing information offered in earlier chapters. Please review the intentions and guidelines for muscle testing and the foundation material before proceeding with *LEAP* level two.

The *life essence* of an individual is greatly affected by mind and emotions. Through *LEAP* testing methods, we determine the *life essence* of the emotional and mental fields, the root cause of the imbalances and the priority healing path, and offer the needed vibrational medicine support.

Our *life essence* awakening and energetic freedom occurs through releasing accumulated emotions and thoughts from the energy fields and therefore opening the inner path to the light of the soul.

The Emotional Field

To review, the emotional field surrounds the physical body about 18-48 inches into the aura. Areas of congestion in this energy field are caused by negative thinking and negative emotions.

The Emotional Field Functions:

- To make sensation possible.

- To act as a bridge between mind and matter, connected by the Silver Cord (the thread of light between personality and soul).

- To express passions, emotions, desires and sensations in consciousness.

- The emotional field is where the pull of duality, such as pleasure and pain, is most deeply felt.

- It is the container for memories of the past and thoughts that are deeply layered by emotions.

- It is most often connected with the root, navel and solar plexus chakras.

- The emotional field is connected, through the heart, to the divine realms where love is realized beyond selfishness. This is the pure love of God.

- When we release the past and acquire stillness of mind and emotions, our deepest emotional healing occurs.

The Mental Field

To review, the mental field is a heart-shaped energy body that covers the emotional field with mental energy entering through the crown center. The mental field changes according to our thoughts; positive thoughts create expansion and beauty and negative thoughts create contraction and pain.

There are two aspects of the mental field, one is the higher mental that is formlessness pertaining to the intuitive plane, or Buddhic consciousness. The other is the lower mental that is manifested as form, pertaining to concrete thought and deep mental conditioning, logic and practical matters.

The Mental Field Functions:

- To serve as a vehicle for concrete thought.
- To develop the power of visualization, concentration and focus.
- To assimilate the results of past experiences, both in this life and beyond.
- To integrate the experiences with the soul plan and to increase wisdom.
- To surrender the hold of the mind and open to the soul plane, or intuitive body.

Keys to Awaken the Emotional and Mental Fields

- Emotional honesty is the art of embracing and accepting feelings even if they are not what you want.
- Joy and contentment are the foundation for all healing.
- Saying *yes* to life and evolving in refined emotions such as gratitude, beauty, aspiration and joy, is the healing path for the emotional body.
- The emotional field is healed when we increase our capacity to expand into a more loving and compassionate consciousness.
- Releasing the past allows spaciousness of being and invites the joy of the moment.
- Awakening to divine love and wisdom brings unity of soul and personality as well as mind and emotions.
- Breathe in honesty and exhale out, releasing all denial.
- Emotional healing occurs when you transform the lower chakras and align them with the spiritual centers.
- Release old contracts that bind you to suffering, and create new healing intentions with your higher self.
- Release stories and drama, along with cords that bind.
- Align with the movement of nature: beauty, change, letting go, death, rebirth, renewal and communion with the great creator.
- Forgiveness of self and others, resting in profound forgiveness.
- Gentle acceptance of self in each moment.
- See all pain as a cry for love and the release of false identification.

- Raise hidden suffering to awareness.
- Accept the pain and allow it to guide you to the root cause, healing the buried wounds, unlocking the cause.
- Accept all with awareness, loving kindness and compassion.
- Release the pattern of seeking love outside of self to discovering the love of the divine self within.
- Enter your life fully, with full agreement to evolve as a spiritual being.
- Come to the altar of the divine, empty, silent and surrendered.
- Allow the shadow self to safely come forward. Embrace the darkness, lovingly and with compassion.
- Reclaim your divine power through letting go of the separate sense of self.
- Know you are the truth, the path, the lighted way.
- Release judgment, the part of us that limits our perception of ourselves and others based on past failure, comparison and opinions.
- Open to the dynamic flow of divine consciousness that is readily available to assist you in your life.
- Look for imbalances of energies which point to where you need to pay more attention.
- See a way out through positive emotions and life affirming goals and intentions.
- Consciously align with your highest good; access the right use of will.
- Change the story of your life to reflect your soul's goal and clear intention; release negative subconscious patterns.
- Heal through awakening to the essence of your true self.
- Learn the art of being in the moment, being totally present.
- Become the observer of your life, seeing all as appearing in the container of witness consciousness.

Grace

God's grace is the beginning, the middle, and the end. When you pray for God's grace, you are like someone standing neck-deep in water and yet crying out for water. It is like saying that someone neck-deep in water feels thirsty, or that a fish in water feels thirsty, or that the water feels thirsty.

Ramana Maharshi

Emotional Honesty, Our Responsibility to the Story

Observe fully, moment to moment. When emotions and feelings appear, remain in witness consciousness. Breathe deeply and stay firmly anchored in the truth of your witness consciousness. Observe the stories and the characters of your life and the emotions and belief systems that are attached to these scripts.

Realize that your true nature is simply the eternal background in which the changing story is appearing. You are, in truth, not your story or the characters, nor the many displays of thoughts and emotions that are appearing in the story. The truth of your being is the peace and awareness in witness to the passing phenomenon of life.

Emotional and mental afflictions emerge as we deepen our healing and transformation, allowing more light to enter our beings. *LEAP* gently assists in the uncovering of frozen emotions, and awakens the ability to observe life honestly. Through quiet observation and attention, with the love and wisdom of the heart, we experience a profound healing and transformation.

LEAP Emotional and Mental Field Analysis

See Soul Dialogue and Healing Intentions Guidelines in
The Sacred Appointment section of this book.

Beginning Procedure for Awakening Mind and Emotions

After completing the opening procedures for all levels (page 132), proceed with the emotional and mental field analysis.

1. Remind your client that you are now accessing a deeper level of the energy fields, the field of mind and emotions. This may bring up feelings that are disturbing, so it is important to keep in mind a vision of the opening soul's goal during the session.

2. Ask your client to please take a moment to reflect on their healing intention. Ask also that they notice any sensations in the body. State the goal and confirm by saying "Is this goal for the highest good at this time?" Test again to confirm. If *no*, then dialogue further to reach the goal.

3. After performing the opening procedures begin the next steps in the emotional/ mental field analysis by testing for which chart will reveal the key emotion.

Emotional and Mental Field Testing Charts

- Chakra Emotions
- Core Emotional Deviations
- Human Limiting Emotions
- Human Expansive Emotions
- Five Element and Meridian Emotions
- Life Fears

This is how I would die into the love I have for you.
As pieces of clouds dissolve into sunlight.

Rumi

Chakra Emotions

Use the lists in this section to determine which chart to use, then proceed with testing the emotions or beliefs on each chart. For time efficiency you can check these emotions in groups of 10-20, then narrow them down to one or two.

Energy test each item on the following list. If the energy test goes weak while touching an emotion it may be an emotion that needs further investigation.

Root Chakra

Balanced
- Trust
- Gratitude
- Life Energy intact
- Connected with Nature
- Flowing with Change
- Secure

Unbalanced
- Self-Centered
- Fearful
- Possessive
- Distrust
- Insecurity

Navel Chakra

Balanced
- Harmonious Feelings
- Sexual Expression
- Creative Life Force
- Considerate and Friendly
- Happily Connected to Life
- Vital Force Balanced
- Good Self-Esteem

Unbalanced
- Unhealthy Sexuality
- Loss of Innocence
- Cannot Express Feelings
- Suppress Needs and Desires

Solar Plexus Chakra

Balanced
- Feelings of Inner Peace
- Deep Reverence
- Gratitude
- Express Positive Energy
- Sense of Wholeness
- Acceptance of Others
- Calm
- Soft-Spoken
- Trusting

Unbalanced
- Aggressive
- Boisterous
- Manipulative
- Opinionated
- Judgmental
- Self-Centered
- Low Self-esteem
- Power Issues
- Distrust
- Insecurity

Heart Chakra

Balanced

- Harmonious
- Surrendering
- Tolerant
- Unconditional Love
- Child Like
- Radiate Love
- Forgiving
- Sincerity
- Compassion
- Wholeness
- Non-judgmental

Unbalanced

- Self-Centered
- Intolerant
- Ungiving
- Non-Receptive
- Judgmental
- Non-Acceptance
- Unforgiving
- Uncaring
- Lack of Self-Love

Throat Chakra

Balanced

- Express Feeling and Truth
- Inner Knowing
- Attending to Silence
- Honesty
- Truthful Speech
- Creativity
- Listening

Unbalanced

- Thoughtless Actions
- Judgment of Self and Others
- Afraid of Silence
- Not Able to Be Alone
- Manipulative
- Self-Expression Blocked
- Offensive Voice

Third Eye Chakra

Balanced

- Clear Perception
- Non-duality
- Clarity
- Intuition
- Reception
- Awareness
- Connected to Source
- One-Pointed, Mindful

Imbalanced

- Overly Intellectual
- Rational
- Inability to Integrate
- Too Mental
- Non-Perceptive

Crown Chakra

Balanced	**Imbalanced**
• Integrated	• Frustrated
• Open to Divine	• Depressed
• Surrendered	• Psychotic
• Knowledge of Unity	• Confused
• Self-Reflective	• Out of Touch With Self
• Masterful	• Anxious
• Whole	• Fearful
	• Not Grounded

Afflictive Emotions
Core Emotional Deviations

1. Anger
2. Crisis
3. Fear
4. Guilt
5. Inertia

6. Irritation
7. Sadness
8. Shame
9. Shock
10. Worry

Use the following lists to determine which emotion needs attention. For time efficiency you can check the emotions in groups of 10-20, then narrow them down to one or two.

Human Limiting Emotions Chart

1. Abusive	34. Cheated	67. Dependency
2. Afraid	35. Childish	68. Depraved
3. Agonized	36. Clingy	69. Deserted
4. Austere	37. Competitive	70. Desolate
5. Awkward	38. Complaining	71. Despair
6. Ashamed	39. Compromised	72. Destroyed
7. Abandonment	40. Conflict	73. Destructive
8. Apathy	41. Contempt	74. Devalued
9. Alienate	42. Control	75. Different
10. Acceptance	43. Cope	76. Difficult
11. Addictive	44. Cowardly	77. Disapproved
12. Agitated	45. Crazy	78. Discordant
13. Aimless	46. Critical	79. Discouraged
14. Anger	47. Criticized	80. Discredited
15. Anguished	48. Cruel	81. Disgrace
16. Anxiety	49. Cynical	82. Disgusting
17. Apprehension	50. Careless	83. Disharmony
18. Arrogance	51. Communicate	84. Dishonored
19. Betrayal	52. Compassion	85. Disliked
20. Bad	53. Confusion	86. Disorderly
21. Baffled	54. Conceit	87. Disorganized
22. Banished	55. Decisions	88. Disrespect
23. Bashful	56. Darkness	89. Distraught
24. Belligerent	57. Delusion	90. Distressed
25. Belittled	58. Debased	91. Disturbed
26. Betrayed	59. Deceived	92. Doomed
27. Bewildered	60. Deframed	93. Doubtful
28. Blocked	61. Defeated	94. Drained
29. Bondage	62. Defiled	95. Dreary
30. Burdened	63. Degenerate	96. Drudgery
31. Bitter	64. Demanding	97. Deceit
32. Blame	65. Demeaned	98. Depression
33. Careless	66. Denial	99. Desire

100. Despondency
101. Disheartened
102. Discouragement
103. Distrust
104. Empty
105. Egotistical
106. Embarrassed
107. Enmity
108. Entangled
109. Envy
110. Estranged
111. Exasperated
112. Excessive
113. Excluded
114. Exhausted
115. Exploited
116. Exposed
117. Easily Influenced
118. Enthusiastic
119. Fanatic
120. Failure
121. Faithless
122. Fatigued
123. Fearful
124. Feeble
125. Fierce
126. Flippant
127. Floundering
128. Foolish
129. Forced
130. Forgetful
131. Forgotten
132. Forlorn
133. Forsaken
134. Fragmented
135. Frantic
136. Friendless
137. Frightened
138. Frustrated
139. Furious

140. Frenzy
141. Glad
142. Grounded
143. Gloomy
144. Greedy
145. Grief
146. Guilty
147. Helplessness
148. Honesty
149. Hopelessness
150. Hostility
151. Harassed
152. Hard
153. Hasty
154. Hateful
155. Hatred
156. Haughty
157. Heartbroken
158. Heartless
159. Hesitant
160. High Minded
161. Hollow
162. Horrible
163. Humiliated
164. Hurried
165. Hurt
166. Hysterical
167. Harshness
168. Identity
169. Identification
170. Ignorant
171. Ignored
172. Immature
173. Immoral
174. Impatient
175. Impossible
176. Impoverished
177. Imprisoned
178. Incapable
179. Incompetent

180. Inconsiderate
181. Inconsistent
182. Incorrect perception
183. Indecisive
184. Indifferent
185. Indolent
186. Ineffective
187. Inefficient
188. Inept
189. Inferior
190. Inflexible
191. Infuriated
192. Injustice
193. Insecure
194. Isolated
195. Instability
196. Intense
197. Intolerant
198. Irritable
199. Irritated
200. Irresponsible
201. Irreverent
202. Inferior
203. Inflexible
204. Inner Conflict
205. Insensitive
206. Insight
207. Jealousy
208. Jeopardy
209. Joyless
210. Judgmental
211. Listless
212. Loneliness
213. Loss
214. Loyalty
215. Lacking
216. Less than
217. Limited
218. Lonely
219. Longing

220. Lost
221. Low Self-Esteem
222. Lustful
223. Lust
224. Manipulation
225. Melancholy
226. Mad
227. Malice
228. Manipulated
229. Mean
230. Merciless
231. Miserable
232. Mistreated
233. Misunderstood
234. Moody
235. Negativity
236. Nerves
237. Narrow Minded
238. Naughty
239. Negative
240. Neglected
241. Nervous
242. Nonacceptance
243. Not enough
244. Nothing
245. No Way Out
246. Optimistic
247. Overwhelmed
248. Obsessive
249. Obscure
250. Offended
251. Opinionated
252. Opposing
253. Oppressed
254. Over-Concerned
255. Over-Powering
256. Overwhelmed
257. Over-Sensitive
258. Panic
259. Paranoid

260. Perfectionist
261. Persecute
262. Pessimistic
263. Phony
264. Pitiful
265. Poor
266. Possessive
267. Powerless
268. Prejudice
269. Pretense
270. Pride
271. Procrastinator
272. Pain
273. Passion
274. Panic
275. Perfection
276. Pleasure
277. Power
278. Projection
279. Quick-Tempered
280. Rage
281. Rational
282. Reckless
283. Rebellious
284. Refusal
285. Regret
286. Reluctant
287. Remorse
288. Repressed
289. Resistant
290. Restrained
291. Restricted
292. Revenge
293. Ridiculed
294. Ridiculous
295. Right
296. Rigid
297. Rude
298. Ruined
299. Repressive

300. Resentment
301. Reserved
302. Respect
303. Restlessness
304. Sadness
305. Selfish
306. Sarcastic
307. Scattered
308. Scornful
309. Self-Centered
310. Self-Condemnation
311. Self-Contempt
312. Self-Conscious
313. Self-Doubt
314. Self-Violence
315. Self-Willed
316. Separate
317. Shy
318. Sinful
319. Slandered
320. Smothered
321. Sorrowful
322. Spiteful
323. Stagnant
324. Stifled
325. Struggling
326. Stubborn
327. Stupid
328. Suffering
329. Suicidal
330. Superficial
331. Suppressed
332. Suspicious
333. Self Importance
334. Sensitive
335. Sexuality
336. Shame
337. Shock
338. Strength

339. Stress
340. Tactless
341. Talk too much
342. Temperamental
343. Tension
344. Terrible
345. Thoughtless
346. Timed
347. Tired
348. Tormented
349. Trapped
350. Troubled
351. Turmoil
352. Timid
353. Tolerance
354. Transformation
355. Trauma
356. Unconditional Love
357. Unworthiness
358. Unacceptable
359. Unappreciated
360. Unaware
361. Unbearable
362. Uncertain
363. Uncomfortable
364. Uncompromising
365. Unconscious
366. Uncontrollable
367. Undecided
368. Understanding
369. Undeserving
370. Undisciplined
371. Uneasy
372. Unfair
373. Unfeeling
374. Unforgivable
375. Unfit
376. Unfriendly
377. Unfulfilled
378. Ungrateful
379. Unhappy
380. Unimportant
381. Unkind
382. Unlovable
383. Unlucky
384. Unmindful
385. Unnoticed
386. Unpleasant
387. Unpopular
388. Unprepared
389. Unprotected
390. Unqualified
391. Unreceptive
392. Unreliable
393. Unresolved
394. Unsatisfied
395. Unstable
396. Unsettled
397. Unsuccessful
398. Unsupported
399. Unsure
400. Untrusting
401. Untrustworthy
402. Unwanted
403. Unwelcome
404. Unwilling
405. Unwise
406. Unworthy
407. Upset
408. Useful
409. Vague
410. Vain
411. Vengeful
412. Victim
413. Vindictive
414. Violence
415. Vulnerable
416. Wallowing
417. Weak
418. Weary
419. Wicked
420. Why Me
421. Willful
422. Withholding
423. Worried
424. Worthless
425. Wounded
426. Wrong
427. Wily
428. Willingness
429. Wisdom
430. Worry
431. Yearning

Emotional Expansion Chart

1.	Accelerated	36.	Centered	71.	Forgiveness
2.	Accepted	37.	Cheerful	72.	Fortunate
3.	Acknowledged	38.	Cherished	73.	Free
4.	Active	39.	Clear	74.	Free flowing
5.	Adaptable	40.	Comfortable	75.	Friendly
6.	Adored	41.	Committed	76.	Fulfilled
7.	Agreeable	42.	Compassion	77.	Full of life
8.	Aligned	43.	Competent	78.	Generous
9.	Allowing	44.	Complete	79.	Genuine
10.	Ambitious	45.	Confident	80.	Glorified
11.	Abundant	46.	Congruent	81.	Good
12.	Admired	47.	Connected	82.	Grace
13.	Angelic	48.	Content	83.	Graceful
14.	Appreciative	49.	Courageous	84.	Gracious
15.	Ascended	50.	Courteous	85.	Great
16.	Aspired	51.	Direction	86.	Grounded
17.	Assertive	52.	Dynamic	87.	Happy
18.	Assent	53.	Eager	88.	Harmless
19.	Attentive	54.	Effective	89.	Harmonious
20.	Attuned	55.	Elated	90.	Healed
21.	Authentic	56.	Elevated	91.	Honest
22.	Aware	57.	Emancipated	92.	Honored
23.	Balanced	58.	Empowered	93.	Humble
24.	Beautiful	59.	Enabled	94.	Independent
25.	Beauty	60.	Encouraged	95.	Innocent
26.	Benevolent	61.	Encouraging	96.	Insight
27.	Blessed	62.	Energetic	97.	Intact
28.	Blissful	63.	Enlightened	98.	Intelligent
29.	Bright	64.	Essential	99.	Intent
30.	Brilliant	65.	Esteemed	100.	Interested
31.	Calm	66.	Faith	101.	Invigorated
32.	Capable	67.	Fearless	102.	Joyful
33.	Careful	68.	Flexible	103.	Kind
34.	Caring	69.	Flowing	104.	Knowledgeable
35.	Celebrate	70.	Focused	105.	Let go

106. Liberated
107. Loved
108. Loving
109. Luminous
110. Magnetic
111. Mastered
112. Merciful
113. Mercy
114. Mindful
115. Moral
116. Moving forward
117. Noble
118. Open
119. Optimistic
120. Orderly
121. Passion
122. Peace
123. Peaceful
124. Perfect
125. Pleasant
126. Powerful
127. Precious
128. Productive
129. Prosperous
130. Protected
131. Pure
132. Purified
133. Purposeful
134. Quiet
135. Radiant
136. Real
137. Reassured
138. Redeemed
139. Regarded
140. Rejoice
141. Rejoicing
142. Relaxed
143. Release
144. Relief
145. Renewed
146. Respectful
147. Responsible
148. Responsive
149. Restful
150. Restored
151. Revere
152. Revered
153. Rich
154. Safe
155. Secure
156. Self-Reliant
157. Self-Sufficient
158. Sensitive
159. Serene
160. Sharing
161. Skillful
162. Spirited
163. Spiritual
164. Stable
165. Steadfast
166. Strong
167. Supported
168. Sustained
169. Teachable
170. Thoughtful
171. Tolerance
172. Tolerant
173. Tranquil
174. Trust
175. Trustworthy
176. Truth
177. Unconditional love
178. Undisturbed
179. Unified
180. Unique
181. Unselfish
182. Unshaken
183. Upheld
184. Valuable
185. Vibrant
186. Victorious
187. Vigilant
188. Virtuous
189. Vital
190. Warm
191. Welcoming
192. Whole
196. Wise
197. Wonderful
198. Worthwhile
199. Yielding

Five-Element Emotions

1.   Fire Emotions (acute)

Small Intestine

Joy	Sorrow	Sadness	Internalization
Neglected	Appreciated	Unappreciated	Lost
Overexcited	Loner	Abandoned	Assimilation
Love	Safety	Closeness	Nourishment
Warmth	Receptivity	Balance	

Emotional Heart

Acute Grief	Shocked	Grow Trust	Betrayal
Deep Hurt	Remorse	Not Lovable	Withholding
Compassion	Disappointment		

Triple Warmer

Despair	Elation	Despondent	Lightness
Heaviness	Humiliated	Hopeless	Balance

Circulation Sex

Calm	Hysteria	Relaxation	Stubbornness
Responsible	Jealousy	Remorse	Gloomy

2.   Wood Emotions (let go)

Gall Bladder

Love/Anger	Rage/Wrath	Self-Righteous	Indignation
Forbearance	Assertive	Helpless	Passive
Proud/Humble	Choice	Resentment	Victim-hood
Martyr	Self-Pity	Second Best	Unforgiving
Bitter	Indecision	False pride	Manipulative

Liver

Rage	Anger	Wrath	Distressed
Resentment	Self-Righteous	Indignation	Transformation
Unhappiness	Happiness	Content	Chronic Grief
Sadness	Isolator	Longing	Feeling Trapped
Separation	Hopeless	Not Belonging	Despair
Disappointed	Frustration	Lost Zeal For Life	

3.   Earth (decision)

Spleen/Pancreas

Faith	Approved	Rejected	Assurance
Anxiety	Confidence	Cynicism	Sympathy
Empathy	Envy	Inadequacy	Self-Punishment
Dependant	Oversensitive	Over-Worried	Low Self-Worth
Low Self-Love	Smothered		

Stomach

(Un)Reliable	Criticism	Contentment	Disappointment
Deprivation	Sympathy	Empathy	Hunger/Nausea
Dislike	Stomach	Hate	Disgust/Doubt
Anxiety	Overload	Smoldering	Broken Power
Stressed Out	Devastation	High Demands	Confusion

4.   Water (chronically)

Kidney

Fear	Anxiety	Creative	Sexual Insecurity
Cautious	Careless	Recklessness	(In) Decisive
(Dis)Loyal	Fear	Guilt	Powerless
Broken Will	Fright	Survival	Disappointment
Demoralized	Bad News	Exhaustion	

Bladder

Peace	Dread	Panic	Terror
Restlessness	Frustration	Impatience	Inner Direction
Confidence	Courage	Shame	Paralyzed
Dependence	Shyness	Hurt	Helpless
Yearning	Embarrassed	Self-Pity	Resignation

5.   Metal (Insight)

Lung

Cheerful	Depressed	False Pride	Haughty
Humility	Modesty	Regret	Scorn/Disdain
Prejudice	Contempt	Grief	(In)Tolerance

Large Intestine

Guilt	Grief	Regret	Release
Self-Worth	Enthusiasm	Depression	Letting Go
Indifference	Apathy	Over-Critical	Controlling
Uptight	Dogmatic	Compulsive	Cynical
Miserly	Narrow-Minded		

Life Fears Chart

Kinesiology can make it possible to uncover hidden fears that affect the flow of your life essence.

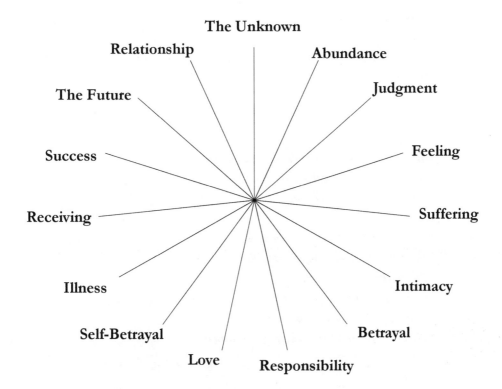

The presence of fear is a sure sign
that you are trusting in your own strength.
W, 77
A Course In Miracles

A thousand eyes with a thousands views,
A thousand hearts with a thousand loves,
Am I.
As the sea that receiveth the clean and impure rivers
And heedeth not
So am I
Deep is the mountain lake,
Clear are the waters of the spring,
And my love is the hidden source of things,
Ah, come hither and taste my love;
Then, as the cool evening
The Lotus is born,
Shalt thou find thy heart's own secret desire
The scent of the jasmine fills the night air;
Out of the deep forest,
Comes the call of a passing day
The Life of my love is unburdened;
The attainment thereof is the freedom of fulfillment.

From Darkness to Light
J. Krishnamurti

L.E.A.P.
Intuitive Field Analysis
& Soul Kinesiology

Your task is not to see love, but merely to seek and find all the barriers
within yourself that you have built against it.
It is not necessary to see what is true, but it is necessary to see what is false.
W, 77
A Course in Miracles

Notes

The Intuitive Field

To review, the intuitive field extends past the mental field about 18 inches. The energy of the intuitive field is radiant and full of color, according to our development. This field holds the essence of our true nature and functions as a vehicle to express the divine laws of love, wisdom and truth. The Bridge of Light, Antahkarana, is constructed in the intuitive field, merging soul and personality into one unified whole. The intuitive, or causal body, is developed through meditation, contemplation and concentration. Below are important points to remember of how the intuitive plane functions and the keys to awakening it.

The Intuitive Field Functions

- The causal plane, or intentional body, holds the essence of our true nature.
- Functions as a vehicle through which the true self expresses the divine laws of love, wisdom and truth.
- The Akashic Records, the stories of our soul, are held in the causal body.
- The Pearls of Existence, our thirst for God or Trishna, are held within the intuitive field.
- The Antahkarana, or Bridge of Light, connects the personality with the soul through the realization of one's true nature.

Keys to Awakening the Intuitive Field

- Discrimination between the real and unreal opens the intuitive plane.
- The quiet mind is the key to all healing.
- Self-recognition, returning awareness to the heart.
- Through centering into the heart and attaining one-pointed thought, one can tap into soul creativity. Found in the intuitive field.
- The breath of the heart and the quiet of the mind awaken intuition.
- Through the release of deep scarring of the past the soul is set free to soar into divine potential. Living in potential is the doorway to joy.
- The doorway to the intuitive plane opens and one receives a glimpse of their true nature. This path, or lighted way, is pure grace that comes when there is willingness, surrender and decision to serve this suffering humanity. As the surrender process deepens there is a new identification with our source. We then live life as a disciple, listening, honoring and devoted to the source.
- The intuitive plane deepens with unification of personality and soul.

Guidelines for Mystical Seeing

- Begin by breathing deeply, allowing all tensions, worry and outward thoughts to be released.

- Feel a deep sense of letting go of the outer eye; turn within and see through the inner eye. Invoke the truth; ask for the Light to be present on your inner journey.

- Release ideas of the personality self; journey deep into the quiet and listen.

- Ask for Guidance. Believe that guidance is there for you.

- Ask for the highest good regarding your questions. Be open to answers that go beyond the rational mind.

- Allow spirit to empower you. Feel the strength of the guidance coming through.

- Stabilize the changing emotions and thoughts of the emotional plane, deepen your stillness to receive the higher good.

- Find your spiritual center within, anchor your breath in the navel center and allow your energies to reach deep into your intuitive energy fields.

- Breathe in a dark blue Prana, the color that invokes spiritual guidance.

The Seven Rays of Divine Light

The seven rays are a person's innate characteristics. Each one of the seven rays is in our makeup but one ray predominates in each of us. This dominant ray is more evolved than others and is considered the individual's ray type. The number seven is deeply rooted in the physical to which the rays correspond. There are the seven centers in the brain, the seven centers of force (chakras) and the seven major glands, which determine the quality of the physical body. The human, in its nature, is a sevenfold being with the potential of seven states of consciousness. Each human being has a particular ray quality which has been swept into manifestation by the impulse of one of these rays. These seven rays exist in the cosmos and are essentially white light, but when they hit the human atmosphere they become a prism of many colors. Everything in the solar system that has a living quality to it belongs to one of the seven rays.

The first, second and third rays are the rays of ***aspect.*** The fourth, fifth, sixth and seventh rays are the rays of ***attribute.***

The first ray is the higher counterpart of the seventh ray, the second is the higher counterpart of the sixth ray, the third is the counterpart of the fifth ray, and the fourth connects and harmonizes higher and lower rays. Rays correspond to chakras.

First Ray Monadic plane, crown center, color white or electric blue, gemstone diamond. The qualities of the first ray are power, will, courage, leadership and self-reliance. The aspirations of the first ray are to conquer, to attain and to find ultimate reality. The weaknesses of the first ray are tyranny, self-will, pride, domination, selfishness and thirst for power. Sources of suffering for the first ray are defeat, degradation, humiliation and displacement. The methods of achieving highest attainment are concentration, will power and discipline.

Second Ray Buddhic plane, heart center, color golden yellow, azure blue, gemstone sapphire. The qualities of the second ray are universal love, wisdom, insight, intuition, a sense of oneness, compassion and cooperation. The aspirations of the second ray are to save, to heal, to illumine, to teach, to share and to serve. The weaknesses of the second ray are sentimentality, sensuality, impracticability and unwise sacrifice that undermines the self-reliance of others and increases their selfishness. The sources of suffering are neglect, heartbreak, loneliness, isolation, exclusion, broken faith, misjudgment and disloyalty.

Third Ray Etheric plane, navel center, color emerald green, gemstone emerald. The qualities of the third ray are creative idealism, comprehension, understanding, mental power, dignity, adaptability and impartiality. The aspirations of the third ray are creative activity and understanding. The weaknesses of the third ray are indecision, seeing too many sides, coldness, cruelty and failure to support in a crisis, deliberate deceit, intrigue and cunning. The sources of suffering are indignity, proven incompetence, darkness.

Fourth Ray Physical plane, root center, color bronze or red, gemstone jasper. The qualities of the fourth ray are stability, harmony, balance, beauty and rhythm. The aspirations of the fourth ray are to beautify. The weaknesses of the fourth ray are moods of exaltation and despair, sensuous behavior, posing, self-conceit, self-indulgence. The sources of suffering are frustration and failure to express perfectly.

Fifth Ray Mental plane, throat center, color yellow, gemstone topaz. The qualities of the fifth ray are analysis, logic, accuracy and patience. Aspirations of the fifth ray are to discover and a thirst for knowledge. The weaknesses of the fifth ray are self-centeredness, shortsightedness, pride, criticism, materialism, separating, one-track mind. The sources of suffering are mental.

Sixth Ray Emotional plane, solar plexus, color red, gemstone ruby. The qualities of the sixth ray are one-pointedness, fiery enthusiasm, devotion, loyalty and sacrificial love. The aspirations of the sixth ray are to serve, to adore, to worship the cause. The weaknesses of the sixth ray are fanaticism, being overemotional, impulsive, intolerant, narrow-minded and blindly devoted to personalities.

Seventh Ray Atomic plane, ajna center, color purple, gemstone amethyst. The qualities of the seventh ray are grace, precision, ordered beauty and activity, chivalry, skill, dignity, careful attention to detail and splendor. The aspirations of the seventh ray are to harness, to synthesize, to make manifest. The weaknesses of the seventh ray are formalism, love of power, using people as tools, extravagance, plausibility, and regimentation. The sources of suffering are humiliation, loss of power, frustration, rudeness and discourtesy.

Awakening Intuition and Opening the Doorway to the Soul

- Begin the Soul Kinesiology Session with invocation and a prayer to healing guides; call in protection and light by spending a few moments in silent prayer, breathing and opening to divine guidance.

- Next, have your client write down their soul's goal or healing intention. Assist him or her to establish their highest priority intention, from their soul's deepest wisdom.

- Perform the pre-checks, such as clarity, switching, readiness, willingness, permission. (See opening procedures for all levels.)

- Energy test and confirm the priority for healing. Now state, "We are now accessing the soul plane to facilitate growth, transformation and healing."

- Please take a moment, and reflect on your healing intention. Notice any sensations in the body. State the goal and confirm by asking, "Is this goal for the highest good at this time?"

Before the soul can see, the harmony within must be attained and fleshly eyes be rendered blind to all illusion. Before the soul can hear, the image (man) has to become deaf to roaring as to whispers, to cries of bellowing elephants as to the slivery buzzing of the golden fire-fly. Before the soul can comprehend and may remember, she must unto the silent speaker be united, just as the form to which the clay is modeled is first united with the potter's mind. For the soul will hear and will remember. And then to the inner eye will speak the voice of the silence.

H.P. Blavatsky

The Voice of Silence

Soul Star

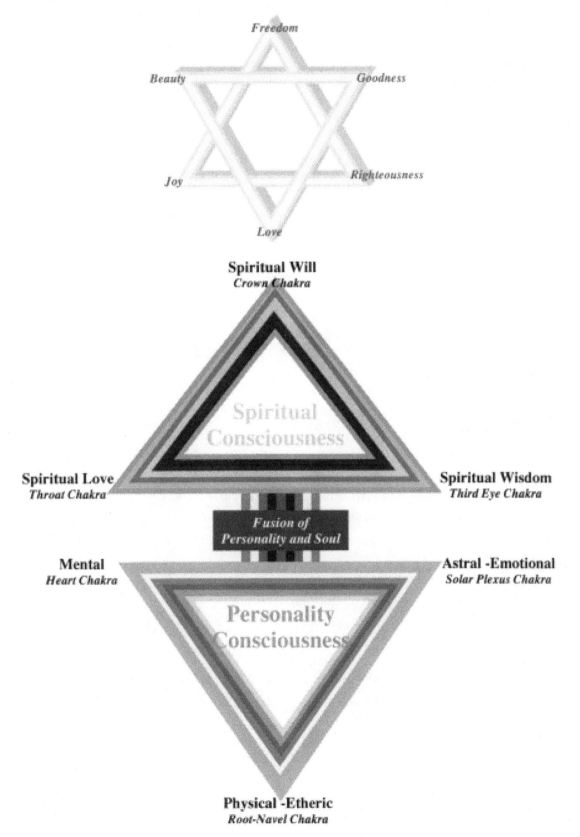

Freedom

Beauty   Goodness

Joy   Righteousness

Love

Spiritual Will
Crown Chakra

Spiritual
Consciousness

Spiritual Love
Throat Chakra

Spiritual Wisdom
Third Eye Chakra

*Fusion of
Personality and Soul*

Mental
Heart Chakra

Astral -Emotional
Solar Plexus Chakra

Personality
Consciousness

Physical -Etheric
Root-Navel Chakra

Seven Ray Chart

Ask permission to determine ray type. Then muscle test each ray and the related chakra. Hold the chakra while making the statement, "This person is ray #___." If *yes*, the test will be strong. If *no*, test the same question regarding each ray type then proceed to test the strengths and challenges. Note your findings. Now, hold neurovasculars while affirming the ray strength, or say a statement of release or soul prayer, such as, "I am willing to release pride and ask spiritual guidance to assist me in being conscious of pride and releasing it for my higher good."

1st Ray of Power and Will – Monadic Plane – Crown Chakra

Hold Crown Chakra. Test. If strong (*yes*), this is the ray type that you are. Test to identify strengths and weakness.

Positive Qualities

		Challenges
___Will to act	___Beingness	___Arrogance
___Will to unify	___Truthfulness	___Pride
___Strength	___Striving	___Ambition
___Fire	___Endurance	___Willfulness
___Renunciation	___Energy/Power	___Hardness
___Self-control		___Anger
___Purification		___Control Issues
___Humility		___Isolation
___Will to Evolve		
___Expression		
___Steadfastness		

2nd Ray of Love and Wisdom – Buddhic Plane – Heart Chakra

Hold Heart Chakra. Test while asking, "Is this person from the 2nd ray?" Test to identify strengths and weakness.

Positive Qualities

		Challenges
___Compassion	___Communication	___Fear
___Serenity	___Endurance	___Indifference
___Faithfulness	___Blessing	___Too Sensitive
___Education	___Unfoldment	___Unhealthy boundaries
___Right Relationship	___Enlightenment	___Selfish
___Understanding	___Sharing	___Mental limitations
___Healing	___Initiation	
___Intuition	___Sanctuary	
___Beatitude		
___Charity		
___Affinity		
___Patience		
___Unselfishness		

3rd Ray of Activity and Adaptability – Etheric Plane – Navel Chakra

Hold Navel Chakra. Test while asking, "Is this person from the 3rd ray?" Test to identify strength and weakness.

Positive Qualities

___Light
___Intellect
___Money
___Relationships
___Energy
___Synthesis
___Accuracy
___Service
___Goals
___Reason
___Organization

___Tolerance
___Adaptability
___Sincerity
___Joy
___Knowledge
___Discrimination
___Vibrant Energy
___Balance

Challenges

___Impractical
___Inertia
___Absent Minded
___Critical
___Selfishly Manipulative
___Intellectual Pride

4th Ray of Harmony Through Conflict – Physical Plane – Root Chakra

Hold Root Chakra. Test while asking, "Is this person from the 4th ray?" Test to identify strength and weakness.

Positive Qualities

___Beauty
___Rhythm
___Light and Shadow
___Agreement
___Confidence
___Balance
___Inspiration
___Inner Vision

___Harmony
___Creativity
___Manifestation
___Stillness
___Purity
___Perception
___Intuition

Challenges

___Compromising
___Procrastination
___Worry
___Moody
___Combative
___Lack of Moral Courage
___Indolence

5th Ray of Concrete Knowledge and Science – Mental Body – Throat Chakra

Hold Throat Chakra. Test while asking, "Is this person from the 5th ray?" Test to identify strength and weakness.

Positive Qualities

___Form
___Intellect
___Thought forms
___Energy
___Reverence
___Accuracy
___Knowledge
___Independence
___Fact

___Perseverance
___Consciousness
___Problems
___Common Sense
___Detachment
___Order
___Mind
___Abstract

Challenges

___Criticism
___Lack of Sympathy
___Unforgiving
___Narrow Minded
___Judgmental

6th – Ray of the Personality, of Devotion, Sacrifice and Idealism - Emotional Plane- Solar Plexus Chakra

Hold Solar Plexus Chakra. Test while asking, "Is this person from the 6th ray?" Test to identify strength and weakness.

Positive Qualities

___Sacrifice	___Devotion
___Love	___Power
___Intuition	___Balance
___Reverence	___Desire
___Forgiveness	___Gentleness
___Gratitude	___Purity
___Strength	___Tolerance
___Serenity	___Suffering
___Detachment	___Mastery
___Self-discipline	

Challenges

___Jealous Love
___Overbearing
___Blind Faith
___Intolerance of
  others' ideas
___Suspicious
___Violent

7th Ray of Ceremonial Order– Intuitive Plane - Third Eye Chakra

Hold Third Eye Chakra. Test while asking, "Is this person from the 7th ray?" Test to determine strength or weakness.

Positive Qualities

___Ceremony	___Rhythm
___Ritual	___Magic
___Sound	___Mastery
___All Seeing	___Glory
___All Knowing	___Order
___Alchemy	___Non-Dual
___Mystery	___Beauty

Challenges

___Dependence
___Poor Judgment
___Perfectionism
___Intolerance
___Superstition
___Pride

Soul Qualities

Use kinesiology testing methods to determine soul qualities you wish to enhance, or for guidance regarding blocks to your spiritual progress. (Suggestion: use *yes/no* method.)

1. Acceptance	20. Faith	39. Openness	58. Aspirations
2. Aspiration	21. Forgiveness	40. Patient	59. Surrender
3. Awareness	22. Goodness	41. Peace	60. Sympathetic
4. Balanced	23. Gratitude	42. Perfection	61. Thoughtful
5. Beauty	24. Greatness	43. Power	62. Tolerant
6. Benevolent	25. Humility	44. Purposeful	63. Truth
7. Bliss	26. Humor	45. Radiant	64. Understanding
8. Channel	27. Impersonal	46. Reception	65. Unity
9. Commitment	28. Insight	47. Redemption	66. Unlimited
10. Compassion	29. Inspiration	48. Self Correcting	Potential
11. Contentment	30. Intelligence	49. Self Inquiry	67. Unconditional
12. Courage	31. Intention	50. Serving	Love
13. Detachment	32. Intuition	51. Silent	68. Compassion
14. Devotion	33. Joy	52. Silence	69. Forgiveness
15. Discernment	34. Kindness	53. Simplicity	70. Vigilant
16. Discrimination	35. Love	54. Solemnity	71. Willingness
17. Elevation	36. Mercy	55. Solidarity	72. Wisdom
18. Enduring	37. Neutrality	56. Spiritual Gift	73. Wise
19. Equanimity	38. Now	57. Spiritual	74. Witness

Soul Weaknesses and Blocks to Spiritual Progress

(Suggestion: use *yes/no* method.)

1. Anger	15. Giving Up	28. Lack of	41. Shame
2. Apathy	16. Greed	Compassion	42. Unforgiving
3. Arrogance	17. Guilt	29. Laziness	43. Unkind
4. Attachment	18. Harmful	30. Limitations	44. Unloving
5. Attraction	19. Immoral	31. Manipulation	45. Vanity
6. Criticism	20. Impractical	32. Negativity	46. Violent
7. Deception	21. Indifference	33. Obstinacy	47. Willful
8. Desire	22. Indolence	34. Pride	48. Worry
9. Dishonesty	23. Inertia	35. Procrastination	49. Wrong Use of
10. Divisive	24. Intolerant	36. Repelling	Power
11. Doubt	25. Jealousy	37. Resentment	
12. Exclusiveness	26. Judgement	38. Revenge	
13. Extravagance	27. Lack of	39. Self-Centered	
14. Fear	Boundaries	40. Self-Cherishing	

Study Questions

1. Explain the opening procedures of LEAP, such as attunement, hydration, set up, *yes/no* answers.

2. Describe how to perform a surrogate test.

3. Describe how you would use a pendulum for energy analysis.

4. What are the tests suggested in the Etheric Field Analysis?

5. How do we identify limited emotions and belief systems through kinesiology?

6. Using kinesiology methods, how do we dialogue with the soul? What does it mean to listen to guidance when testing?

7. Write a review of the emotional and mental field testing processes as they are offered in LEAP.

8. Write your understanding of Intuitive and Soul Kinesiology. Share your perceptions regarding opening the doorway to the soul.

Awareness cleansed by mind to a polished mirror.

The presences came near, and I knew

that was everything and I nothing.

Lalla - Naked Song
by Coleman Barks

Notes

Part Four
Kinesiology Counseling
The Sacred Appointment

You who are the source of all power
Whose rays illuminate the whole world
Illuminate also my heart
So that it can do your work.
Anonymous

Kinesiology Counseling

Ask assistance from guides to reveal the core issue and gently allow it to come up for healing. Once a core issue has been identified, offer periods of silence so your client can observe the life story. Hold the neurovascular points on your client's forehead to assist them in understanding the issue. (See emotional stress release technique.) Ask if the system is ready to create a new and positive decision based on a clear vision of the primary cause of suffering.

Suggested Questions for Guidance

- What does the system need for it to come into balance? (i.e. release of the past, letting go of a relationship, reframing a childhood trauma, working with the emotions of forgiveness, gratitude and self-love.)
- Do we need more information?
- Do you need to speak about this issue?
- Then ask further questions such as, "Do we have permission for deeper investigation?

Guidelines for Sacred Dialogue

The Life Essence Analysis for the etheric, emotional, mental and spiritual energy fields identifies areas of the body/mind in need of healing or transformation. Use the following guidelines for questions to ask and suggestions for dialogue with your client for the release of disturbed energy patterns.

Next, follow the opening procedures for testing and offer a glass of water before beginning this dialogue session. Create a sacred dialogue to open the system to greater levels of awareness and to release limited emotions and self-limiting belief patterns.

Devotion Invocation

"We turn attention to the divine source and, with gratitude, we give thanks for this opportunity to become an instrument of source healing, to bring to this moment healing, compassion, light and willingness."

Heart Reading to Begin a Session

Turn inward to your heart, allowing the breath to silence and open your consciousness to receive information for the highest good. Listen carefully to the impressions and feelings that come to you.

Guided Inquiry

1. Ask for permission, and for the help of the healing guides in revealing the source of any energy disturbances or obstacles to the Soul's Goal.

2. Ask for the Soul's Goal, Life Intention, or Affirmation. Write it down. (See Soul Affirmations Form.)

3. Ask permission to check the chakras that hold information regarding the healing intention.

4. Determine the priority chakra involved and the subtle energy field.

5. When the emotional field is the priority, ask for guidance regarding the emotion. Test which chart to use, then test the emotions in groups of ten.

6. When the mental field is involved, also check to see if the emotion that has become a belief needs to be identified. (Example: the "I feel unworthy" emotion becomes the "I am unworthy" belief.) Also test to see if the Conscious Choice therapy chart should be used.

7. Ask if a relationship is involved. (See Influencing Factors Chart).

8. Ask if a time frame that holds the key to the healing is involved (i.e. Influencing Factors Chart).

9. Remember to recheck the chakras during a balance session. Often, a new chakra will appear weak, revealing hidden issues. Several chakras may be uncovered.

10. During a balance session relationships and time frames can change. Dialogue can unravel the story so you understand when to test for influencing factors.

Summary of Questions to Ask During a LEAP Level 2 or Level 3 Session

*   Do we need to look at an emotion?
*   Is there a core belief that needs to be healed or transformed?
*   Do we need to look at the Block to Spiritual Progress Chart?
*   Do we need to look at a time frame that holds the key to the core issue?
*   Do we need to investigate a past-life pattern?
*   Do we need to inquire regarding another chakra?
*   Do we need to look into a relationship?
*   Do we need to look at the Life-Style Chart?
*   Is a referral needed?

Deepening the Inquiry

Suggested Questions:

*   Can we heal the essence of this pattern and bring forth your soul's gifts and divine purpose?

*   How would you feel if your life were to change so that you could truly bring forth your soul's intention?

*   Assist your client to reveal the hidden fear of the life problem. Remember, energy disturbances often stem from a part of our being that calls in a crisis in order to reach a desired goal.

*   Invite your client to see what he or she truly wants. The nature of the desire or want often holds the key to transformation. The core desire is always for happiness but often, because of our low self-esteem, we try to attain something that is not for our highest good and therefore we battle with the universe. In reality, life usually points us to what our true heart's desire is and the highest good for our life.

*   How are these patterns of your life connected with your family's patterns?

*   Use negative statements to help uncover the issues, such as "*I am not worthy.*" When a negative statement tests strong, the body believes it to be true. Other examples of negative statements are, "*I am not loved, I will never be worthy, I will not attain my dreams, I'm not good enough, It's too late for happiness.*"

*   Most negative statements are connected to a lack of self-esteem that expresses in self-judgment or lack of self-love. Work with guidance to help release these deep-seated beliefs.

Toward Balance and Completion of a LEAP session

Always create a way out by bringing in a visionary affirmation and allowing the subconscious mind to agree with the possibility or soul's goal. Next, ask whether the system is 100% willing to receive the gifts of the affirmation and 100% willing to release the obstacles to receiving the gift of this affirmation. Ask these questions separately. Obstacles may indicate sabotage or *energy culprit* interference.

How would your life be changed if you were to reach the soul's goal? List your visionary goals here. Examples of visionary goals include:

*   I will be free.
*   I have more energy.
*   I am more joyous.
*   I am lighter.
*   I am happier.
*   I can begin anew.

An Example of the Balancing Process

Assume answers to testing questions below are *yes*. If *no*, ask for clarification. Ask guidance to locate the source of the energy block, breathe, and wait in silence.

1.   Do we have permission to work with the emotion or fear that is causing the energy disturbance?
2.   Is this emotion related to a particular relationship?
3.   Do we have permission to look at the relationship?
4.   If *yes*, go to the relationship chart.
5.   Test which relationship is involved and note it on the analysis form.
6.   Do we need a time frame?
7.   Reference the time frame chart and test.
8.   Do we need to look at a particular chakra?
9.   If *yes*, check the chakras again until all disturbed chakras are identified.
10. Do we need to look at a particular subtle body that is involved?
11. If *yes*, ask which subtle body until all have been identified.
12. From this picture invite your client to see the story and the origin of the disturbance.
13. Ask permission to inquire further. Test to verify you are on the right track.
14. Invite the client to ponder what gift is revealed from this story or what might be revealed through the release of it.
15. Ask if the client is ready to release the story.
16. Ask the client to think of a phrase or affirmation to reframe this story.
17. Work with the emotion or conscious choice that tests strong. Then create a soul affirmation with the positive emotions or new choices.
18. Invite them, from their witness consciousness, to see where their investment is. What do they want from the situation? Be very honest. Ask them to trace back into the story and take responsibility for the self-gain and desire patterns that are the root of the problem and may be at the core of the disturbance.

After a balancing session, recheck the life essence and any other areas of imbalance. And ask your client to rate the level of disturbance. Schedule more time or further sessions as needed.

The Divine Light Mantra

I am created by Divine Light

I am sustained by Divine Light

I am protected by Divine Light

I am surrounded by Divine Light

I am ever-growing in Divine Light

Principles of Transformation

- Our inner being is molded by our willingness to stay with our inner process of awakening.
- Integrity is a quality of being, a state of being whole and undivided.
- Request guidance for healing all unprocessed memories.
- Clear your mind of mental accumulations, giving spaciousness to your being.
- Realization of our higher mind is to see that nothing is broken, nothing needs to be fixed. We just return to the wholeness of our true nature.
- All fear is a result of the belief in our separate ego self.

Empowerment Process

1. Observe where you have given yourself away, lost yourself in relationships in the pursuit of something.
2. See where and with whom the loss of yourself has occurred. See your need in the situation. Learn the lesson of the action involved and then call yourself back into your heart.
3. Do this for every event, age, and relationship that created an experience in which you gave up your sense of self.
4. Do you see where you can take responsibility regarding this?
5. Can you see a recurring pattern in other aspects of your life?
6. Is it possible that this pattern was there before birth?
7. What gifts are being held or locked up by this pattern?

Options for Direction of Inquiry

After learning these preliminary protocols, there are many ways to use and benefit from muscle testing. Start with the simple question of whether a certain food item would be nourishing to the body then move on to deeper questions about the direction of the life path. Generally, when asking about the life path, emotions or belief systems, etc. it is good to first ask permission to test regarding a particular question. For example, "Do I have permission to ask about x?" Sometimes a person may not be ready to hear the answer to a certain question. We need to trust the wisdom of higher guidance in these matters. A few ideas for direction of inquiry include:

Therapy Localization: Place one hand on the area that is affected and do an energy test using the other hand. A muscle that tests weak while you are holding or touching the affected area indicates the area needs a healing or balancing. To test other areas or organs of the body, place hands over the area in question and test.

Food Affinity Testing: Hold a food or supplement in one hand and test for strength or weakness. This is an easy way to determine what foods are good for the body.

LEAP: *Life Essence Awakening Process.* Proceed to the next section for Life Essence Awakening – Etheric Field Analysis. Once experienced with this process, proceed to the following sections for Emotional, Mental and Intuitive Field Analysis.

Candles of Awakening

Below are some pointers that will help you remember that the time shared in a *LEAP* session is for self-inquiry and self-realization. This work is an awakening process that removes the veils that shroud our true nature, bringing about a renewal of being and a deep connection with the source of life.

The most beloved teacher of our true reality, Nisargadatta Maharaj, offers us many pointers to our true reality. The following quotes are borrowed from his acclaimed book and modern spiritual classic *I Am That,* which is highly recommended for anyone who is interested in spiritual awakening.

- Let go of your attachment to the unreal and the real will swiftly and smoothly step into its own. Stop imagining yourself as being or doing this or that and the realization that you are the source and heart of all will dawn upon you. With this will come great love, which is not choice or predication, nor attachment, but a power which makes all things love-worthy and lovable.
- Love says: "I am everything." Wisdom says: "I am nothing." Between the two my life flows.
- You will never be satisfied until you find out that you are what you are seeking.
- The mind turned inward is the self; turned outward, it now becomes the ego and all the world.
- There is only life. There is nobody who lives a life.
- The state of witnessing is full of power, there is nothing passive about it.
- Suffering is due to non-acceptance.
- In order to let go of something you must first know what it is.
- Love is the meaning and purpose of duality.
- To live in the known is bondage, to live in the unknown is liberation.

The Breath of Emptiness

Gently bring your attention into the heart. Breathe deeply, allow your heart to return to its natural state of innocence, a deep release of the past. Letting go of all psychological accumulations, you can sense the emptiness of the heart. Your heart has the deep teaching of silence; breathing allows this teaching to come forth. The heart's inner work is to let go of suffering and return to joy. Offer your life to your Sacred Heart and allow your heart to guide you to a renewal of body, mind and spirit.

Prayer Water

- Use a glass bottle with a glass dropper in the cap. Fill it with water.

- With open palms over this bottle of water, infuse it with your clear intentions. Mantras, prayers, affirmations and loving thoughts all work well.

- With deep gratitude, thank the water for holding the intention and allow the vibration to fully enter the water.

- Take the water like homeopathic drops, under the tongue, about three times a day, 10 drops each time. You can also use the pendulum or muscle test to see how many drops to take.

- For a more powerful effect, have many people pray into the water and then the drops can be taken or given to an individual in need.

Life Essence Analysis Opening Procedure: Summary

The *Life Essence Analysis* forms available in this section are very helpful as a reminder of the procedures as well as convenient for note-taking during the session.

1.   Use the Soul's Goal Journal Form to begin a session.
2.   Review client questionnaire. Discuss goals for healing and intention for the session. Explain the *LEAP* process and Life Essence. Handouts may help.
3.   Have the subject sign the Client Release Form.
4.   Attunement process: Call in Healing Guides, Opening Invocations, Prayers, etc.
5.   Check for hydration.
6.   State intention and ask permission to test.
7.   Check for switching.
8.   Check for clarity. Try some test questions.
9.   Optional: test for priority level/field of inquiry.
10. Proceed to Life Essence Awakening Analysis for appropriate level.

Recheck a few of these initial tests after the session to confirm progress and to check the Life Essence after each session.

Suggested Invocation for a LEAP Session

At the beginning of a healing session an invocation will summon guides and create protection. Here are samples of invocations.

*   To the supreme God, thank you for making me Thy divine healing instrument. Let my entire being be filled with compassion for others who are suffering.
*   To my spiritual teachers, angels and healing guides, thank you for your divine guidance, love and compassion.
*   I am created by divine light, I am sustained by divine light, I am protected by divine light, I am surrounded by divine light, I am ever-growing into divine light.

> *Not words, nor fear, nor habit, but communication of the heart is the*
> *most immutable and most eternal manifestation. Thus will the*
> *Rainbow Bridge draw closer to the shore. Not the withered leaf of*
> *autumn, but the flaming heart shall cross all bridges.*
> ***Agni Yoga Society, Heart***

Notes

Forms for Further Balancing

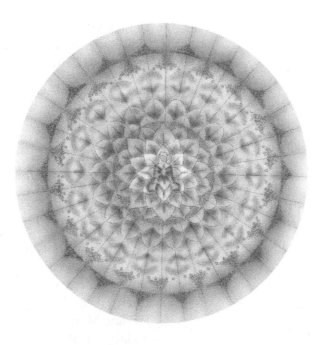

- Priority Healing and Testing Charts
- Life Essence Analysis Flow Chart
- Influencing Factors or Energetic Interferences
- Life-style Questions
- Soul's Goal Forms
- Soul Affirmation Cards

Testing Charts for LEAP Sessions

Etheric Field Testing Charts
Life Force Grounding
Aura Scan
Shen Alarm Points
Endocrine Gland Test
Chakra Test

Etheric Field Revitalization Treatments
Shen Revitalization
Spinal Cleanse
Pain Body Release
Meridian Chi Massage
Lymphatic Massage
AuraTouch
Chakra Balancing

Emotional and Mental Field Charts
Chakra Emotions
Meridian Emotions
Core Emotions
Limited Emotions
Expansive Emotions

Emotional and Mental Field Treatments
Chakra Balancing
Parashakti Alignment
Conscious Choice Affirmation Therapy
Emotional Freedom Technique
Emotional Stress Release
Using EFT Points for meditative treatment

Intuitive Field Charts
Blocks to Spiritual Progress
Soul Qualities
Seven Ray

Intuitive Field Awakening
Guidelines for Building the Bridge of Light
The Path of Ascension
Principles of Awakening
Seven Ray Color Healing

Vibrational Remedy Tool Box
Bach Flowers
Chakra Vibrational Support
Color Healing
Essential Oils
Flower Essences
Soul Ray Remedies
Stones and Crystals

Energy Field Wellness Charts
Life-style Chart
Nutritional Chart
Allergies
Supplements

Energy Field Self-Care
Breathing
Chakra Balancing
Energy Field Protection: Grounding,
     Shielding, Protection, Cleansing
Energy Exercises
Energy Tune-Up
Healing Mudras
Sound, Chanting, Prayer

Influencing Factors
Energetic Influences
Emotional Influences
Belief Systems
Relationships
Timeline Influences
Past-Life Patterns
Self-Sabotage Patterns
Life-Style Questions
Energy Field Congruency – Test for
     conflict between energy fields.

Life Essence Analysis for all levels   Name _____   Date _____

Soul's Goal _____

Healing Intention _____

Prechecks: O Attunements   O Hydration   O Permission   O Switching   O Clearing

1. Rate over all Life Essence

___ Etheric ___ Emotional ___ Mental ___ Spiritual

Rate of Pain/Discomfort/Disturbance _____

Life Force Grounding- Does this system need L.F.G? O Yes   O No

Check the Chakras and note which Subtle Body needs attention.

___ Etheric ___ Emotional ___ Mental ___ Spiritual

Determine the Priority Energy Field for the healing session. _____

Test if there are any energetic influences. _____

2. Etheric Field Analysis

Soul Goal or Healing Intention _____

Rate- Etheric Life Essence _____

Rate- Pain Discomfort _____

Check Life Force Grounding _____

Check Alarm Points _____

Check Endocrine Gland- Etheric Chakras _____

Aura Scan _____

3. Testing Charts

Life Force Grounding _____

Chakras _____

Endocrine Glands _____

Alarm Points _____

Aura Scan _____

4. Etheric Field Revitalization Treatments

Shen Revitalization _____

Spinal Cleanse _____

Pain Chasing _____

Meridian Energy Massage _____

Auricular Exercise _____

Lymphatic Massage _____

Aura Touch _____

Chakra Balancing _____

Optional Treatments _____

5. Emotional and Mental Field Analysis

Souls Goal or Healing Intention _____

Emotional and Mental Field Life Essence _____

Level of Disturbance _____

Life force grounding _____

Alarm points _____

Astral/Emotional or Mental Chakra

Emotions _____   Beliefs _____

Aura Scan _____

6. Emotional and Mental Field Testing Charts

Chakra Emotions _____

Core Afflictive Emotions _____

Limiting Emotions _____

Expansive Emotions _____

Five Element Meridian Emotions _____

Related Fears _____

Conscious Choice Therapy _____

7. Emotional and Mental Field Treatments

Chakra Balance _____

Emotional Stress Release _____

Tapping _____

Forgiveness _____

Judgment Balance _____

Conscious Choice Affirmations _____

8. Intuitive and Soul Kinesiology Analysis

Soul's Goal or Healing Intention _____

Soul Vital Force _____

Level of Disturbance- Soul Crisis _____

Tests to reconfirm balancing _____

Life Force Grounding _____

Soul Chakras _____

9. Testing Charts

Soul Qualities to Enhance _____

Soul Weakness or Blocks to spiritual progress _____

Seven Ray Test- Hold Chakra Determine Ray Type _____

The Path of Ascension _____

The Parashakti Alignment _____

Soul Chakra Balancing/ Energy Field Congruency _____

Qualities and Guidance for Spiritual Awakening _____

10. Intuitive Field and Soul Healing

The Energy of Atma and Building the Bridge of Light _____

The Path of Ascension- Walking with Presence _____

Pathways of the Sacred Heart _____

Soul Ray Color Affirmations _____

Gifts of the Lighted Way to release blocks to your spiritual progress _____

11. Energetic Interference- See Chart

Life Style   _____

Relationship   _____

Time Line   _____

Past Life Pattern   _____

Soul Loss   _____

Discordant Energy   _____

continued, next page

Life Essence Analysys

12. Energy Field Congruency

Ask if the subtle bodies are in agreement with the
healing intention or goal.

O Etheric/ Emotional _____
O Emotional _____   Mental _____
O Mental/ Spiritual _____
O Emotional/ Spiritual _____

13. Optional Testing or Support Charts Tests for Energy Field Kinesiology

(if strong, see appropriate chart)

Life Style _____
Energy Exercises _____
Energy Field Self Care _____
Breathing _____
Nutrition _____
Supplements _____
Allergies _____
Vibrational Remedies _____
Color _____
Sound _____
Essential Oils _____
Bach Flowers _____
Flower Essences _____
Referral _____
Soul Remedies _____
Energy Wellness _____
Life Style Chart _____
Living Meditations _____

Notes:

Life Essence Etheric Analysis

Name _____   Date _____

Soul's Goal _____

Healing Intention _____

Prechecks: ○ Attunements   ○ Hydration   ○ Permission   ○ Switching   ○ Clearing

Overall Tests:	Before	After
Life Essence		
Etheric Field		
Emotional Field		
Mental Field		
Spiritual Field		
Energy Field Priority		

Pain/Disturbance: 1-10	Before	After
Overall		
Specific area I		
_____		
Specific area II		
_____		

Life Essence Grounding:	Before	After
Right		
Left		
Cross		
Cross		
(Write "B"alanced or "W"eak)		

Meridian Check / Alarm Points: Over+/Under-

	Under	Over		Under	Over
Lung			Spleen		
Heart			Kidney		
Circ. sex			Large Intestine		
Stomach			Triple Warmer		
Liver			Small Intestine		
Gall Bladder			Bladder		
Conception			Governing		

Endocrine Glands:
(Write "B"alanced or "W"eak)

Reproductive	____
Adrenals	____
Pancreas	____
Thymus	____
Thyroid	____
Pituitary	____
Pineal	____

Etheric Tests: Vital Force Index

Chakras:	Strong/Weak	SB	Open/Closed	Before	After	Notes
Root						
Navel						
Solar Plexus						
Heart						
Throat						
Third Eye						
Crown						

Aura Scan and AuraTouch
(Write "B" alanced or "W"eak)

Head/Neck	____
Chest	____
Abdomen/Pelvic	____
Legs	____

Remedies/Treatments:

Referrals:

Notes:

Life Essence: Emotional/ Mental Field Analysis Name _____ Date _____

Soul's Goal _____

Healing Intention _____

Pre-checks: ○ Attunements   ○ Hydration   ○ Permission   ○ Switching   ○ Clearing

---

Rate Feeling of Disturbances between 1-10

Before _____

During _____

After _____

Soul crisis: ○ Yes   ○ No

Field Vitality & Priority:

	Before	After
Etheric Field Life Essence	_____ %	_____ %
Emotional Field Life Essence	_____ %	_____ %
Mental Field Life Essence	_____ %	_____ %
Spiritual Field Life Essence (circle priority)	_____ %	_____ %

Life Essence Grounding:

	Before	After
Right		
Left		
Cross		
Cross		

(Write "B"alanced or "W"eak)

Chakra Information:

Chakras:	Strong/Weak	Open/Closed	SB	Chakra Congruency	Notes
Root					
Navel					
Solar Plexus					
Heart					
Throat					
Third Eye					
Crown					

New Goal/Intention (in process)

Emotional Field Disturbance:

Core Chakra (s) _____

Core emotion _____

Time frame: past   present   child   teen   adult
              life   life   age ___   age ___   age ___

Notes _____

Relationship _____

Notes _____

Mental Field Disturbance:

Core Chakra (s) _____

Core belief system _____

Time frame: past   present   child   teen   adult
              life   life   age ___   age ___   age ___

Notes _____

Relationship _____

Notes _____

New Soul Goal/Affirmation:

Remedies/Treatments:

Referrals:

Notes:

Life Essence: Intuitive and Spiritual Field Analysis Name _____ Date _____

Soul's Goal _____

Healing Intention _____

Pre-checks: ○ Attunements   ○ Hydration   ○ Permission   ○ Switching   ○ Clearing

---

| **Rate Feeling of Disturbances between 1-10** | **Field Vitality & Priority:** | | **Life Essence Grounding:** | |

Rate Feeling of Disturbances between 1-10

Before _____

During _____

After _____

Soul crisis: ○ Yes   ○ No

Field Vitality & Priority:

	Before	After
Etheric Field Life Essence	_____ %	_____ %
Emotional Field Life Essence	_____ %	_____ %
Mental Field Life Essence	_____ %	_____ %
Spiritual Field Life Essence (circle priority)	_____ %	_____ %

Life Essence Grounding:

	Before	After
Right		
Left		
Cross		
Cross		

(write "B"alanced or "W"eak)

Intuitive and Spiritual Chakra Influence:

Chakras:	Strong/Weak	Open/Closed	Chakra Congruency	Energy Field Congruency
Root				
Navel				
Solar Plexus				
Heart				
Throat				
Third Eye				
Crown				

Intuitive and Spiritual Disturbances:

Core Chakra (s)_____

Spiritual qualities to increase_____

Time frame: past   present   child   teen   adult
                life   life   age __ age __ age __

Notes_____

Relationship_____

Notes_____

Influence Ray:

1st Monadic _____

2nd Buddic _____

3rd Etheric _____

4th Physical _____

5th Mental _____

6th Emotional _____

7th Spiritual _____

New Soul Goal/Affirmation:

Remedies/Treatments:

Referrals:

Notes:

The truth in you remains
as radiant as a star
as pure as light
as innocent as love itself.
T,65
A Course in Miracles

Influencing Factors or Energetic Interferences Chart

Directions for Inquiry Regarding Energetic Influences or Disruptions

(Refer to Soul Dialogue Guidelines)

_____ Mom	_____ Dad	_____ Brother	_____ Sister
_____ Son	_____ Daughter	_____ Grandmother	_____ Grandfather
_____ Grandson	_____ Granddaughter	_____ Stepmother	_____ Stepfather
_____ Stepson	_____ Stepdaughter	_____ Stepsister	_____ Stepbrother
_____ Aunt	_____ Uncle	_____ Niece	_____ Nephew
_____ Cousin	_____ Friend	_____ Teacher	_____ Other

Timeline/Age:

A. Past

__ 0-5	__6-10	__11-15	__16-20	__21-25
__26-30	__31-35	__36-40	__41-45	__46-50
__51-55	__56-60	__61-65	__66-70	__71-75
__76-80	__81-100			

B. Present

__0-5	__6-10	__11-15	__16-20	__21-25
__26-30	__31-35	__36-40	__41-45	__46-50
__51-55	__56-60	__61-65	__66-70	__71-75
__76-80	__81-100			

Past-Life Chart

A. Cellular memory: What percentage of the vital force is held by past lives?

__10%	__30%	__60%	__70%	__80%
__90%	__100%			

B. Soul memory: What percentage of the vital force is held in the past of this life?

__10%	__30%	__60%	__70%	__80%
__90%	__100%			

Life-style Questions

Test *Yes* or *No* to determine which ones need attention.

1. Activism
2. Addictions
3. Alcohol
4. Allergies
5. Alone
6. Attitude
7. Automobile
8. Behavior
9. Caffeine
10. Career
11. Cell Salts
12. Change Geographical Locality
13. Change Job
14. Change Partner
15. Change Residence
16. Chaos
17. Children's Issues
18. Choice of Products
19. Codependence
20. Computer
21. Creative Outlets
22. Daily Emotions
23. Daily thoughts
24. Devotion
25. Diet
26. Drugs
27. Energy Drain
28. Energy Field Wellness Charts
29. Environmental Toxins
30. Exercise
31. Family Ties
32. Fitness
33. Follow Joy
34. Garden
35. Geopathic Stress
36. Guru
37. Health Questions
38. Hobbies
39. Home
40. Integrity
41. Internet
42. Life Shocks
43. Life Style Testing Charts
44. Love
45. Manipulation
46. Mealtimes
47. Medication
48. Medicine
49. Meditation
50. Minerals
51. Money
52. Moving
53. Music
54. Nature
55. Need for Clear Intention
56. Need for Meditation
57. Need for Prayer
58. Need for Quiet
59. Need Referral
60. Need to be alone
61. Need Vibrational Support
62. News
63. Non-scheduled time
64. Nutrition
65. Order
66. Organization
67. Outdoor
68. Over Caring Issues
69. Parents Issues
70. Personal Products
71. Products
72. Radio
73. Reading Material
74. Relationship to Higher Power
75. Relationships
76. Relaxation Techniques
77. Rest
78. Rhythm
79. Romance
80. Sabbatical
81. Sacred Space
82. School
83. Services
84. Simplicity
85. Sleep
86. Soul Mate
87. Soul Rest
88. Soul Search
89. Spiritual Growth
90. Spiritual Practice
91. Sports
92. Sunlight
93. Supplements
94. Support
95. Teacher
96. Television
97. Therapist Choice
98. Trips
99. Vacation
100. Vitamins
101. Walking

The Soul's Goal

Name _____ Date: _____

Opening Affirmation

_____

_____

Priority Chakra(s) _____

Subtle Body_____

Time-Frame _____

Vital Force and Cellular Memory Held by the Past

_____

Related Emotion or Belief System

_____

Relationship _____

The Way Out, The Path of Return

_____

_____

The Soul's Goal or Living Affirmation

_____

_____

Chakra involved with Soul's Goal

Root	Navel	Solar Plexus	Heart	Throat	3rd Eye	Crown
Yes	Yes	Yes	Yes	Yes	Yes	Yes
No	No	No	No	No	No	No

Subtle Body involved with Soul's Goal

Etheric	Yes	No
Emotional	Yes	No
Mental	Yes	No
Spiritual	Yes	No

Notes:

_____

_____

_____

_____

The Soul's Goal Journal Page

Name _____Date:_____

Opening Affirmation

_____

_____

_____

_____

_____

_____

_____

_____

_____

_____

_____

_____

_____

_____

_____

_____

_____

_____

_____

_____

_____

_____

_____

_____

_____

_____

Soul Affirmation

_____

_____

_____

Soul Affirmation

_____

_____

_____

Soul Affirmation

_____

_____

_____

Soul Affirmation

_____

_____

_____

Soul Affirmation

_____

_____

_____

Soul Affirmation

_____

_____

_____

Soul Affirmation

_____

_____

_____

Soul Affirmation

_____

_____

_____

Soul Affirmation

_____

_____

_____

Soul Affirmation

_____

_____

_____

Cards to be used for sessions - Give to client for home use

Practitioner Notes

Practitioner Notes

What most of us need, almost more than anything, is the courage and humility really to ask for help, from the depths of our hearts; to ask for the compassion of the enlightened beings, to ask for purification and healing, to ask for the power to understand the meaning of our suffering and transform it; at a relative level to ask for the growth in our lives of clarity, peace and discernment and to ask for the realization of the absolute nature of mind that comes from merging with the deathless wisdom mind of the master.

Sogyal Rinpoche

Part Five

LEAP into Vitality, Joy and Faith
Healing and Transformation Methods

Deep within you is everything that
is perfect, ready to radiate through
you and out into the world.
W,63
A Course in Miracles

Leap into Vitality!

Etheric Field Revitalization

Using etheric field treatments will help the vital energy grow strong and balanced. After completing the Life Essence Analysis in the previous section, use kinesiology to determine the most beneficial treatments. If many treatments show up as beneficial, you can do a priority test to see which treatment modality is best for your client. To do this, place index finger and thumb (either your hand or your client's hand) together, so the finger pads touch and ask what is the priority treatment for today. Muscle test for *yes* or *no*. Proceed with the direction of the treatment and remember to test the vital force after the session as well as to see if any further balancing is needed. You can also check to see if the energy needs advanced balancing in the emotional, mental or spiritual fields.

Note: descriptions of pressure point locations and treatment methods are intended primarily for support of those who have had some hands-on training. Instructions from the book alone may not be sufficient to give an effective treatment.

Life Force Grounding Treatment

Hold or press the tender point on the inside corner of one eyebrow (Bladder 1-Eyes Bright) and at the same time, with the opposite hand, press the lateral, outside tender point on the pubic bone (Stomach 30-Rushing Chi) on the same side of the body. Repeat on opposite side and then diagonally.

If the life force needs further balancing, hold base of lower back near the coccyx, behind the ears on each side and then check vital force again. Wait for pulses to come into rhythm.

Suggested Affirmation

I connect deeply with Earth energies while opening to the divine.

Etheric Revitalization Treatment

Client Lying on Back – Yin Treatment: Use pillow under knees, if needed.
Breathing in through your nose or mouth, visualize a beautiful energy of white light flowing from the crown chakra. Encourage your client to breathe deeply and to visualize this energy. Visualize the crown center opening to the healing presence, the light and truth of perfected energy coming in through the crown, flowing down the spine, and gently bathing the chakras. This energy flows down the back side of the body and through the feet, connecting you with the great healing energy of Mother Earth. Use deep breathing throughout the Etheric Revitalization Treatments.

1. Hold the neurovascular points on the forehead.

These points are found in the middle of the forehead halfway between the hairline and middle of the eyebrow.

Suggested Affirmation: I relax into beingness, letting go of

all concerns, worries and stories of life.

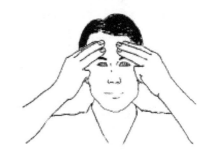

2. Hold Lung 1 points.

Measure four fingers width from the arm point and four fingers down from the collarbone. Use the breath to assist in releasing any pain.

Suggested Affirmation: Letting go, I breathe in humility and contentment.

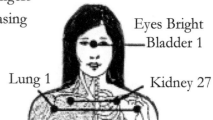

Eyes Bright
Bladder 1

Lung 1

Kidney 27

3. Kidney 27 – Elegant Mansion

In the hollow below the collarbone next to the breastbone.

Suggested Affirmation: I move forward with love. (Release fear.)

4. Rib Points

Hold points along area where rib points curve, directly below nipples.

Suggested Affirmation: I release all blocks to my natural state of joy.

5. Abdomen Release

Use deep pressure counter-clockwise around navel. Pause when painful, encourage deep breathing.

Suggested Affirmation: I breathe in contentment, peace and gratitude.

Rib Points

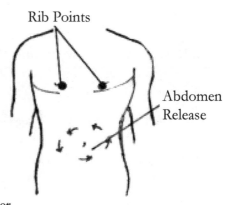

Abdomen
Release

6. Hold Spleen 10

Located three fingers width above the border of the kneecap along the inside of the leg where a hollow tender point exists.

Suggested Affirmation: I release all feeling of separation.

7. Hold Spleen 9

Located at the top of the shin bone on the inside of the leg, three fingers width below the kneecap. (See diagram next page.)

Suggested Affirmation: I have confidence and faith in my life.

8. Spleen 6 – Three Yin Crossing

Four fingers width above inner anklebone, along the middle inside of the top of the leg.

Suggested Affirmation: My life is a river of grace, where all streams are connected to the source.

9. Kidney 1 – Revitalization Point

On the bottom of the foot, at the middle third of the sole between the second and third metatarsal bones.

Suggested Affirmation: My vitality is renewed through spirit.

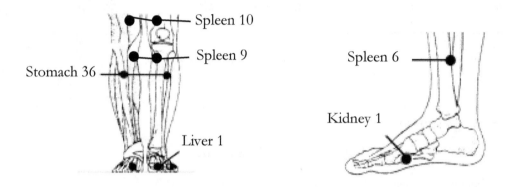

Client turns and lies on Stomach – Yang Treatment: Use pillows as needed and continue to assist the client in the breathing process.

10. Stomach 36

Four fingers below kneecap, one finger width outside of shin bone, in hollow of knee.

Suggested Affirmation: I consciously release patterns of worry and I breathe in great peace.

11. Bladder 54 – Commanding Middle

Located in the center of the crease behind the knee. Press gently, according to the client's guidance.

Suggested Affirmation: I flow through life with ease.

12. Gall Bladder 31 – Wind Market

Directly below middle finger when arm is alongside the body.

Suggested Affirmation: I let my will be the will of my highest good.

13. Bladder 47 – Sea of Vitality-Kidney Revitalization

Four fingers from the spinal column at waist level. Hold thumbs pointing toward back along the waist while fingers point forward. The points are near where the thumbs meet the back muscles. (See diagram next page.)

Suggested Affirmation: I receive the abundant life energy and allow it to flow freely.

14. Bladder 38 – Vital Diaphragm
Between shoulder blade and spine at the level of the heart.

Suggested Affirmation: I let go of patterns of judgement of myself and others.

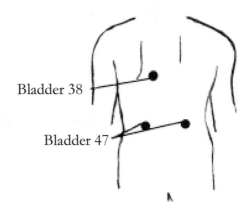

Bladder 38

Bladder 47

15. Hold Hoku – Large Intestine 4 and 11
Upper edge of webbing between thumb and index finger when they are brought together. Hold this and Large Intestine 11 – The point at outer end of elbow crease.

Suggested Affirmation: Breathing out, I practice letting go. Breathing in, I affirm my trust in life.

Back of Hand
Large Intestine 4   Large Intestine 11

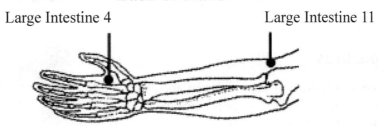

16. TW 15 – Heavenly Bone.
Located one finger width above inside tip of shoulder blade.

Suggested Affirmation: I openly communicate my truth with others.

17. SI 10 – Shoulder Blade.
In the middle of the shoulder blade, below the spine of the scapular spine, about two fingers width.

Suggested Affirmation: I release all blocks to my natural state of joy.

18. Gall Bladder 21 – Shoulder Well.
On either side of the head, between neck and shoulder joint.

Suggested Affirmation: My will reflects a gentle letting go and acceptance of life.

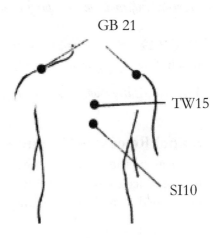

GB 21

TW15

SI10

19. Bladder 10 – Heavenly Pillow. Located halfway between the base of the skull and the base of the neck, between the third and fourth cervical vertebra and about two to three fingers width outside of the spine.

Suggested Affirmation: The ocean of life dissolves any separation I feel.

20. Gall Bladder 20 – Gates of Consciousness. Below the base of the skull in the hollows between the large neck muscles, two to three inches apart.

Suggested Affirmation: I open the door of my heart to the unknown mystery of life.

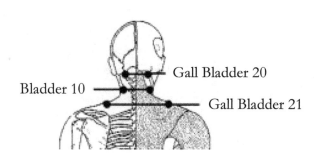

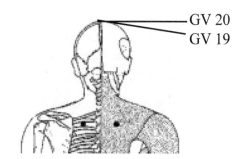

21. Gall Bladder 36

Halfway between spine and upper edge of shoulder blade on both sides of back. Governs resistance, especially to colds and flu.

Suggested Affirmation: I flow through life with ease.

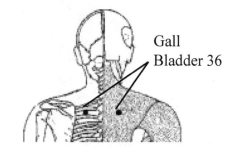

22. GV 20 Head Release – 100 Meeting Point.
Baby's soft spot. Place left fingers behind left ear, right fingers behind right ear. Move fingertips to top of head with a feather-light touch, then feel for hollow area toward the back of the top of the head.

Suggested Affirmation: I express myself according to my truth and co-create with the dance of life.

23. GV 19 – Posterior Summit.
In a hollow, 1" posterior from GV 20.

Suggested Affirmation: I let go and open to the divine, calling truth to guide my being.

Spinal Release – Opening the Channel of the Sushumna.

Move along the spinal column inch by inch, vertebra by vertebra, pressing points on each side to give space to the spinal column. Pause with the breath when the pain is strong. This, performed by itself, is a treatment called the Spinal Cleanse.

Suggested Affirmation: I invite space and movement into my life.

Pain Chasing – Meridian Pain

1. Rate the pain on a scale between one and ten.
    (See pain chart in Etheric Analysis section.)

2. Begin by assisting the client in the deep breathing process. When breathing, put attention on the pain. On the exhalation of the breath, focus on the area of pain.

3. Locate the area of pain along the meridian. Hold the are of pain, using the angle of the finger deep in the point.

4. Hold another point along the same meridian, toward its end. Hold this point until the pain releases.

5. Visualize the breath assisting the pain to move out of the body.

6. Tapping along the meridian while holding the point can be very effective.

7. Continue to hold the point until pain is reduced.

8. You can move pain out of an effected meridian by brushing the pain in the direction the meridian flows.

9. Evaluate pain chart again. Work on other meridians if necessary.

Figure Eight Movements

Trace a figure 8 or infinity sign around the areas of pain. You can do this in any direction. This helps disrupt the energy pattern of the field that is stuck in a pain loop.

Shen Meridian Massage

Practice Shen Massage with your clients, or for self-care. It is invigorating, centering and very healing. Try ending a healing or counselling session with a Shen Energy Massage.
(See Meridian Diagrams in Meridian section.)

Central – Start at the pubic bone and move up the midline to the lower lip.

Governing – Start at the tailbone, go up the spine and over the top of the head, over the nose to the upper lip.

Stomach – Start under the pupil of the eye, move straight down to the jaw, circle up around the face to the neurovascular points, drop straight down over the eye to the clavicle, go out to the side directly over the nipple, straight down over the chest, jog in at the stomach and out at the hips, down the leg (outside knee) and off the second toe.

Spleen – Start on the outside tip of the big toe (medial side), go up the inside of the leg, veering to the outside of the chest and up to the arm crease.

Heart – Start at the armpit, go straight down the inside of the arm, over the palm along the path of the little finger, over the palm and off the tip of the little finger.

Small Intestine – Start at the outside tip of the little finger, go up the back side of the arm to the back, trace the edge of the shoulder blade, then go up the side of the neck to the earlobe, over the cheek and then back to the ear.

Bladder – Start at the inner corner of the eye, go over the head and down the back alongside the spine and around the curve of the gluteus maximus. Then start again at the neck, go out to mid-shoulder, down the back and back of leg, behind the anklebone and out to the little toe.

Kidney – Start on the ball of the foot, go up the arch and just back of the ankle bone, loop back on the inside of the heel, continue straight up the inside of the leg, up the chest right next to the midline, to the inner end of the collarbone.

Circulation Sex – Start just outside the nipples and go up around the arm crease, down the middle of the inside of the arm and out to the middle finger.

Triple Warmer – Start at the ring finger, ascend along the outer surface of the arm to the lateral border of the neck, around the ear and end at the eyebrow.

Gall Bladder – Start at the outer corner of the eye, back to the ear, then loop up and forward, coming down back behind the ear. Return to the frontal eminence, then go down the back of the head, behind the shoulder, forward on the ribs, half-circle backwards to the waist, forward on the hip, then down the side of the leg and out the fourth toe.

Liver – Start on the inside (lateral side) of the big toe next to the second toe. Forward on the edge of the ribs about halfway to the center.

Lung – Start on the upper chest just outside the shoulders, down the inside of the top of the arm, through the palm to the thumb.

Large Intestine – From the top of the index finger go up the outside top of the arm, over the shoulder, to the front of the neck, then up to the corner of the mouth, under the base of the nose, end at the crease next to the flare of the nose.

Auricular Exercise

Along the earlobes are points that correlate to the organs and meridians of the entire body. For this technique, pull earlobes out with fingers pressing all along the points, this brings energy into the whole system.

Lymphatic Massage

The Lymphatic System is part of the overall circulatory system. It is comprised of lymph vessels, nodes and capillaries. It has a system of valves that allow the lymph fluid to flow in one direction. The primary function of the lymph system is to remove wastes from the tissues. This is an absolute essential function without which we would die within 24 hours.

The Lymph system, with its pumping action, flows in one direction towards the heart. The lymph flow is fairly slow and this is necessary in that this system processes and breaks down large bits of matter that cannot be passed directly into the blood system. Being slow, it sometimes clogs up the body.

Neurolymphatic Points (NL), while related to the flow of the lymph, are not lymphatic vessels or nodes. The NL's are reflex points which affect changes in the lymph flow. In general, the stimulation of the neurolymphatic reflexes helps the body to turn on the mechanism that aids the flow. The NL's correspond to particular muscle groups and can be used to facilitate balance and healing in those muscles. A simple image is to think of the NLs as switches that turn up or down the lymph flow. This makes it easier to understand why a muscle will respond so quickly to the stimulation of the NL's.

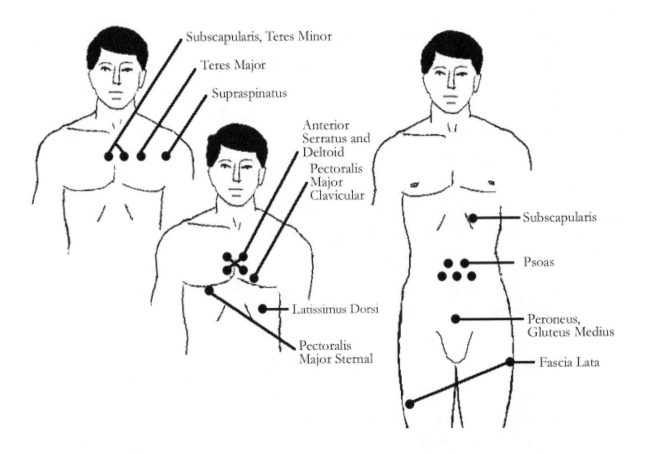

Lymphatic Massage Points

- Teres Minor - Along the ribs, between 3rd & 4th and 4th & 5th thoracic ribs, on the back.

- Teres Major – On the front of the chest in line with where the arms attach to body.

- Supraspinatus – Along the area where the arms are attached to the body.

- Anterior Seratus – Just above breast area at the four corner points of an imaginary square centered on the chest.

- Pectoralis Major Clavicular – Along the underside of the breasts, in soft tissue area.

- Pectoralis Major Sternal – On the ribs, where the ribs surround the solar plexus area.

- Latissimus Dorsi – On the left side of the body, thoracic ribs 7th & 8th.

- Subscapularis – Between ribs 2 and 3 near the sternum (breast bone).

- Psoas – One inch above and one inch below the navel, about two inches out.

- Peroneus Gluteous Media – Upper edge of the pubic bone.

- Fascia Lata – Along upper lateral sides on the outside of the legs, from hips down to the knees.

AuraTouch

Open the palm chakras by rubbing your hands together and sensing the energy there. Create an energy ball in which to focus your attention. Hold the palms together two to three inches apart and move them back and forth. When you have your healing vortex ready begin by scanning your client's aura. Move the palms of your hands down the front of the body, asking for information. If your hands feel magnetically drawn to an area, allow them to receive the information. The following guidelines will assist your scanning and reception.

Does it feel hot, congested, tight? Is there pain? These are signs that there is too much energy in a particular area causing and imbalance.

Does it feel cool, weak, loose? Is there a pain in a different part of the body? These are signs that there is not enough energy, which can also be the cause of an energy imbalance. Check for referral pain or related pain located, for instance, in the neck and lower back.

After scanning the aura, go back again and work with what you have perceived. For weak energy, visually bring in more heat through colors of red to orange, directing energy into an area. For excess energy, use your hand to pull energy out of the congested area, visualizing the calming color blue.

AuraTouch can be used for the following purposes:

- Scanning for information in an analysis.
- Finding out if there are any cords, tears, congested areas, weak or excess energy areas and where they are.
- Releasing energy built up in an area or strengthening an area.
- Clearing the aura and reconnecting it with divine energies.
- Renewing and rejuvenating the aura through the use of color, sound and projections of white or healing light.the emotional field. If strong, move your hand out to the tips of your client's fingers and test while touching the tips of the fingers. If the muscle is strong, while testing as far out as the tips of the fingers, it indicates a healthy emotional field and mental field.

The seeker is he who is in search of himself. Give up all questions except one: Who Am I?

After all, the only fact you are sure of is that you are sure. The I am *is certain. The* I am this *is not. Struggle to find out what you are in reality. To know what you are, you must first investigate what you are not. Discover all that you are not: body, feelings, thoughts, time, space, this or that. The end of the search is when you come to this understanding and you realize you are a limitless being.*

Sri Nisargadatta Maharaj

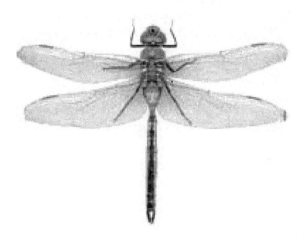

Chakra Balancing - Our Healing Hands

Our hands are nature's way of giving us the ability to heal, comfort and direct love to areas of physical, emotional or mental pain or discomfort. The palm chakras are often portrayed in images of Christ healing. The palm chakras are given to us for use in helping others or ourselves heal our energy. For review, we open our palm chakras by simply rubbing our hands together and sensing the energy. Create a vortex of healing energy and apply it to the chakras that need healing.

Clearing the Chakras

For clearing the chakras, place your palms above each chakra and move it in a counter-clockwise motion. This will remove static energy and clear negative buildup. Flick your hands after the motion to remove the energy or just open your palms upwards towards the heavens and consciously offer it over to spirit to transform or recycle this energy in the highest and best way. After you clear a chakra, move your hand clockwise on the chakra for a longer duration than was used for the counterclockwise movements. The number of these movements depends on how the chakras feel. Listen to your intuition. Clockwise motions can help to open and energize the chakra.

Note: The chakras are tools for transformation. We balance them through a simple clearing motion (as explained above), use them to gain understanding of our issues, and map our healing course. One may balance them on one level in one session, but the imbalance may soon return again until the issue/imbalance on another level/field is healed.

Mantra of the Heart

Gate, Gate, Paragate, Parasamgate, Bodhi Svaha

Gate means gone, Gone from suffering to the liberation of suffering

Gone from forgetfulness to mindfulness

Gone from duality to non-duality

Parasamgate means gone all the way to the other shore

Bodhi – The light of the mind

Svaha – The city of joy

LEAP into Joy!

Emotional and Mental Energy Field Balancing

Energy Field Psychology

The Life Essence Awakening Process for emotional and mental field healing uses kinesiology to determine deep emotions and beliefs that are not in harmony with our natural flow of energy. The subconscious mind and emotions are expressed through the root, navel and solar plexus chakras. These are the life centers that hold the context of our experience as a personal self.

In life, disturbed and unresolved mental and emotional patterns resurface and affect our behavior, choices and relationships. Our challenges and difficulties often display these underlying and recurring disturbances so they can be healed and transformed.

During a *LEAP* session, we ask for divine guidance for help in locating the source of energy disturbances and the hidden gift of the lesson. The pain we hold in what is known as the Pain Body, or our inner energy fields, is often from a deep lack of self-love that expresses itself in self-betrayal, self-denial and self-defense. As we awaken and take a greater responsibility for the light of our soul, we learn to understand the cause of our energy disturbances. What is often revealed at the core of all disturbances is a deep misperception and mistaken identification with the wounded aspects of our self. Through self-forgiveness and profound acceptance these energy afflictions are healed, released and transformed.

The *Life Essence Awakening Process* for the emotional and mental fields assists the participant in shifting attention from the wounded self to the realization of the true self within. This change in perception is the profound outcome of turning within and deeply loving and caring about our inner being which, leads us to take the action necessary to release our energetic afflictions and mistaken identification.

The techniques offered in *LEAP* into Joy, invites healing and transformation to our mind and emotions, leading us to a new life of inner freedom, joy and love and helping us attain harmony and alignment in our body, mind and soul.

Using kinesiology methods, determine which is the priority treatment for the emotions that were identified by *LEAP* in the previous chapter.

Life Essence Awakening
Healing and Transformation Processes

Emotional Stress Release Technique

The emotions or beliefs that have been identified through the muscle testing guidelines throughout this work can be released in a gentle, meditative way through holding the neurovascular points on the forehead. These points are located halfway between the hairline and the eyebrow, in the pulse points, on the middle of the forehead. You will feel a small indentation on these points. (See diagram below.)

When an emotion is particularly charged with energy, the pulses will feel stronger than normal. Simply place your hands, using a feather light touch, on these points. Have your client do deep breathing while allowing the emotion to float through the sky of awareness. Just witness and refrain from all judgment. Through quiet observation, the emotions will release and the pulses will synchronize and become calmer. While holding these points you can also work with the positive affirmation that is the antidote to the painful emotion being experienced. Affirmations with words such as acceptance, forgiveness, and release are suggested for most effective balance.

Neurovascular Points for Emotional Stress

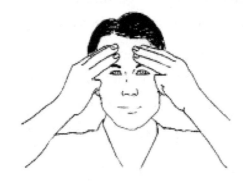

Emotional Freedom Technique *by Gary Free*

Offered by permission. Visit www.emofree.com for a complete listing of teaching videos, EFT Certification and more. (See diagram, pg 224, for Tapping Procedures.)

Tapping meridian points, along with affirmations, is an effective way to release stress from the energy fields. The seventeen points offered in the Emotional Freedom Technique will help you release suppressed emotions and beliefs and experience an overall renewal of your life force.

Step One – Dialogue with client to determine emotional or mental stress. Use charts that test strong, for further clarity. Rate the disturbance between one and ten. (See the guidelines at the front of this section on how to rate disturbances).

Step Two – Tap on the meridian points five times using the tapping sequence affirmation given on pg. 225. After you have done this, see if the disturbance has subsided.

Step Three – Rate the disturbance again, to determine if it is lessened.

Step Four – If the disturbance remains, tap up to three more times and then rate again.

Step Five – For persistent disruption, tap the points for psychological reversal.

Step Six – Hold neurovascular points while the client does deep breathing and sees the disturbance as if on a movie screen. See the story connected with the disturbance and remain in observation. You may also use the tapping procedure to enhance this powerful technique. Use muscle testing to determine other areas of healing that need attention. Psychological reversals are a disruption in the energy field that could be called the *energy culprit*. Work with sacred dialogue suggestions to assist in bringing forth any hidden energies.

The Emotional Freedom Technique

Rate stress level, once in the beginning of the session, and one or two times more during and at the end of the session. Tapping the acupoints stimulates and changes the body's energy flow, releasing disturbances in the field.

Use a scale of 1-10. (Zero means that the issue does not bother you and you are neutral and relaxed.)

One – Absence of stress.

Two – Slight discomfort, mild irritation.

Three – Unpleasant feeling.

Four – Tolerant of stress, but uncomfortable.

Five – Very uncomfortable but not completely out of control.

Six – Extremely uncomfortable, life is altered.

Seven – Severe emotional pain.

Eight – Very disturbed, crisis.

Nine – Increasing to almost intolerable.

Ten – Extreme Crisis

Following, you will find some important points to remember while tapping.

The Sore Spot

There are two sore spots and it doesn't matter which one you use. They are located in the upper left and right portions of the chest and you find them as follows: Go to the base of the throat, about where a man would knot his tie. Poke around in this area and you will find a U-shaped notch at the top of your sternum (breastbone). From the top of that notch go down three inches toward your navel and over three inches to your left (or right). You should now be in the upper left (or right) portion of your chest. If you press vigorously in that area (within a two inch radius) you will find a "sore spot." This is the place you will need to rub while repeating the affirmation. This spot will be sore when you rub it vigorously because lymphatic congestion occurs there. Rubbing the spot disperses that congestion. Fortunately, after a few episodes the congestion is all dispersed and the soreness goes away. Then you can rub it with no discomfort whatsoever. To treat psychological reversals, you can tap or rub on the point, clockwise.

The Karate Chop Point

The Karate Chop point (abbreviated KC) is located at the center of the fleshy part of the outside of either hand, between the top of the wrist and the base of the baby finger or – stated differently – the part of your hand you would use to deliver a karate chop. Instead of rubbing it as you would the Sore Spot, you vigorously tap the Karate Chop point with the fingertips of the index finger and middle finger of the other hand. While you could use the

Tapping Sequence

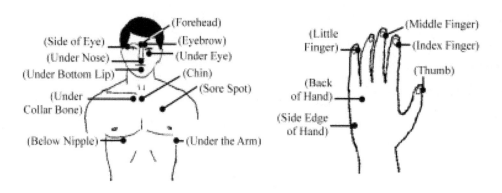

karate chop point of either hand, it is usually most convenient to tap the Karate Chop point of the non-dominant hand with the two fingertips of the dominant hand. If you are right handed, for example, you would tap the karate chop point on the left hand with the fingertips of the right hand.

The Basic Tapping Sequence Setup

Repeat this affirmation three times while continuously rubbing the Sore Spot or tapping the Karate Chop point: "Even though I have _____ (specify energy disturbance), I deeply and completely accept myself." Next, tap about seven times on each of the following energy points while repeating the reminder phrase at each point. (See tapping chart.)

1. EB = Beginning of the eyebrow. Trauma, frustration, restlessness.
2. Forehead. Neurovascular points, about halfway between the hairline and the eyebrow, where the indentation on the forehead is, or about one inch up from the eyebrow. (As shown in the description of Emotional Stress Release in this section.) These are strong emotional points to hold, or tap gently, while saying affirmations or tapping statements. For depression, anxiety, trauma and painful memories.
3. SE = Side of the eye. Anger.
4. UE = Under the eye. Anxiety, nervousness.
5. UN = Under the nose. Embarrassment.
6. Ch = Chin. Shame.
7. CB = Beginning of the collarbone, on the chest between, and slightly down from, the collarbone points. Immune system, energy improvement.
8. UA = Under the arm. Nervousness, self-esteem.
9. BN = Below the nipple. Where rib cage ends. Sadness and unhappiness.
10. Th = Thumb. Helps with tolerance and arrogance.
11. IF = Index finger. Located on either index finger, on the side of the fingernail closest to the thumb. Helps to release guilt.
12. MF = Middle finger. On either middle finger. For treating jealousy and addictive cravings.
13. LF = Little finger. Inside tip of either hand, where the fingernail joins the cuticle. Helps to release anger.
14. KC = Karate Chop. Side of hand located on the little finger side of either hand, the palm crease that is closest to fingers. Important point for sadness and psychological reversal.

15. BH = Back of hand. Points between the little finger and ring finger knuckles, in the direction of the wrist. For pain, depression, and loneliness. Important point for psychological reversals.

After performing the tapping sequence above, the next procedure helps the body to assimilate the Emotional Freedom Technique (EFT) process. This is called the 9 Gamut actions or, brain balancer. In this procedure you will tap on the back of the hand between the little finger and ring finger while following the nine steps below.

1. Eyes closed.
2. Eyes open.
3. Eyes hard down right while holding the head steady.
4. Eyes hard down left while holding the head steady.
5. Roll eyes in a circle as though your nose were at the center of a clock and you were trying to see all the numbers in order.
6. Repeat as item five, but reverse the direction in which you roll your eyes.
7. Hum two seconds of a song such as Happy Birthday. This stimulates brain activity.
8. Count rapidly from one to five.
9. Hum two seconds of a song again.

Meditative Point-holding for Emotional Release

At some point you may want to simply hold the tapping points, while saying the affirmations and doing deep breathing. This is an alternative to tapping, for times when you may want a more meditative experience. This is a wonderful healing technique that is also very effective, calming and balancing.

Psychological Reversal

When the mind and emotions are not in agreement and there is a conflict between the personality and the soul, there is most likely a psychological reversal occurring. This is an energy war between mind and heart that creates conflict between actions and thought. For example, you want to be happy but are choosing to be miserable. Maybe you don't feel worthy of what you want from life. When you work on your goal something blocks you from attaining it and you behave in a manner that is self-destructive. These blind spots prevent you from seeing and implementing solutions. You know you have the ability to change, but cannot. Energy Reversal occurs due to switched or reversed electromagnetic energies in the meridians, due to layering of issues.

To correct this energy disruption, tap the Karate Chop point approximately five times. This will change the psychological reversal. If it does not, tap up to 15 times more. It is helpful to repeat your soul affirmation while tapping these points.

Other corrections for switching are explained in the opening procedure for Life Essence Awakening Analysis, and include Cross Crawl, Cooks Hook-Ups, Figure Eights, Zip Ups, Eye Rotations with Affirmations, drinking water, deep breathing, rubbing Kidney 27 and navel, and rubbing above and below the lip and around the navel.

Eye roll

This aspect of the treatment reduces levels of stress through tapping on the back of the hand between the ring finger and little finger while you slowly move your eyes, looking down at the floor then looking up at the ceiling in one continuous circular motion.

Collarbone Breathing Exercise

Place two fingers of your right hand on your right Collarbone point. With two fingers of your left hand, tap the Gamut point continuously while you perform the following five breathing exercises:

1. Breathe halfway in and hold it for seven taps.
2. Breathe all the way in and hold it for seven taps.
3. Breathe halfway out and hold it for seven taps.
4. Breathe all the way out and hold it for seven taps.
5. Breathe normally for seven taps.

Place the two fingers of your right hand on your left Collarbone point and, while continuously tapping the Gamut point, repeat the five breathing exercises. Bend the fingers of your right hand so that the second joints, or knuckles, are prominent. Then place them on your right Collarbone point and continuously tap the Gamut point while doing the five breathing exercises. Repeat this by placing the right knuckles on the left Collarbone point. You are now halfway done. You complete the Collarbone Breathing Exercise by repeating

the entire procedure using the fingertips and knuckles of the left hand. You will, of course, be tapping the Gamut point with the fingertips of the right hand.

The Parashakti Alignment Process

Through our healing and transformation, we awaken to the essence of our true nature. We are building an inner bridge between our personality and soul, and opening the gateway to our Intuitive and Spiritual Energy Fields. Our inner guide appears and takes us by the hand through the narrow passageway of life's duality. The duality is simply the tendencies of the mind that are locked in desire and veil our spirit. The softening of the mind assists us to awaken and open our reflective consciousness. The lower centers of the root, navel and solar plexus are the container for our subconscious thoughts, desires and emotions. In purifying this aspect of our being we attain alignment with our soul's evolving love. When the first three chakras of our personality nature are aligned and integrated with the higher chakras of our soul we become unified in Light Consciousness.

Crown Chakra

The Crown chakra is the awareness in which all is appearing, the master power that reconnects us with our divine source. Through integration and unification of our soul's experience, the thousand-petaled lotus blossoms in radiant beauty.

Root and Third Eye Chakras

When the Root and Third Eye chakras are in alignment, our foundation for life is strong and we are able to master our personal will and surrender to the highest good. Duality is transcended as we walk the middle path between opposites, remaining deep at rest in the unchanging nature of life.

Navel and Throat Chakras

Our Navel chakra (the center of physical creativity) is aligned with our Throat chakra (the center of spiritual creativity), and we are unified in our expression as spiritual beings. Our emotional expression is connected with our true vision and our soul's purpose and we create life with divine intention. We return often to the silence of our true nature through prayer and communion. Afflictive emotions such as opinions, judgments, criticism, ego-positioning and wrong use of power are transformed through deep surrender.

Solar Plexus and Heart Chakras

The Solar Plexus chakra, in harmony with the Heart chakra, brings healing and release of our lower emotional nature. The energy of the solar plexus, once used for personal gain and power, now serves a higher purpose. Our sense of self is infused with the divine attributes of the Sacred Heart and the personality and the soul merge. The heart is the temple of our intuition to which we turn quietly and receive divine light and guidance. The opened heart floods our being with intuition and compassion which, in turn, nurtures our entire being.

Questions for the Parashakti Alignment Process

Open the balance by asking for the soul's goal or healing intention. Write it down on the form provided. (See the Sacred Appointment section.)

1. Ask if the chakras are aligned, congruent and in agreement with the soul's goal or healing intention.

2. If weak, note which chakras are not aligned. Look at the emotions, beliefs and psychological aspects of the chakras. Create a dialogue between them to assist the alignment process. An example dialogue would be, "Are the Solar Plexus and Heart chakras in agreement with the soul's goal, or healing intention?"

3. Test. If weak, ask what emotions or beliefs are involved (see charts).

4. Identify the energy block that is preventing the two chakras from being in alignment with the healing intention.

5. Ask: "How is this serving me? What would it be like for me to give up this energy block?" (See chakra emotion charts in Chakras section.)

6. Through dialogue with the energies, you can discover the aspects of your being that are held in fear and insecurity and then infuse them with the highest healing energy of love. This is supported by unconditional love, acceptance and compassion.

7. Ask what emotions or beliefs would strengthen your life essence to accomplish the release of the disturbance. (See chart of positive emotions or spiritual qualities.)

8. Test the charts. Create an affirmation using these positive qualities.

9. Test. If strong, end with "I am 100% willing to accept the gift of balance, and to release the need for the problem." "I am 100% willing to release obstacles to this gift." "I am 100% willing to release the need for the problem."

10. Test. If both are strong, the balance is complete. Confirm the soul affirmation and say a blessing of gratitude for the balance.

Conscious Choice Therapy

After determining the rate of the vital force from the previous analysis and that Conscious Choice Therapy will strengthen the vital force, proceed with the dialogue.

A suggested dialogue:

"I choose self-love and ...

1. ... ask that the obstacles in my mental field are cleared by this choice." Test. If strong, proceed with the healing affirmation.
2. "I am 100% willing to choose self-love now and I let go of all obstacles to choosing self-love."
3. "I am 100% willing to receive the gifts of choosing self-love." Test. If weak, use soul dialogue guidlines to determine what is blocking the conscious choice.

To Review see Consciouse Choice Chart or use the following choices:

"I choose ...

1.	Abundance	17.	Joy
2.	Acceptance	18.	Letting Go
3.	Beauty	19.	Life
4.	Blessings	20.	Love
5.	Compassion	21.	Peace
6.	Conscious Awareness	22.	Present Time
7.	Death	23.	Right Perception
8.	Devotion	24.	Self-Love
9.	Dignity	25.	Service
10.	Forgiveness	26.	Timelessness
11.	Freedom	27.	To Be True
12.	God	28.	Understanding
13.	Goodness	29.	Wisdom
14.	Gratitude		
15.	Health		
16.	Integrity		

I am that I am
Exodus 3:14

A man is called the Knower of the Self who casts away all desires of the mind and is satisfied by the Self and the Self alone. A man is called Enlightened by the Self whose mind is not disturbed by pain, whose cravings for pleasure have disappeared, who is free from passion, fear and anger, and who, under any condition, remains detached. The good and evil cannot disturb him and he neither praises nor condemns nor hates. Thus he is well established in the light of Self-Knowledge.

Bhagavid Gita 2:55:58
H. Saraydarian translation

LEAP into Faith!

Soul Rejuvenation and Intuitive Field Healing

The Life Essence Awakening Process for the Intuitive and Spiritual energy fields, *LEAP* into Faith!, is a research program that endeavors to understand spiritual principles and energy alignment with the divine to facilitate deep and profound transformation.

The *LEAP* Intuitive and Soul Kinesiology and Analysis will assist you in identifying blocks to your spiritual progress as well as soul qualities to enhance and awaken your soul's light. *LEAP* into Faith! is an invitation to your soul to bring about self-realization and reconnection with your divine source.

To review, the *Life Essence Awakening Process* for the emotional and mental energy fields identifies disturbed energy patterns that prevent you from living to your true potential. Through deep transformation, these patterns are healed and released and a new life is possible, one with clear intentions and inspiration from the light of the soul. The lower energy fields are stabilized and held steady in the light. The energy fields, when transformed, become a great vehicle to express your soul's higher intention as well as to increase the power of visualization and spiritual invocation. The next level of healing and transformation occurs through opening to the higher realms, the intuitive and spiritual energy fields. Through the purification process of the lower energy fields you are now able to access a greater light to assist you on your journey home. *LEAP* into Faith! facilitates the unification of your personality and soul, aiding you in attaining a deep sense of wholeness, unity consciousness and spiritual well-being.

Most humans are imprisoned and controlled by their lower natures and often live a life of suffering. The path of spiritual evolution is a serious one that requires one to let go of the lower tendencies of the mind and increase the soul qualities of love, wisdom and spiritual will. The first step for those serious about radical change in consciousness is to let go of our identification with the false nature of the self.

The Energy of Atma and Building the Bridge of Light

The highest expression of the divine realms is Atma, the omnipresent pure consciousness of God, beyond time and form. This sacred force is reached through building the Bridge of Light, when the soul and personality become one unified whole. It is within this divine realm that the will-aspect of spirit is expressed, directing you to your divine purpose.

The energy of Atma impresses upon your soul deep feelings of inspiration and spiritual creativity. Upon rising to this divine plane, you are bestowed with the spiritual gifts of power, inspiration, light, love, and wisdom.

When the personality and soul are unified, the energy fields become instruments of the soul and you are guided by a higher will. From this, a deep peace is realized within your heart and you walk with great care and harmlessness. Through the awakening process, you accept being a disciple of truth and your life is lived in service to the evolution of consciousness for the benefit of all beings.

Now a student in the art of mystical seeing, you see the truth of life and increase your ability to discern between the real and unreal. You realize that you are the awareness or witness of the changing nature of life. Compassion deepens when detachment is achieved as you hold dear the eternal and unchanging essence within your heart as a most precious jewel.

The purified mind lives free from the pulls of duality and the activity of judging, rejecting, liking and disliking. Resting deep within your spiritual heart, life is lived in peace, free from the obstacles of the ego self. The lighted way opens the doorway to the celestial energy fields where you live in the vibration of spiritual will, love and wisdom.

The higher calling of the soul is a magnetic force that pulls you out of the darkness of ignorance and suffering. This calling, or whisper, can be heard when the mind is silent and surrendered to guidance. This most sacred guidance reveals the mystery of life and the unification process between spirit and matter. You have now embarked on your path to joy.

The path of the lighted way opens when you have aligned your lower energy fields with the light of the soul. The soul becomes the still pond in which ripples come and go, and life is

seen through the inner eye of clear perception. You walk in life more fully with the great vision of your soul's purpose.

Pathways of the Sacred Heart

The Path of Surrender

As you embark upon the Path of Surrender there is no more holding of anything that obscures the vision of your true self. Your sincerity is clear and devoted to wholeness and unity. Your spiritual practice becomes one of letting go, allowing the truth of your being to emerge. This is true surrender.

Know that, through surrender, your inner guide appears and the light of your true essence is strengthened. You turn inward to the presence residing within your heart, and offer all to this sacred force. Your life becomes a garland of roses, in which all experiences are devoted to the inner altar of your heart.

On your golden platter of offerings, you freely put everything, your darkest secrets and human errors, releasing all burdens, once and for all. Offer your entire human history on this sacred platter.

Your relationship to life becomes unconditional, as your surrender deepens. The temporary, passing nature of life teaches you about detachment and guides you to hold steadfast to the eternal, unchanging essence of life.

In this most beautiful and gracious act of consciousness, you now begin taking full responsibility for the evolution of your soul. Through your evolving love, you deepen the connection with your divine source, creating a ground of being that is unshakable.

You welcome the Sacred Presence within to release and transform the story of your being. The transformation of your story creates a new life, one of service and the expression of love, truth and beauty for the good of all concerned.

The Path of Devotion

Devotion is the natural action that stems from the silence of your heart. The love within your heart, when unbounded, is equal to the love of the creator and the love for all of life. You are capable of this love when you turn within to the silence of your heart.

Devotion that is expressed from your true essence brings a deep sense of unity, where the worshipped and the worshipper become one unified sacred force. Devotion from the silence of the heart is simply an unmistakable recognition of the sacred essence of God within all of life.

Upon the realization of your true nature, you experience the love of God, the supreme devotion of the sacred essence of life. Devotional inquiry becomes the foundation for your life, when knowing God as your true self becomes your life task.

In physical manifestation you have the distraction of the body, mind, emotions and senses. You know, deeply, that your attention must turn inward to meet your true and unchanging nature. This turning is the supreme action of devotion. In this turning you find the eternal source for all of life. You are this unity, an integral being of light. You are the manifestation of the divine and you must remember your source at all times. This remembering is an act of devotion.

The Path of Service

Suffering is what all humans experience through the school of life. Because much of the suffering that is experienced is a result of the seeds you have planted for self-centered gain, there comes a time when you need to take responsibility and turn to a path of harmlessness for yourself and others. The art of inquiry reveals the source of suffering and leads you to self-understanding. The first question to ask yourself is, Who Am I? This flame of inquiry leads you to find out who you truly are, and ends the cause of suffering. Deep within the silence of your heart, your answers await in the wellspring of truth. This silence is the fountain of peace where all life's actions come from divine order and harmlessness. In this silence there is no longer a separate individual who is contributing to sorrow.

The eternal truth of life leads you to find your inner light, beyond the effects of opposites. You see that where there is pleasure there is pain, and these dualities are a display of mental positions and judgments, the result of a pleasure-seeking mind. The middle path is the path of silence, where the duality of life ceases and there is only *being*.

Service is living and being in your truth. In the silence of your heart, your true nature resides. The love of your true nature will guide you to serve where it is needed. You

become a vehicle of divine love, allowing it to flow when needed; an unconditional love that is beyond personal gratification and self-gain. Your devotion to your true nature fills your inner cup. From this sacred chalice of love all things come.

The Path of Ascension – Walking with Presence

Alignment with Purpose – The Sacred Contract to Evolve

Joyfully agree to walk the Path of Ascension, the journey to evolve in love. Ask to be accepted as a Disciple of Truth.

Alignment with Truth – The Authentic Use of Ego

Your intention for truth is the fuel for your journey. Ask that all aspects of your being be in agreement with your intention for truth.

Alignment with a Higher Power – Right Use of Will

Surrender all self-centered activity, power, thoughts and emotions that feed your separate sense of self. Become an empty vessel of the light. Allow the power of spirit to fill you, offer everything to spirit, in deep devotion.

Alignment with Unconditional Love, Compassion, and Acceptance – Releasing All Judgement

Return to your sacred temple with empty hands and open arms, releasing attachments and ego positions and receive the abundant love of spirit. Come to the altar of the divine free of judgment, doubt, fear and self-centered love.

Alignment With Silence and Harmlessness – Reception to a Higher Guidance

From the depth of your being, ask that all actions, expressions, thought, words and deeds come from the wellspring of your Sacred Heart. Take the vow of harmlessness. Live from deep surrender and allow all actions to emerge from your true nature of silence.

Alignment with Pure Perception – The Art of Seeing Clearly

Hold steady the point between duality, the swaying between the senses of pleasure and pain. Remain true to this sacred light that is accessed through stillness. Live the truth, live the inquiry, live the divinity, and live the love.

Alignment with Glory – The Art of Surrender

Surrender all separation; know you are whole and one with the divine source. Accept the crown of glory as you deepen your surrender. Take your rightful place as a beacon of light in the manifested world. The path of mastery leads to deeper and deeper surrender, the emptiness of self. You stand in the center of your being, on your own sacred ground as a spiritual warrior of truth.

Gifts of the Lighted Way

Through using the *yes/no* method of Kinesiology, (or muscle testing) you can determine which *Soul Qualities* or *Gifts of the Lighted Way*, you would like to enhance on your spiritual path. After discovering which qualities are needed, you can create affirmations and spiritual intentions using kinesiology to test whether or not your whole being will support these qualities. Below is an example of a simple testing procedure for *Gifts of the Lighted Way*. If you need more information, review the testing guidelines in the Kinesiology Counseling section of the book.

Sample Dialogue

- Say: *"I call in acceptance for all things on my life path."* Test strong (yes), you believe this to be true. Test weak (no), this does not hold true for you.

- If weak (no), follow the guidelines for sacred dialogue in the Kinesiology Counseling section of this book.

- If strong (yes), say: *"This system is 100% willing to accept the gifts of acceptance."* Test.

- If strong again, say: *"This system is 100% willing to release all obstacles to having acceptance in their life."* If the answer is, once again yes, the affirmation will support the evolution of the body, mind and spirit. If the answer is no, again read the Kinesiology Counseling section for further guidance.

Gifts of the Lighted Way Soul Qualities

Use kinesiology to determine qualities that are lacking and qualities that are developed. Qualities of having or being:

Accepting	Expanded		Renewed
Alive	Faith	Loving	Responsible
Attentive	Flowing	Magical	Serenity
Autonomy	Focused	Masterful	Simple
Awakened	Freedom	Mindful	Stillness
Aware	Fullness	Non-Afflictive	Strong
Beauty	Grace	Non-Invasive	Supportive
Benevolent	Grateful	Non-Judgmental	Surrendering
Certainty	Generosity	Non-Reactive	Tenderness
Compassionate	Gentle	One-Pointed	Tranquil
Concerned	Giving	Oneness	Transcendent
Confident	Good Listener	Open-Minded	Transformed
Conscious	Goodness	Peace	Truth
Contemplative	Gracious	Perceptive	Unified
Contentment	Harmless	Perfection	Understanding
Conviction	Honest	Positive	Unlimited
Courageous	Impersonal	Power	Uplifting
Dedicated	Infinite	Practical	Value
Devoted	Innocence	Presence	Vigilant
Discernment	Intelligent	Pure Will	Vitality
Discriminating	Intentional	Quiet	Wholeness
Enchanting	Joyous	Receptive	Wise
Equanimity	Kindhearted	Rejuvenated	Wondrous

Soul Ray Color Affirmations

Energy test to find which qualities and colors strengthen the energy fields. Then create and use soul affirmations along with visualization of the ray color or by using colored glasses. (Colored glasses are available through Life Essence Foundation.)

First Ray of Power

Monadic Plane – Hold the crown chakra and visualize blue, or use the colored glasses in white or blue. Create a soul affirmation after testing which qualities need enhancement.

Beingness
Courage
Endurance
Energy and Power
Humility
Renunciation
Self-control
Self-reliance

Steadfastness
Strength
Striving
Truthfulness
Will
Will to Act

Will to Evolve
Will to Express
Will to Harmonize
Will to Unify

Second Ray of Love and Wisdom

Buddhic Plane – Hold the heart center and visualize, or use colored glasses that are, golden yellow or azure blue. Create soul affirmations and use them to enhance the following qualities.

Beauty
Blessing
Communication
Compassion
Cooperation
Endurance
Enfoldment
Enlightenment

Consciousness Expansion
Faithfulness
Healing
Insight
Intuition
Magnetism
Oneness
Patience

Righteousness
Serenity
Tolerance
Understanding
Unselfishness
Wisdom

Third Ray of Activity and Adaptability

Etheric Plane – Hold the navel chakra while visualizing, or using colored glasses that are, green. Create soul affirmations after determining what qualities need improvement.

Accuracy
Adaptability
Balance
Common Sense
Comprehension
Dignity
Discrimination

Energy
Idealism
Intellect
Intuition
Joyousness
Knowledge

Light
Service
Sincerity
Synthesis
Tolerance
Understanding

Fourth Ray of Harmony Through Conflict

Physical Plane – Hold the root chakra while visualizing, or using colored glasses that are, bronze or red. Create soul affirmations after determining the qualities that are needed.

Agreement	Harmony	Purity
Balance	Inner Vision	Rhythm
Beauty	Intuition	Serenity
Confidence	Manifestation	Stability
Creativity	Perception	

Fifth Ray of Concrete Knowledge or Science

Mental Plane – Hold the throat chakra while visualizing the color yellow or wearing yellow glasses. Create a soul affirmation after testing which qualities are in need of strengthening in the energy fields.

Accuracy	Detachment	Order
Balance	Energy	Perseverance
Connection	Independence	Reverence
Consciousness	Intelligence	Thoughtfulness

Sixth Ray of Devotion

Emotional Plane – Hold the solar plexus chakra and visualize the color red or wear red glasses. Create a soul affirmation using the qualities below that strengthen the energy fields.

Austerity	Inclusiveness	Sacrifice
Balance	Intuition	Self-discipline
Detachment	Love	Serenity
Devotion	Loyalty	Strength
Forgiveness	Mastery	Tenderness
Gentleness	Purity	Tolerance
Gratitude	Reverence	Trust

Seventh Ray of Ceremonial Magic

Atmic Plane – Hold third eye chakra while visualizing the color purple or using the purple colored glasses. Create an affirmation that strengthens the energy fields from the seventh ray qualities below.

Alchemy	Glory	Sharing
Beauty	Initiation	Sound
Ceremony	Magic	Teaching
Color	Order	Guiding
Discipline	Rhythm	

Study Questions

1. Explain your understanding of the etheric field treatments and the balancing effect they have in the *Life Essence Awakening Process*. Why is it called *LEAP* into Vitality?

2. What are the important points of Energy Field Psychology and the transformation and release of emotions?

3. Describe the treatments offered in *LEAP* into Joy! – Emotional and Mental Field Kinesiology. How can they help you to feel lighter and more joyful?

4. How do you use the testing charts in this level to determine the treatment that is most effective?

5. Explain the following treatments: Emotional Stress Release and Emotional Freedom Technique.

6. What is the importance of letting go of judgment in healing discordant emotions and belief systems?

7. What are the significant points in the *LEAP* into Faith! section of this book?

8. Explain your understanding of Building the Bridge of Light.

9. What are the aspects of ascension and walking with presence in your life?

10. Share your understanding of the principles of awakening, surrender, devotion and service.

I wearied myself searching for the friend with efforts beyond my strength

I came to the door and saw how powerfully the locks were bolted.

And the longing in me became that strong, and then I saw I was gazing from within the Presence. With that waiting, and in giving up all the trying, only then did Lalla flow out from where I knelt.

Lalla – Naked Song
by Coleman Barks

Part Six
Vibrational Medicine
An Energy Healer's Toolbox

*Rise up nimbly and go on your strange journey to
the ocean of meanings. The stream knows it can't
stay on the mountain. Leave, and don't look away
from the sun as you go, in whose light you are
sometimes crescent, sometimes full.*

Rumi

Bach Flowers and Flower Essences

Dr. Edward Bach first developed the Bach Flowers in 1930 as treatment for the causes of illness in the emotional and mental energy fields. Dr. Bach believed that illness could not be treated effectively without taking emotional, mental and spiritual influences into consideration. His work with flower essences was based on the premise that the heart and soul held the answers to tuning negative emotional and health states to positive states.

Dr. Bach defined thirty-eight different emotional states, along with seven states of mind. He discovered that correcting beliefs, attitudes and conditioning can stop the onset of disease. The mental components that lay at the root of a problem can be corrected through flower remedies which illuminate negative aspects of the personality and encourage the positive expression of energy.

The remedies balance disturbances in the emotional, mental and spiritual bodies to prevent physical illness. Dr. Bach realized that illness was a symptom of disharmony between soul and personality. He believed all beings had a divine purpose and illness was a message for people to see their error in perception and find their true purpose.

Some of the core soul issues that Bach felt were the cause of illness are impatience, a critical attitude, grief, excessive fear, terror, bitterness, lack of self-esteem, indecision, over-enthusiasm, doubt, ignorance, denial or repression, resentment, restlessness, apathy, indifference, weakness of will and guilt.

The positive soul virtues of love, wisdom, courage, joy, strength, vigilance, harmlessness, forgiveness, understanding, acceptance and compassion are encouraged through the flowers. They reconnect the personality with the soul and create an energy alignment between the lower fields and the spiritual fields.

Flower essences are made from flowers found all around the world. Blossoms are picked in their prime and floated in vats of pure distilled water, which are exposed to sunlight. The subtle essence of the flowers is transferred by means of the light into the water. Brandy, vinegar or glycerine is added as a preservative.

In choosing a remedy, let the state of mind guide you to the choice of which remedies are needed. Observe the state of mind for any change in the thought process. It is important to note these changes before disease appears so that treatment can prevent the onset of disease. When an illness has been present for a long time the mood of the sufferer will act as a guide to finding the correct remedy.

Guidelines for Using Flower Essences

Take 2-4 drops under the tongue, four times a day or every hour. Doses can be taken in water, milk, juice or any other liquid and may be taken every few hours – for more severe symptoms, every half-hour. For long-standing conditions take every 2-3 hours. Up to seven Flower Essences can be mixed in a dropper bottle and administered as above either under the tongue (sublingualy) or in a small amount of water.

Rescue Remedy

Rescue Remedy is a combination of Clematis, Cherry Plum, Impatiens, Rock Rose and Star of Bethlehem. It is effective for sudden shock, emotional upheaval, stress, loss, grief or any disturbance. This mixture can assist in relieving urgent symptoms within 20 minutes. This remedy has a calming effect and works well for people, animals and plants. Take up to five drops either under the tongue or in water.

How to use Bach Flowers – Self Kinesiology Testing

Soul Dialogue is an exploration that reveals which Bach Flowers will be beneficial to your healing and transformation path. This inquiry can identify soul issues related to the present, future or past and identify remedies to assist in releasing blocks that prevent you from living to your full potential.

To perform the test, hold the selected remedy in one hand, preferably near the solar plexus. With the other hand, test a muscle. If the muscle tests strong, then the remedy will be supportive of the healing path.

O Ring Test

Press the thumb and pinky finger of one hand together to form an O. Bring the tips of the thumb and forefinger of the opposite hand together to form a second O interlocking with the first and attempt to pull the first circle apart. When the fingers stay connected, or strong, a *yes* answer is indicated. When they can be pulled apart, the answer is a *no*. See section on self-testing methods for more options and for information on pendulum testing.

Preparation of Flower Remedies

First, decide from which flowers you wish to prepare an essence, then pick them fresh. Place flowers in a clear glass bowl filled with spring water. Now place the bowl in the early morning sunlight. The essence of the flower will infuse the water with healing vibrations. Put a preservative in the essence such as brandy, vinegar or glycerin and pour into a glass bottle with a glass dropper in the top. Pound the stoppered bottle against your palm 100 times to infuse the healing energies into the water.

Using a glass dropper, mix one ounce of water to each four drops of concentrated flower essence. Take four drops, four times daily, either under the tongue or in juice, water or milk.

Essences assist with recurrent issues and deep-seated emotional and mental patterns. They also assist in deep transformation and consciousness change and support your healing intention. Through releasing negative, recurring thoughts, they change self-destructive tendencies and break the habits of worry, fear and anxiety. Flower essences also release toxic emotions such as resentment, guilt, grief, hatred and victimhood. They also release mental conclusions and limiting belief systems, opening doors to new possibilities of freedom and well-being.

The Bach Flowers - Healing Benefits and Disturbances

* Indicates one of the original 12 Bach Flowers

Aspen

Healing Benefits: Increases peace, trust, faith and fearlessness.

Disturbances: Sudden and vague fears of unknown origin, worries, nervousness, anxiety, bad dreams, sweating and trembling.

Agrimony *

Healing Benefits: Increases joy and cheerfulness.

Disturbances: Repression and denial of feelings of pain and discomfort. For those who seek excitement, loneliness, who are distressed by arguments, avoid conflict, are worried and restless.

Beech

Healing Benefits: Increases tolerance, understanding, strong convictions and high ideals.

Disturbances: Intolerance of others, overly critical, lacking in humility, over-strong convictions, finding fault with others, judgmental, arrogant and extremely prejudiced.

Centaury *

Healing Benefits: Helps to develop self-determination, wisdom and a strong sense of self.

Disturbances: Weak-willed, cannot stand up for oneself, behaves like a doormat and cannot say no. For those who constantly try to please others, who fear telling the truth, do not like to make waves or displease in any way. Effective for issues of co-dependency and feelings of victimhood.

Cerato *

    Healing Benefits: Promotes inner trust, wisdom and commitment.

    Disturbances: Self-doubt, foolishness, continuously needing advice, lack of self-trust and lack of confidence in own judgment.

Cherry Plum

    Healing Benefits: Promotes courage, balance and calmness under any situation.

    Disturbances: Suicidal thoughts, fear of insanity, violent impulses, nervous breakdown, desperate situations, constant frictions, deep despair.

Chestnut Bud

    Healing Benefits: Helps in being observant, learning life's lessons, gaining knowledge and wisdom from life's experience.

    Disturbances: Failure to learn from experiences, lack of observation, repeating mistakes and lack of humility.

Chicory *

    Healing Benefits: Helps develop selfless-care and concern for others, and giving without thought of return.

    Disturbances: Possessiveness and selfishness, oversensitivity, easily offended, feelings of rejection, needing constant attention and dislike of being alone.

Clematis *

    Healing Benefits: Helps us to feel inspired, hopeful and idealistic, and to be down to earth, realistic and actively interested in life.

    Disturbances: We feel indifferent, faint, lethargic, unhappy, often daydreaming and prefer to be alone. Extreme disturbance is coma.

Crab Apple

    Healing Benefits: Cleansing for mind and body, helps us put things in perspective. Good for self-control and for increasing harmony and balance.

    Disturbances: Feelings of despair, of being unclean and of disgust or shame.

Elm

    Healing Benefits: Increases efficiency and intuition, as well as the ability to follow an inner call, and cultivate a feeling of service, faith and confidence.

    Disturbances: Being overwhelmed, having too much responsibility, exhaustion, depression, weakness and debility.

Gentian *

    Healing Benefits: Makes us confident that we can conquer all obstacles, fearless in pursuit of our goals and creates great conviction of purpose.

    Disturbances: Discouragement, despondency, depression, lack of faith, negative outlook, long term or recurring illness and long convalescence.

Gorse

Healing Benefits: Engenders positive faith and hope and feelings of great strength, uninfluenced by the opinions of others.

Disturbances: Hopelessness, despair and a feeling that pain is too much to bare.

Heather

Healing Benefits: Selflessness, understanding and a willingness to help others.

Disturbances: Self-centeredness, self-concern, obsessed by personal problems, sometimes weepy, saps the vitality of others, dislikes being alone and is a poor listener.

Holly

Healing Benefits: Produces vibrations of divine love. Imparts generosity, great rejoicing, understanding and tolerance.

Disturbances: Negative thoughts and emotions such as jealously, envy, revenge and suspicion. Sometimes causes feelings of aggression and greed. For those who suffer from inner unhappiness and an absence of love.

Honeysuckle

Healing Benefits: Helps us to let go of past, becoming present-centered. Helps us put memories into perspective and to extract essential value from them.

Disturbances: Lives in the past, homesick, regretful, fearful of the future and experiences a loss of interest in the present.

Hornbeam

Healing Benefits: Clears and increases mental vitality and strengthens our ability to deal with life.

Disturbances: Weariness and mental fatigue, doubts own strength, feels life is burdensome and is self-preoccupied and tired all of the time.

Impatiens *

Healing Benefits: Promotes relaxation, patience, tolerance and gentleness.

Disturbances: Over-assertive, irritable, impatient, nervous, accident prone, feels mental tension through frustrations and other pressures.

Larch

Healing Benefits: Helps us to release fears, to feel capable, not discouraged, and willing to take risks. Helps us live life with an "I can" attitude.

Disturbances: Lack of confidence, convinced of failure, harbors feelings of being "not good enough" or not capable, chronic low self-esteem and a feelings of inferiority.

Mimulus *

Healing Benefits: Brings courage, equanimity, humor and lightness. Increases understanding and faith.

Disturbances: Fear of unknown things, stage fright, stammering, nervousness, secret fears, shyness and timidity.

Mustard

Healing Benefits: Provides inner serenity, peace, joy and cheerfulness.

Disturbances: Deep depression, intense gloom, melancholia, hopelessness and an overwhelming sense of doom.

Oak

Healing Benefits: Helps us develop courage, stability, reliability, inner strength, common sense, patience and bravery.

Disturbances: Despondency, hopelessness, grave difficulties, illness and disconnection with self.

Olive

Healing Benefits: Brings forth revitalization, renewed interest in life, quietness, peace and clarity of mind.

Disturbances: Complete exhaustion, difficult convalescence, long illness, mental fatigue and a loss of vital force.

Pine

Healing Benefits: Helps us to develop responsiblility, great perseverance, humility and sound judgment.

Disturbances: Self-reproach, guilt, self-blame, self-criticism. Takes on blame of others, overly hard working and perfectionist.

Red Chestnut

Healing Benefits: Helps us to project positive thoughts of safety and care for others, encouragement and the ability to remain calm in an emergency.

Disturbances: Anxiety for others, negative thoughts, fearful, fretful and worried.

Rock Rose *

Healing Benefits: Gives us great courage, a willingness to take risks for others and great inner strength.

Disturbances: Terror, fear, extreme shock, panic, trauma, acute threats, natural disaster and sudden illness.

Rock Water

Healing Benefits: Flexibility, peace and joy, relief from strictness and the ability to adapt. Not easily influenced by others.

Disturbances: Depression and denial, over-concentration on self, hard taskmaster, self-denial, martyrdom and uptightness.

Scleranthus *

Healing Benefits: Good for children, calmness, determination, poise and balance.

Disturbances: Uncertainty, unreliability, indecision, hesitancy. Indecision when confronted with two conflicting emotions. Example: joy/sadness, energy/apathy, optimism/pessimism, laughing/crying, etc.

Sweet Chestnut

Healing Benefits: Gives us full control of our emotions, strong character, faith and miracles.

Disturbances: Great anguish, mental despair, at the limit of endurance, exhaustion, depression and finding life too difficult.

Star of Bethlehem

Healing Benefits: Releases trauma, brings peace and faith.

Disturbances: Grief, sudden shock, fright of an accident and loss of a loved one. A remedy for crisis of any kind.

Vervain *

Healing Benefits: Helps build great courage and ability to face danger. Promotes calm, wise and tolerant behavior.

Disturbances: Tenseness, anxiety, stress, fanatical, argumentative and high strung.

Vine

Healing Benefits: Helps us to be capable, confident, assured, balanced and flexible and gives us the ability to help others in self-knowledge.

Disturbances: Domineering, inflexible, opinionated, demanding, expects obedience, aggressive pride, greedy for authority, knows better than anyone, arrogant and needs power.

Walnut

Healing Benefits: Idealistic. Helps to protect us from the effects of change and is helpful for transitions and life changes. Relieves stressful situations and helps us be more idealistic.

Disturbances: Oversensitive, affected by others, influenced by others.

Water Violet *

> **Healing Benefits:** Helps us to be silent, gentle, tranquil, wise, independent, self-reliant and capable. Brings peace, calm and blessings to those around us.
>
> **Disturbances:** Proud, aloof, disdainful, condescending, mentally rigid and tense.

White Chestnut

> **Healing Benefits:** Promotes peace and quiet, self-control and clarity of mind.
>
> **Disturbances:** Argumentative, worried, troubled by distressing thoughts, sleepless and lacking concentration.

Wild Oat

> **Healing Benefits:** Helps us to live life feeling useful and with great happiness. Gives us clarity in life, direction and vocation.
>
> **Disturbances:** Uncertainty regarding path in life, indecision, unclear, despondent, dissatisfied, frustrated, depressed and unable to find happiness.

Wild Rose

> **Healing Benefits:** Showing a lively interest in life, ambitious and purposeful.
>
> **Disturbances:** Resignation, apathy, resigned to illness, surrendered, hopeless, weary, and lacking in vitality.

Willow

> **Healing Benefits:** Exhibiting optimism and faith, taking responsibility, able to remain neutral and releasing bitterness from the past.
>
> **Disturbances:** Resentment, bitterness, self-pity, blames others, begrudges life, irritable, not interested in affairs of others, ungrateful and alienating.

Chakra Vibrational Support

Bach Flowers and Chakras

Root Chakra

Cherry Plum – Letting go

Clematis – Grounding

Gorse – Integration

Pine – Taking responsibility

Sweet Chestnut – Trusting yourself

Navel Chakra

Crab Apple – Getting rid of what
    you can't digest

Elm – Turning your ideas into reality

Mimulus – Enjoying freedom
    within a fixed structure

Oak – Surrender

Rock Water – Discipline with release

Vervain – Accepting others

Wild Rose – Taking part in life
    joyfully and fully

Solar Plexus Chakra

Aspen – Overcoming fear

Hornbeam – Being able to achieve
    personal goals

Impatiens – Patience

Larch – Self-awareness

Scleranthus – Balance within yourself

Star of Bethlehem – Ability to act from
    inner joy

Heart Chakra

Centaury – Service

Chicory – Overcoming distance

Heather – Unconditional love

Holly – Free-flowing love, energy

Honeysuckle – Living in the here and now

Red Chestnut – Ability to express
    true love

Rock rose – Overcoming ego limitations

Throat Chakra

Agrimony – Fusing thinking and feeling

Mustard – Trusting yourself even in difficult
    times

Wild oat – Communicating from your
    deepest soul

Willow – Making space for creativity

Third Eye Chakra

Beech – Tolerance

Cerato – Following your inner guide

Chestnut Bud – Being open to learning
    from life

Gentian – Acceptance

Olive – Trusting, cosmic harmony

Vine – Accepting authority

Walnut – Being able to listen to your
    inner voice

White Chestnut – An aid to mediation

Once all other chakras are in balance,
the crown chakra is also in balance.

California Flower Essences

Can be purchased through Flower Essence Society

PO Box 459, Nevada City, CA 95959

(See Guidelines for Using Flower Essences.)

Agrimony Assists in getting in touch with deep soul disturbances and helps to increase emotional honesty.

Aloe Vera Creative activity becomes balanced and centered in vital life energy. Increases harmony and mental rejuvenation. Relieves impatience.

Alpine Valley For women, acceptance of one's femininity, grounded in a deepened experience of the female body.

Angel's Trumpet Spiritual surrender at death or at time of deep transformation, opening the heart to the spiritual world.

Angelica Increases angelic connections and spiritual rejuvenation. Brings divine protection and guidance. Awakens perceptions, assists one to have courage and inner strength.

Arnica Conscious embodiment, especially during shock or recovery from deep-seated trauma.

Aspen Brings a sense of inner trust, confidence, strength and protection from astral influences.

Baby Blue Eyes Childlike innocence and trust, feeling at home in this world, at ease with oneself, supported and loved; connected with the spiritual world.

Basil Integration of sexuality into a sacred wholeness.

Black Cohosh Courage to confront, rather than retreat from, abusive or threatening situations.

Blackberry For manifesting creative inspiration and for opening to new levels of consciousness.

Black-eyed Susan Awakens consciousness making it capable of acknowledging all aspects of the personality. Helps release resistance to looking at our emotions.

Bleeding Heart Loving others unconditionally, with an open heart. Emotional freedom. Good heart healer. Helps heal broken relationships and brings peace, harmony and balance to the heart.

Borage Heart remedy, especially for the feelings of heaviness in the heart. Excellent all-purpose formula.

Buttercup Helps soul realize and sustain inner light. For those who feel inadequate.

Calla Lily Clarity about sexual identity.

Calendula Awakens the healing power of words.

California Poppy Increases intuition, helps one to see the aura.

California Wild Rose Promotes love for earth and human life and enthusiasm for doing and serving.

Chaparral Brings about psychic awareness. Detoxifies the system.

Canyon Dudleya Balances psychic and physical energies.

Cayenne Ignites and sparks the soul to assist in initiating and sustaining emotional development.

Chamomile Promotes emotional balance. Helps release tension from stomach and solar plexus areas. Subdues small emotions.

Chrysanthemum Shifts ego identification from one's personality to a higher spiritual identity.

Corn Alignment with the earth, especially through body and feet; grounded presence.

Columbine Increases self-appreciation, self-love and personal power.

Comfrey Repairs soul damage.

Cosmos Promotes integration of ideas and speech; ability to express thoughts with coherence and clarity.

Deerbrush Promotes gentle purity, clarity of purpose and sincerity of motive.

Dandelion For dynamic and effortless energy; lively activity balanced with inner ease.

Dill Aids in experiencing and absorbing the fullness of life.

Dogwood Allows grace-filled movement, physical and etheric harmony. Clarifies emotions and turning to spiritual sources.

Easter Lily Promotes inner purity of soul, especially the ability to integrate sexuality and spirituality.

Echinacea A fundamental remedy for many soul and physical illnesses.

Evening Primrose Helps to open the heart.

Fairy Lantern Releases emotional blocks that occurred in childhood.

Fawn Lily Promotes integration of spirituality in the world.

Filaree Assists one to put life in perspective and promotes cosmic understanding.

Five Flower Formula Promotes calmness and stability in an emergency. Consists of cherry plum, clematis, impatiens, rock rose and star of bethlehem.

Forget-me-not For awareness of karmic connections.

Fuchsia Promotes emotional vitality and the ability to express feelings.

Garlic Heals fragmented souls.

Gentian Good for life setbacks, discouragement, disheartenment, need for solutions. Increases trust.

Golden Ear Drops Helps one to remember emotional disturbances from the past.

Golden Yarrow Promotes opened, balanced, inner protection, integrity of health and well-being.

Golden Rod Promotes well developed individuality or personal power.

Gorse For deep abiding faith.

Heather Promotes inner tranquility, emotional self-esteem.

Hibiscus Brings soul dignity for women, helps heal sexual trauma.

Holly Aids in feeling love and extending love to others.

Honeysuckle Helps us to be fully in the present, learning lessons from the past.

Hornbeam Promotes energy, enthusiasm and involvement with life's work.

Hound's Tongue Aids thinking in terms of wholeness, integration of spirit and world.

Impatiens Promotes patience, acceptance, flowing with the pace of life.

Indian Paintbrush Makes one lively, energetic and able to express spirituality.

Indian Pink Helps us to remain centered and focused under stress.

Iris Inspires artistry, building the Bridge of Light between spirit and matter. Symbolizes hope and eternal spirit.

Lady's Slipper Integrates spiritual purpose and daily work.

Larch Promotes self-confidence, creative expression and spontaneity.

Larkspur Brings charismatic leadership abilities.

Lotus Brings inspiration and healing, opens up intuition, reconnects us with our divine source, and affects the crown chakra.

Lavender Soothes nerves and over-sensitivity to psychic and spiritual experiences.

Madia Focuses concentration and promotes clear thinking.

Mallow Opens heart and promotes sharing and friendliness.

Manzanita Integrates the spiritual self with the physical world.

Mariposa Lily Helps us develop nurturing and caring attention for others.

Milkweed Promotes healthy ego, strength, independence and self-reliance.

Morning Glory Brings sparkling vital force, putting one in touch with life.

Mimulus Aids in developing courage and the confidence to face life's challenges.

Mountain Pennyroyal Promotes strength and clarity of thought.

Mountain Pride Helps us to take a stand in the world and be a spiritual warrior.

Mugwort Awakens greater awareness of spiritual influence, brings in more consciousness.

Mullein Strengthens our sense of inner consciousness, truthfulness and uprightness. Helps us in being true to ourselves.

Mustard Promotes emotional equanimity, helping us find joy in life.

Nasturtium Brings glowing vitality and radiant energy.

Nicotiana Brings emotional well-being, peace, inner strength and stability.

Oak Balances strength, life acceptance and knowing when to surrender.

Olive Revitalizes through connection with one's inner source of energy.

Oregon Grape Promotes trust in the goodness of others, develops loving kindness.

Peony Assists the heart center to open and increases deep love of self and unconditional love for others. Opens one to the presence of God within.

Penstemon Brings great inner strength in the face of outer hardships.

Peppermint Promotes mindfulness and waking clarity.

Pine Helps to release guilt and blaming self for the mistakes of others.

Pink Monkey Flower Provides emotional openness and honesty.

Pink Yarrow Promotes compassion and openness to the feelings of others.

Poison Oak Promotes emotional vulnerability.

Pomegranate Brings sense of warmhearted feminine creativity.

Pretty Face Promotes beauty that radiates from within.

Purple Monkey Flower Provides sense of inner calm, trust in spiritual guidance, release from fear.

Pine Promotes self-acceptance, self-forgiveness and freedom from guilt and shame.

Quaking Grass Brings harmonious soul consciousness and a balanced life.

Queen Anne's Lace Strengthens spiritual insight and visualization and integration of mind and emotions.

Quince Balances masculine and feminine powers.

Rabbitbrush Maintains flexible state of mind.

Red Clover Cleanses, balances and helps us maintain a strong sense of self-awareness.

Red Chestnut Promotes caring for others and inner peace, calmness and trust in the unfolding of life's events.

Rock Rose Enhances self-transcendence, courage, inner peace and tranquility when facing great challenges.

Rock Water Brings flexibility and flowing reception in following spiritual guidance.

Rose Awakens love and inspiration, helping us attune to the angelic hierarchies.

Rosemary Stimulates mental faculties. Aids purification of body, mind and emotions.

Rhubarb Good for boundary issues, insecurity and vulnerability.

Sage Increases understanding of true self, stimulates the mind.

Sagebrush Deepens awareness of our inner self and helps us let go of false images.

Saguaro Brings awareness of ancient memories, assists in our ability to learn. Gives us clarity in relationship to authority and guidance.

Saint John's Wart Opens one to divine guidance. Releases hidden fear from past lives. Good for dispelling depression.

Scarlet Monkey Flower Good for emotional honesty.

Scotch Broom Promotes positive and optimistic feelings in the world; also caring, encouragement and perception.

Self-Heal Excellent for soul healing and balance; enhances self-healing powers, self-confidence and self-acceptance.

Shasta Daisy Integrates thinking and analytical aspects of the mind.

Shooting Star Helps one to find right connection with earthly life, helps us to feel at home on earth.

Snapdragon Helps soul for greater creative focus.

Star Thistle Releases fear of "lack." Promotes inner sense of abundance.

Star Tulip The "listening remedy," opening one to guidance from a higher realm.

Star of Bethlehem Brings soothing, healing qualities and a sense of inner divinity.

Stinging Nettle Eases all emotional stress. Nettle helps as a tonic for the kidneys, lungs and nervous system.

Sunflower Promotes expression of individuality. Balances ego, helps with self-esteem.

Sweet Chestnut Deep courage and faith, knowing and trusting the spiritual world.

Sticky Mountain Flower Heals challenges with intimacy.

Sun Flower Brings light to the soul.

Sweet Pea Helps soul come into contact with feelings of shame.

Tansy Helps with being decisive, reduces lethargy and procrastination, and aids in decision making.

Tiger Lily Increases feminine forces. Helps alleviate symptoms of menopause.

Trillium Increases energy for selfless service.

Trumpet Vine Assists with verbal expression.

Vervain Increases ability to practice moderation, tolerance and balance.

Vine Promotes selfless service, tolerance, strong will and leadership.

Violet Awakens one to the spiritual side of manifestation.

Walnut Helps free one from limiting influences, transitions in life, gives courage to follow one's own path.

Water Violet Enables us to share our gifts with others and aids us in becoming quiet and self-contained.

White Chestnut Promotes inner quiet, calm and a clear mind.

Wild Oat Works as an expression of inner calling, outward life experiences and one's true goal and values.

Wild Rose: Aids those who have given up hope.

Willow: Promotes acceptance, forgiveness, taking responsibility and flowing with life.

Yarrow: Assists in conditions such as environmental illness, allergies, psychosomatic diseases, psychic shielding, boundaries and protection.

Yellow Star Tulip: Brings empathy and receptivity to the feeling experienced by others.

Yerba Santa: The "Holy Herb" harmonizes breath with feeling.

Yarrow Special Formula:

General tonic and strengthener to help us meet harsh technological and environmental challenges in the modern world. Use before and after exposure to radiation and when subjected to forces of geopathic stress, strong electromagnetic fields and other forms of environmental toxicity. Use to strengthen the immune system. Helps during times of extreme stress with core issues of integrity and identity. For those with pronounced sensitivity during traveling and in large crowds. This formula acts on an etheric level.

Zinnia: Promotes child-like playfulness, makes us joyful in the light and gives us a profound sense of self.

Essential Oils and Healing Fragrances

Ancient Egyptians have used essential oils daily since 1500 BC. Oils such as myrrh, frankincense, sandalwood, rosemary and hyssop have been used for anointing and healing the sick for centuries. Essential oils, like flower essences, change the frequency of negative patterns that are locked into the energy fields.

Changing belief systems, becoming conscious of held patterns, seeing a new direction, releasing and reprogramming the subconscious, and letting go of limitations and labels are all assisted through the use of essential oils as well as flower remedies.

Emotions and belief systems are basically frozen energy that needs to be resolved and released. Giving the energy system a different message, such as the positive side of the emotion, brings more vitality into the energy field and provides a goal or healing path to travel through. When the mental field is connected with the higher spiritual energy fields, it has a strong impact on the emotional field. The higher impressions of truth, honesty, aspiration, trust and clarity are more powerful than the negative self-limiting emotions and beliefs. Through working with a soul's goal or healing intention, the self-limiting energy will be released.

Through *LEAP*, patterns are identified in the energy fields that cause disturbances and energy drains. Usually the pattern is connected to a desire pattern that has been implanted in the emotional field or a belief system about something one wants. When these discordant energy patterns are understood one can work with the soul's truth to find a wiser way to be in life – for example, releasing desires that are for self-centered gain, for the greater good of all concerned. Through understanding life's problems in the light of the soul, there is a greater thrust in removing obstacles to being in the light. The light brings a great joy and peace to one's life. Once negative patterns are identified, one discovers a goal healing intention to assist in their release. The vibrational remedy that supports this energy release is chosen through kinesiology testing. When the discordant energy pattern is identified, the way out, or healing intention, becomes the soul affirmation. Through sacred dialogue the healing intention draws the negative energy out of its frozen or stuck state.

Put goals and affirmations in the present time, using "I" statements such as "I am____," or "I will____," affirming and being in the present time with the new reality. Creating a new reality means envisioning how you want it to be and believing you can transform your reality to this new vision.

LEAP believes you can reach for optimal health in body, emotions and spirit through increasing your vitality, joy and faith. Faith is a spiritual vibration that transforms fear, doubt and feelings of hopelessness into invocation, conviction and trust in life's plan.

Disturbed vibrations appear in a subtle body before disease manifests; negative thought patterns produce negative energies and negative patterns. Identification and release allows the universal consciousness to work through energy fields.

Through understanding that life's suffering points to unrealized lessons and soul gifts, we can work with patterns of suffering, understand the lesson and receive the gift it imparts.

Essential Oils – Nature's Fragrant Garden

Aromas are pure fragrances for healing body, mind and spirit. You can use the aromas in the form of incense, flower essences, and essential oils, or soaps, candles, and sachets. Aromatherapy is used externally and most are diluted with a base oil or carrier oil. Some of the carrier oils that can be chosen are sesame, coconut, sunflower, canola, mustard, sweet almond, avocado, calendula, carrot, hazelnut, jojoba, olive, peanut and wheat germ.

Steps to Release Emotional Stress

Use kinesiology to identify the emotion (see the Emotional Healing section.) Create an affirmation, or soul's goal, that increases the positive emotion that you want to receive from the balance. Ask for a gift of the spirit or soul lesson. Use the emotional stress release technique and apply oils at the emotional points on the forehead, chakras, alarm points, hands or feet. They can also be applied to the points specified in the etheric revitalization treatment.

1. Identify and feel the emotions.
2. Inhale the fragrance of the oil.
3. Identify the positive emotion or healing intention.
4. Apply the oil to a specific area.
5. Create a new life-affirming affirmation.
6. Apply the oils to the ayurvedic acupressure points.

Ayurvedic Acupressure Points

Third Eye (between eyebrows).

Heart Chakra (chest center).

Between the navel and pubic bone.

Neurovascular Points for Emotional Stress

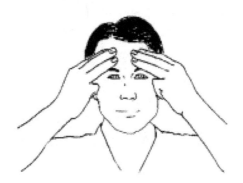

Emotional Stress Release Points

On the forehead, divide the space in two. The emotional stress release points are halfway between the eyebrow and the hairline in the hollow of the forehead. (See Emotional Stress Release in Emotional Healing section for more details.)

Use the testing procedures in the book to clear and find a strong indicator muscle. When an emotion is identified, muscle test. If the arm goes weak that indicates it is the target emotion that needs releasing. Always ask if it is the priority, or first, emotion that needs releasing. To deepen this test, you can check the chakras or alarm points to determine the area of the body that is holding the cellular memory or discordant pattern. Identify the emotion or belief system that is calling for healing, change and transformation.

1.   To find the chakra involved, hold a hand above each chakra and ask: "Is this the chakra involved?"
2.   Ask if the stress has to do with a relationship, time frame, situation or pattern.
3.   While holding the points with the specific oil, close your eyes, breathe in one continuous breath and allow the story to unfold as if on a movie screen.
4.   Discover the soul affirmation through dialogue; this affirmation is the positive side of the emotional or mental pattern. An example is, "I release all fear and allow joy and lightness to enter my body, mind and emotions."
5.   Say, "I am willing to see and release the obstacles that are created by this story." Muscle test. If *yes*, move to the next step.
6.   Say "I am willing to accept the gift of _____." (See the gift, such as freedom, joy, love, forgiveness.) Muscle test; if *yes*, then repeat and test again.

Using Energy Field Kinesiology, identify the emotion and the chakra that the emotion is related to on the belief pattern. Create a healing intention or soul affirmation and then apply the oil to the emotional points, the frontal eminences. Hold the points while stating the affirmation, and visualize the story that the emotion or belief is attached to, as if on a movie screen. Wait for the pulses to synchronize and then retest. If the arm is strong, it indicates the emotion or limiting belief has been diffused or released. Always work with the soul dialogue. A summary of the procedures follows.

How to Use Essential Oils

Oils can be applied to chakras, alarm points, and emotional stress points and the point at the base of the neck called the release point. They can also be applied to points on the feet, such as K1, and to many points on the hand. Apply to the hand and rotate clockwise to activate.

Bathing:

Using oils in the bath helps unlock congested pores, eases muscle tension and fatigue, quiets the mind and calms the spirit. After running a warm bath, add eight to ten drops of your chosen oil and relax in the bath for at least ten minutes.

Suggested bath oils: bergamot, chamomile, frankincense, geranium, jasmine, lavender, mandarin, neroli, rose, tangerine, ylang ylang. Add vegetable or olive oil for dry skin.

Bath Therapy: Put seven drops from a flower essence or essential oil bottle in the bath water in the morning, before noon. For best results soak for 30 minutes. Water is a conductor for electrical force. It activates the aura, cleanses the energy fields and releases karmic patterns.

Massage

Choose specific oils to suit the condition and temperament for the massage. Add ten to twelve drops to one ounce of massage oil.

> **Inhaled as a vapor:** Use two to three drops. Put hot water into a bowl, add the oil, cover your head with a towel, lean over bowl and inhale. Breathe in deeply.
> **Diffusers:** Use candles or electric diffusers. Diffusers should be made of clay or glass.
> **Humidifiers:** Add one to nine drops to the water.
> **Room Sprays:** Four or more drops, per one cup of water.

Essential Oil Recipes

20 to 60 drops base oil per 100ml.
5 to 15 drops per 25ml.
2 to 3 drops per teaspoon.
25ml (12-13 drops per 1 fluid ounce base oil).

Vaporization/Inhalation

Inhale the essential oil by putting six to seven drops onto a tissue or cotton ball; take deep breaths for maximum benefit.

Anointing

Use myrrh, frankincense, jasmine, rose or lavender on the third eye along with stating the soul affirmation out loud.

For protection use rosemary, juniper and vertiver. Put on solar plexus and move the energy with a counter-clockwise motion. It is wonderful to use specific oils on the chakras, or on any area of the body that needs attention.

Over-thinking and Worry

Sandalwood, lemon, frankincense, myrrh

Depression and Fear, Nervous tension

Chamomile, orange, bergamot

Disempowerment and Indecision

Ginger, juniper

Clarity of Mind

Rosemary

Anger and Frustration

Orange, bergamot, grapefruit, peppermint, chamomile, yarrow, lavender, oil of rose

Impatience and Intolerance

Bergamot, lavender, peppermint

Mental Fatigue

Rosemary, tea tree, laurel

Tension and Agitation

Chamomile, sweet orange, bergamot

Relaxation and Rejuvenation

Frankincense, lemon, peppermint

Anxiety and Apprehension

Basil, bergamot, clary sage, frankincense, geranium, grapefruit, jasmine, juniper, lavender, neroli, orange, patchouli, rose, sandalwood, vanilla, verbena, vertiver, ylang ylang, thyme

Nerves

Angelica, basil, bergamot, camphor, cypress, jasmine, lavender, melissa, neroli, patchouli, chamomile, rose, rosewood, sandalwood, tangerine, vertiver, ylang ylang

Lack of Confidence and Self-esteem

Rosemary, Jasmine, Rose

Low Morale

Thyme, Pine, Cedarwood

Lack of Self-worth

Rose, jasmine

Anxiety and Depression

Lavender, rose

Sudden Fear
Geranium, vertiver, rose

Calming
Jasmine, ylang ylang

Vulnerability
Pine, thyme

Resistance to Change
Cypress and juniper

Chronic Indecisiveness
Clary sage, bergamot, orange

Frustration and Negativity
Bergamot, orange, neroli

Bitterness
Chamomile, bergamot

Lonely and Forlorn
Marjoram, rosemary, myrrh

Overattachment
Frankincense, myrrh

Joylessness
Jasmine, ylang ylang, orange

Abandonment
Rose, neroli, ginger

Depression
Basil, bergamot, camphor, chamomile, clary sage, geranium, grapefruit, Jasmine, lavender, neroli, patchouli, rose, sandalwood, ylang ylang

Nervous Tension
Chamomile, orange, bergamot, lavender

Meditation Burners and Diffusers
Angelica – Connects with the divine, frankincense, lavender, rose
Juniper – Psychic cleanser
Rosemary – Spiritual protection, rosewood, sandalwood

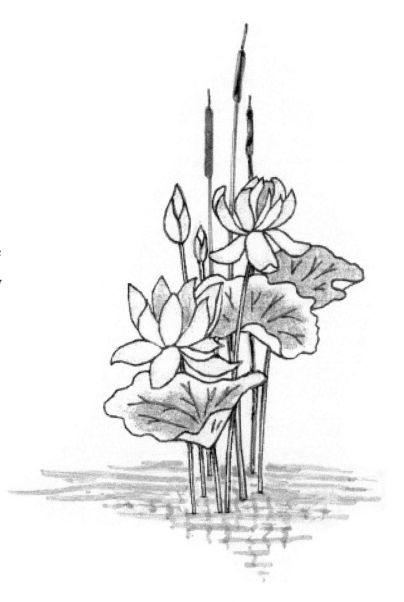

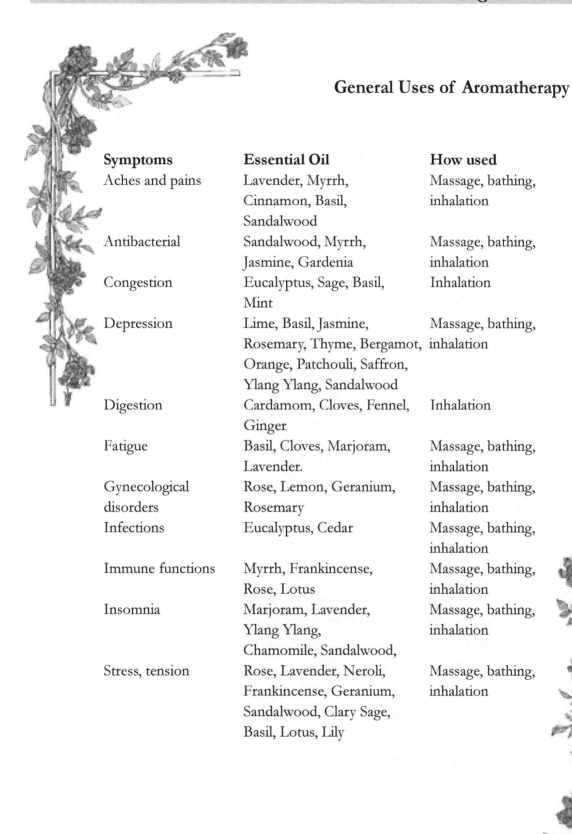

General Uses of Aromatherapy

Symptoms	Essential Oil	How used
Aches and pains	Lavender, Myrrh, Cinnamon, Basil, Sandalwood	Massage, bathing, inhalation
Antibacterial	Sandalwood, Myrrh, Jasmine, Gardenia	Massage, bathing, inhalation
Congestion	Eucalyptus, Sage, Basil, Mint	Inhalation
Depression	Lime, Basil, Jasmine, Rosemary, Thyme, Bergamot, Orange, Patchouli, Saffron, Ylang Ylang, Sandalwood	Massage, bathing, inhalation
Digestion	Cardamom, Cloves, Fennel, Ginger	Inhalation
Fatigue	Basil, Cloves, Marjoram, Lavender.	Massage, bathing, inhalation
Gynecological disorders	Rose, Lemon, Geranium, Rosemary	Massage, bathing, inhalation
Infections	Eucalyptus, Cedar	Massage, bathing, inhalation
Immune functions	Myrrh, Frankincense, Rose, Lotus	Massage, bathing, inhalation
Insomnia	Marjoram, Lavender, Ylang Ylang, Chamomile, Sandalwood,	Massage, bathing, inhalation
Stress, tension	Rose, Lavender, Neroli, Frankincense, Geranium, Sandalwood, Clary Sage, Basil, Lotus, Lily	Massage, bathing, inhalation

Essential Oils Chart

Angelica Supports and connects the energy fields with the soul. Opens intuition and helps one realize deep inner self. Puts one in touch with angelic realms, enhances meditation. Detoxifies the body, rebuilds vital force. Good for headaches and to stimulate the glandular system.

Bay Helps heal the heart and throat chakras and the illnesses associated with them. Good for the immune system. Helps heal and balance the lung meridians.

Basil Cleanses the colon. Antiseptic. Stimulating. Reduces fever and virus. Increases devotion and intuition. Helps with confidence and courage. Helps lift depression.

Bayberry Used for clearing the astral and mental bodies. Clears the entire auric field. Balances the spleen and heart chakras.

Bergamot Relaxing. Antiseptic. Stimulating. For courage and harmony. Eases depression, anxiety, anger, tension and worry. Brings in more light to situations.

Camphor Opens the mind, senses, and lungs. Increases perception and the effects of meditation. Alleviates headaches. Good for devotional ceremonies, brings in more light. Good for boosting confidence and for discernment. Helps with nervous ailments.

Carnation Used to increase the metabolic system. Balances and removes negativity in the energy field. Clears and balances the meridians, protects and strengthens the aura.

Cedar Encouraging, balancing. Helps with anxiety, emotional imbalance, stress. Supports the nervous system.

Cedarwood Relaxing, aid for diabetes, arthritis, and edema. Good for cleaning the air, for harmonizing and for opening psychic centers. Calms aggression, anger and fear. Relieves bronchitis and urinary tract disorders. Counters dishonesty.

Chamomile A soothing tonic for nerves and restlessness. Helps support the endocrine system and the kidneys. Releases emotional toxins. Helps calm the stomach and relieve indigestion. Excellent for calming agitated children.

Cinnamon Good for meditation, healing and protection.

Clary Sage Eases stomach cramps. Helps weak digestion, bronchitis, asthma, menstrual cramps, PMS, headache, nervousness, paranoia, fear, depression. Brings clarity and balance, eases tension, anxiety, worry and grief. Boosts confidence.

Clove Very cleansing and antiseptic. Helps strengthen spleen and heart meridians. Used for protection and to release negative energy. Good for eyesight, nervousness and memory. Strengthens the kidneys.

Cypress Bolsters weak connective tissue. Controls heavy menstruation, bleeding from cuts, excessive coughing. Aids concentration, prevents nervous breakdown, squandering of energy and uncontrollable sobbing. Offers peace and comfort, eases anxiety. Enhances physical vitality.

Eucalyptus Good for purification, health and vitality, aids concentration. Dispels rage and confusion. Healing oil strengthens and balances all meridians. Used for all respiratory illness and to support the immune system. Balances the heart chakra and releases the pain of the past. Helps with all kinds of disturbing emotions. Cleanses and purifies negative energy from the aura. Helps alleviate grief and anxiety.

Frangipani Brings light and ease to the aura. Balances the throat chakra. Used for meditation.

Frankincense Used more commonly in meditation and for all sacred rituals. Cleanses and balances the aura. Purifies emotional and mental patterns. Evokes inspiration, faith, inner strength and stability. Awakens and balances the crown chakra, and the base chakras. Promotes deep stillness, peaceful sleep, connection with spirit and inner guidance.

Gardenia Works with the emotional plane to bring healthy boundaries. Stabilizes and strengthens all emotional conditions.

Geranium Good for emotional health and easing depression. Fresh, harmonious and healing. Strengthens liver. Effective for alleviating menopause problems, endometriosis, diabetes, blood disorders and throat infections. A good nerve tonic, works as a sedative. Helps in cases of uterine and breast cancer.

Ginger Good for detoxifying the physical body. Tonic and stimulating. Promotes great confidence and courage. Beneficial for colds, sore throat, fever and also aids with digestive problems.

Grapefruit Helps with depression, brings light and vibrant energy into the system. Stimulates and clears the mind, strengthens the physical body, energizes the nervous system, promotes digestion.

Jasmine Assists in opening the heart and crown chakras and helps to integrate the energy fields. Stimulates creativity and imagination. Inspires grace and brings the essence of peace to one's being. Eases depression. Helps with back pain, frigidity, impotence, joint and muscle pain, depression, fear, low self-confidence and emotional suffering. Can be an antidepressant or an aphrodisiac. Heals breast and uterine infections.

Juniper Protecting, purifying, honoring. For anxiety, stress, fear and uncertainty. Helps arthritis, poor circulation and indigestion. Works as a blood purifier and promotes well-being and inner strength. Clears negative energy from the environment and from the aura. Strengthens the immune system.

Lemon Energizing, brings vitality to body, mind and spirit. Stimulates clarity of thought. The color yellow strengthens and supports all mental processes. Works to balance the solar plexus chakra and the organs and conditions associated with it. Will ease depression, confusion, and acts as a tonic for the immune system. Eases nervous disorders. Cleanses, invigorates and balances the meridians. Joyous, purifying, strengthening. Helps with emotional confusion, fragility. Stimulates clarity of thought. A good antiseptic.

Lavender Awakens the crown chakra, opens one to intuition and guidance, clears negative energy from the aura and the environment. Increases peace of mind and emotional balance. Helps to heal inflictive emotions such as impatience, worry and shock. Good for all infections and speeds up healing processes. Treatment for burns and scalds. A natural antibiotic, antiseptic, antidepressant, sedative, and detoxifier. Promotes healing, strengthens the immune system and stimulates circulation. Good for the nervous system, for anxiety, depression and PMS. Acts as a natural sedative.

Lilac Works with the brow chakras to bring clarity. Heals and balances all other chakras. Opens one to the magical aspects of nature such as angels and fairies. Supports memory and intuition.

Lily Calms heart, nerves and emotions. Good for stomach, lungs and for relieving dry cough. Increases faith, devotion and virtue.

Lotus Calms mind and heart. Affects deep sleep. Increases love, faith, devotion, and compassion. Opens crown and ajna centers. Symbol for self-realization.

Magnolia Works with the heart and throat chakras, and the organs associated with them.

Myrtle For love and beauty. Alleviates despair. Helps with short-sightedness, distraction, coughs, colds, infections, bronchitis.

Mint Stimulating; clears the mind, head and sinuses.

Musk Heals and balances the root and naval chakras. Strengthens the Kundalini flow of energy. Purifies the blood stream. Revives those who are in exhaustion or collapse. Strengthens heart and reproductive system. Awakens the senses.

Neroli Opens the heart, brings a sense of inner joy, inspiration and creativity. Helps to transcend negative emotions and boosts confidence and self-esteem. Relieves emotional stress, anxiety, headaches, nervous heart, PMS, fear, anxiety, depression, shock, insomnia, subconscious fear, hopelessness. Brings courage.

Orange Assists the solar plexus chakra and rejuvenates the body-mind system. Promotes mental clarity, and helps to resolve deep emotional issues. Helps to increase confidence, trust and harmonious feelings. Relaxes and calms the nerves. Helps with weak digestion, gall bladder, heart muscle, bladder, kidney disorders, fever, sadness, need for warmth, self-consciousness, anxiety, nervousness.

Patchouli Awakens the yin, or inactive meridians. Balances base and spleen chakras. Aligns all centers with the heart center.

Pennyroyal Protects the aura. Releases negative thoughts. Strengthens spleen and solar plexus chakra and heals conditions such as headaches, nervous conditions and skin conditions.

Peppermint Purifies and energizes the environment. Clears the air, helps direct vital energy. Antiseptic, cleansing and purifying. Stimulates the mind. Alleviates fatigue and exhaustion. Good for stomach disorders, asthma and bronchitis.

Pine Healing, energizing, protecting; good for general fatigue, poor circulation and respiratory tract infections.

Rose Works to heal and balance the heart. Helps bring about love and healing with the crown and heart chakras. Works to increase the vibration of love.

Rosemary Balances the solar plexus chakra and heals unresolved emotions. Stimulates brow and crown chakra. Brings clarity to the mind. Antiseptic and stimulatant. Benefits blood, heart and circulatory system. Also helps to relieve headaches and emotional tension. Promotes menstruation.

Patchouli Earthy and peaceful, helps in grounding by strengthening the navel and root chakras. Brings a deep sense of emotional centeredness and stability.

Peppermint Promotes energy, enthusiasm and joy of life, awakening the inner child. Releases negative thinking in the aura and environment. Inspirational, clears the mind, stimulates thinking and perception and aids in discernment. A tonic for the body, mind and spirit. Excellent for headaches and stomach disorders and helps to support the immune system. A natural stimulant.

Rockrose Fights infection, speeds healing of wounds. Good for chronic skin disorders, eczema, psoriasis, cystitis, menstrual cramps and swollen lymph glands. Soothes emotional coldness and emptiness.

Sage Cleanses, protects and awakens intuition. Releases toxins and tension from the body. Balances the heart and solar plexus chakras. An overall tonic.

Sandalwood Enhances healing on all levels. Opens palm chakras for healing. Brings connection with spirit and increases concentration. Relaxing, antiseptic and very good for heart and lungs. Cleanses kidneys, reduces fever, irritability and anxiety. Promotes meditation.

Tangerine Good for the second chakra, helping one to open and receive love and strengthen relationships. Assists in adapting to changes. Relaxes nervous tension and is excellent for use as a massage oil or bath oil.

Tea Tree Speeds up all healing processes. Provides protection, courage, health, strength. Alleviates exhaustion and fatigue. Good as an immune stimulant, antiseptic, antiviral, antibacterial and antifungal. Useful for many conditions, such as candida, infection, ringworm, sunburn, acne, athlete's foot and toothaches.

Thyme Excellent for the immune system. Activates the thymus gland. Is calming and relaxing. Good for the lung meridian. Balances the third eye and crown chakras.

Tuberose Healing fragrance for the crown chakra. Good for all meridians. Brings peace of mind and relaxation to all areas of the body. Helps strengthen the emotional body. Increases inspiration and intuition. Good for love relationships.

Vetiver Oil of tranquility. Brings a deep sense of inner stability. Helps with grounding and feeling connected to inner earth. Calms extreme nervousness and is good for stress, disconnectedness, anorexia and depression.

Violet Helps to relieve pain. Balances stomach meridian and bladder. Heals and balances the solar plexus chakra. Used in bathing for creating a sense of well-being.

Wintergreen Works with the spleen, solar plexus and heart chakras to promote healing. Aligns all the energies. Brings a positive attitude towards oneself and promotes health on all levels.

Wisteria Promotes good vibrations. Opens up the heart and throat chakras. Strengthens the will and the immune system.

Yarrow Good for confusion, depression, ambivalence, menopause and meditation.

Ylang Ylang Helps to overcome sexual issues. Inspires creativity and appreciation of beauty, opening the heart and calming the nerves. Helps release negative emotions. Good for high blood pressure, PMS, fear, anger, rage, low self-esteem, impotence, nervous depression and nervous headaches.

Chakra Fragrances

Root – Cloves, Cedar, Jasmine, Rose, Patchouli, Myrrh, Musk

Navel – Ylang Ylang, Sandalwood, Jasmine, Rose

Solar Plexus – Peppermint, Lemon, Rosemary, Carnation, Lavender, Cinnamon, Marigold, Chamomile, Thyme, Juniper, Vertiver

Heart – Attar of Roses, Bergamot, Clary Sage, Geranium, Melissa

Throat – Sage, Eucalyptus, Frankincense, Lavender, Sandalwood, Chamomile

Third Eye – Rosemary, Juniper

Crown – Sandalwood, Jasmine, Rose, Lavender, Frankincense

Applications

Palm Chakras – Put in center of palms of hands

Foot Chakras – Put on soles of feet

Eight Chakra – Spiritual center, higher self. Spray with a spritzer around top of head. Frankincense, Lavender, Neroli, Angelica

Color Healing

History

Since the beginning of human life we have been exposed to color. The ancient cultures of Egypt used color rooms with light that refracted through colored gemstones for healing. East Indian culture used colored gemstones prescribed by Ayurvedic medicine, sometimes using pulverized gemstones in therapies.

European culture used the doctrine of four humors from the Greco-Renaissance periods. Each humor was assigned a color; red for blood, black and yellow for bile and white for phlegm. The Chinese compiled the Nei Ching medicine text, which records color diagnoses, over 2000 years ago.

The Importance of Color

Color is a great cosmic force and power that influences us on a deep, cellular level. Color affects every aspect of our lives and dominates our senses even if we are blind. It gives us information about the environment and affects our mental and physical well-being. Mentally, it affects our perception of heat and cold; physically it affects our large and small muscle activity and also our blood pressure, respiration and heart rate. Each color has seven intrinsic elements.

- Color manifests in the physical world.
- Color gives life essence or soul power.
- Color heals the emotional and mental energy fields.
- Color unifies and harmonizes.
- Color is deeply healing and transforming.
- Color opens the third eye, bringing inspiration and intuition.
- Color is nature's instrument for spiritual or higher consciousness.

Color is related to the seven rays and awakens our energy fields (see part three for guidance on seven ray balancing).

The application of color healing takes in the essence of color and releases discordant energy. It is a powerful tool to use with *LEAP*, along with life intention work and energy field healing. The aura holds the colors of the seven rays, the spectrum of our universal energy.

The Meaning of Color

Red represents the body and sexuality.

Orange represents the life force or metabolic body.

Yellow represents the solar plexus and emotional energies.

Green represents ego and the connections between the ego and higher self.

Turquoise represents the higher mental or spiritual self.

Blue represents the causal body and motivation.

Violet represents the higher self.

Magenta represents the spirit self and the eternal being.

The Aura and Chakra Energies

The aura and chakra energies work together to create and maintain life. There are seven colors that correspond to the seven chakras.

Red – Base chakra; relates to passion, life energy, sexuality and creativity.

Orange – Sacral (adrenals); relates to physical movement, etheric health, well-being, joy.

Yellow – Solar plexus (nervous system); center of recognition and self-worth.

Green – Heart; relates to love, harmony and balance.

Blue – Throat, thyroid; relates to creative expression through sound, communication, truth.

Violet – Third eye (pituitary gland); relates to creative visualization. Gathers instruction from the higher self.

Magenta – Crown (pineal gland); relates to the eternal, spiritual self, connecting us to cosmic consciousness.

Color Therapies

There are many methods of color therapy used to promote healing and transformation. Color can profoundly affect the energy fields. Each color of light has its own wavelength and specific energies. For example, blue is peacemaking, yellow is uplifting, red can spark positive action and green stabilizes and centers our energy as well as improves self-esteem.

- *LEAP* uses kinesiology to determine the colors that are needed to balance the energy fields.

- A variety of methods can be used to infuse the energy field with the healing color that is most strengthening.

- Colored water, colored glasses, crystals and colored essences are used.

Methods of Treatment

Color infused water (see resource manual.)

Colored water may be held or applied to the body to uplift, to heal and to balance the energy fields.

Color Slides or Colored Glasses (see resource manual.)

Color slides can be used, along with a pen light, to apply color to areas in need of attention.

Colored Lamps

Colored light rays are focused on the body, especially on the back, along the spine and nervous system. Color applied through a color healing lamp permeates the cells of the body helping to rejuvenate the system.

Color Breathing

Vital energy (or prana) introduced to the body with color breathing is a powerful tool for healing. Color healing is done with deep rhythmic breathing along with visualizations. The universal life spirit is always available through the breath, bringing power and healing transformation to the energy fields.

Color Breathing Meditation

To work with color breathing, simply begin at the root chakra and breathe in the color red along with the affirmation that feels right for that chakra. (See chakra charts for suggested affirmations.) Then move up through the chakras with the breath and the related color. This exercise is very healing and energizing.

Radiate Color Healing Light

The recipient of this healing light sits comfortably. A few moments of breathing and affirmation will set the tone for this session. The healer stands in front of the person and concentrates on the color that the person needs. An affirmation can be shared here, such as "I consciously send blue to this person," or, "I transmit blue, calming energy to restore his/her energy fields to peace and harmony."

Using the directions from the AuraTouch method, you can do an energy massage with any color that tests reveal the person might need. After working with colors, do a final sweeping of the aura with white light along with an affirmation of gratitude.

Color Charged Cloths

Take a piece of colored cloth or silk the size of a postcard and lay it on the area of the body or chakra that needs the particular color remedy. (See color chart for guidance.)

Colors and Their Healing Properties

Colors are absorbed through the eyes and skin; they energize the nerves and stimulate the mind. To stimulate mental fire, use bright colors; to calm, use blue. White or blue reduces; green heals and balances. Colors provide emotional strength and can facilitate creativity. Psychological disease can be healed through color. Color also stimulates digestion and circulation, improves vitality, increases overall physical activity and energizes the blood. Gems and colored lamps strengthen the aura and the astral body. Color also affects the mind. The astral plane is constantly changing according to the emotions and feelings, and therefore has within its realm a wide variety of colors, thoughts and desire patterns. Colors are an important tool in diagnosing the psychological condition of a person and assist in the understanding of emotions and thought patterns within the aura.

The energy fields appear to be composed primarily of energy expressing itself as color. The shade of color that dominates the chakras and subtle bodies are an indication of an individual's health. The aura consists of seven layers of colored light that surround the physical body of an individual; the vibrations of light and color represent the total makeup, the etheric body, emotional field, mental field and spiritual field.

Red Brings strength and courage, releases negativity and generates vitality. It also strengthens the life force, will and sexuality, increasing circulation and overall energy. It increases the metabolism, strengthens the blood, stimulates and warms the body. It also awakens physical life force and is used to clear any disease or illness of the body. Too much red can overstimulate. It is considered the "great energizer" because of the effect it has on the physical constitution. It corresponds to the root chakra, giving vitality and strong creative energy to the body. Treatment with red stimulates the root chakra, releasing adrenaline into the bloodstream, and can reverse dormant or sluggish conditions. Spiritually, red strengthens willpower and creates courage.

Orange The healing energy of purification strengthens the etheric body, helps all muscular systems, creates harmony in one's sense of self, increasing wisdom and creativity. Assists any imbalance of the spleen, pancreas, stomach, intestines and adrenals. It also helps with food assimilation and depression and revitalizes the entire physical body. Orange stimulates the etheric, removes congestion and increases the flow of prana. It brings joy and happiness to one's being, affecting the health aura and creating a balance between the physical and mental bodies. Orange is an energizer bringing creative energy to the body. Called the "wisdom ray," orange works to heal the physical with vitality, while at the same time cultivating inner wisdom. It controls the navel chakra and assists it in the assimilation, distribution and circulation of prana.

Yellow Brings wisdom, opening the mind to expanded consciousness. It is good for intellectual development, strengthening the mind and awakening the left hemisphere of the brain. Yellow calms the solar plexus, brings positive energy, awakens confidence and optimism and helps heal the stomach, gall bladder and entire elimination system. It is effective in the treatment of headaches and a help in learning. Yellow rays have magnetic qualities and are awakening, inspiring and vitally stimulating to the higher mental body through the solar plexus chakra. It is the color of searching for the wisdom of God.

Green Brings nurturing, harmony, beauty and healing. Strengthens and stimulates the heart chakra. Heals emotional pain, neutralizes nervous energy, calms, soothes and brings balance and healing to the body, mind and spirit. It is good for healing and visualization with the breath, brings abundance and prosperity and promotes growth. Green helps things grow, so one must be careful how it is used in healing. It brings compassion, faith, peace and hope as well as soothes the mind and heals the nervous system. Due to its general healing effect, green is used to decrease inflammation and fevers. Green indicates harmony and balance of the mind and body. It is a combination of yellow (wisdom) and blue (truth), and has a healing and rejuvenating nature.

Rose Acts upon the nervous system. Vitalizes and removes depression and symptoms of debilitation. Increases the will to live.

Blue Opens the throat chakra. It brings a clearer way of communication and expression of truth and is used to increase creativity and self-expression. Blue instills self-confidence and connection with inner wisdom. Used in meditation, the color blue brings peace and calmness, enabling devotion, prayer and spiritual healing. Helps with the respiratory system and ear, nose and throat conditions. It also calms energy imbalances and helps reduce high blood pressure. Works well with children's diseases. Awakens intuition, self-expression, and inspiration. The color of truth, perfection and devotion, blue is related to the throat chakra, which is considered to be the greatest creative center in the body.

Indigo Brings deep inner wisdom; opens up intuition, connecting us with the inner teacher. Assists in expressing inner knowing, reveals the mystical nature of life. Indigo indicates devotion and clear, logical thought. Related to the third eye or ajna chakra, it deals with expansion of consciousness.

Violet   Penetrates negative energy and releases it, opening one to experience total transformation and connection with the divine in life. Helps release stress and brings balance and healing to all conditions. Helps balance the crown chakra prompting purification on all levels. Brings inspiration and humility, balancing the physical and spiritual worlds. Violet rays increase the effect of meditation tenfold.

Pink   Produces healing vibrations, opening one to the gifts of spirit. Pink within the aura denotes a quiet and refined person who likes a peaceful life.

White   Offers protection; strengthens and purifies the entire energy system. Beginning and ending color therapy with white amplifies the effect of other colors. Purifies the mind for serenity and peace.

Black   For protection, grounding and strengthening.

Aqua   Used primarily for healing, but also sedates the system and helps calm all aspects of the body and mind.

Brown   Grounds and stabilizes.

Gold   Strengthens and amplifies. Awakens our inner healer.

Silver   Increases intuition and balances female and male energies.

Chakra Healing with Color - Methods of Treatment

Root Chakra

Stimulated by Green, Indigo and Violet.

Soothed by Red, Orange, Yellow and Blue.

Red – Life, physical self, physical plane.

Energizes vitality, creativity, power and courage. Stimulates nerves.

Navel Chakra

Stimulated by Red.

Calmed by Blue and Yellow.

Orange – Health, vital self, physical plane.

Healing, wisdom. Circulates prana, strengthens etheric.

Solar Plexus Chakra

Stimulated by Red, Orange, Yellow and Violet.

Calmed by Blue and Indigo.

Yellow – Wisdom, emotional plane, power self, self-awakening, inspiring, stimulating, wisdom, digestive process. Increases intellect and power of reason.

Heart Chakra

Stimulated by Red, Orange, Indigo and Violet.

Soothed by Yellow, Green and Blue.

Green – Energy, healing self, mental plane, whole self, harmony, balance. Stimulates heart, releases tension and negative energies.

Throat Chakra

Stimulated by Red.

Calmed by Blue, Indigo, Green and Yellow.

Blue – Inspiration, peaceful self, mental plane, healing self.

Truth, perfection, devotion, creativity, peace, calming, intuition. Connects us with the higher mental body.

Third Eye Chakra

Stimulated by Orange and Red.

Indigo – Intuition, inspired self, buddhic plane.

Devotion, clarity, expansion of consciousness. Cools, strengthens thyroid and parathyroid. Purifies blood stream, heals emotional plane.

Crown Chakra

Needs no stimulation, calmed by White and Gold.

Violet – Spiritual power, spiritual self, logic plane.

Meditation, inspiration. Purifies blood, stops the growth of tumors.

Perelandra Soul Ray Essences

Like flower essences, the Soul Ray Essences work directly with both the electrical and central nervous systems. By taking the correct essences, we immediately balance the electrical system, stabilize the nervous system and stop the domino effect that leads to illness.

The Soul Ray Essences are liquid, pattern-infused solutions, each containing a specific imprint that responds in a balancing, repairing and rebuilding manner to imbalances in our systems. These patterns are angelically created, then released and infused into a water solution. To determine if a Soul Ray Essence is needed, use the kinesiology testing methods provided in Part Three.

What They Do

1. Balances and stabilizes the body as it identifies, processes and integrates its ability to function in a broader, more expanded range.
2. Balances the sensory system of each level the individual is opening to, stabilizes the system within those levels, and supports the full, expanded system as it functions as a unit.
3. Balances and stabilizes the interplay and interrelationship among various pertinent levels of the central nervous system.
4. Restores the balance and stability of the electrical system on each level that the individual is opening to. Addresses the electrical system on each of those levels as an independently functioning system.
5. Balances and stabilizes the interplay and interaction between various pertinent levels of the electrical system.
6. Supports, balances and stabilizes the interplay and interrelationship between pertinent levels of the brain. As a result, this facilitates the useful sharing of experiences and information between the appropriate levels of the brain, as well as the corresponding physical body changes that must take place for support.
7. Balances and stabilizes the refracted soul heart links and, as a result, solidifies the sense of home base.
8. Provides the support needed for understanding who we are and our relationship to the many different levels and activities we participate in. Provides the internal support for maintaining that balance.

Information for ordering Soul Ray Essences is provided in the Resources section.

The Healing Power of Crystals and Gemstones

Crystals and gemstones have been used for thousands of years for correcting disorders in the physical body and energy fields. In the past, many valuable stones were crushed and reduced to ashes to produce medicines which were ingested orally. Gems may be kept in water, so that the water absorbs their vibration, and are then used as liquid remedies. The healing energy of gems is the energy of white light with specific healing properties.

Crystals bring more beauty and light and change the energy of an area. Light reflected off a crystal brings healing and greater harmony. Crystals bring messages of great wisdom as well as energy that heals and transforms. They have the power to receive, contain, project, emanate and reflect vibrations. Through using crystals it is possible to awaken one's dormant energies and to remove energy blocks. They also help align the energy fields with the greater universal energy fields. Through this alignment our energy fields are raised to a much higher level and we then develop intuition and a deep connection with the source of life. Crystals are mirrors of our soul and can be powerful tools on our transformation path, reflecting our true nature and our soul's gifts.

Crystals, the most highly evolved in the mineral kingdom, are symbols of radiant white light energy. All crystals are expressions of light and energy and each has their own rate of vibration.

Crystals Come in Seven Specific Shapes

1. Isometric (cubic) example - fluorite
2. Tetrajonal (four sided) example - wolfinite
3. Hexagonal (six sided) example - emerald
4. Triginal (three sided) example - quartz
5. Othorhombic (lozenge shape) example - topaz
6. Monolinic (simply inclined) example - azurite
7. Trilinic (three inclined) example - turquoise

How crystals are used:

- As remedies
- Worn as a talisman
- For pendulums
- For laying on of stones
- For meditation
- Can be held or worn to absorb properties
- Can be placed in visual range to aid in focusing
- For aura cleansing and balancing
- In jewelry as an aid in maintaining mental clarity, improving concentration and emotional stability. Used to clear away emotional debris and to enhance healing abilities.

Care and Cleaning

Place crystals where they can reflect their light and radiate their beauty. Cleanse new stones by soaking in sea salt water for at least three hours.

Recharging

Keep in a well-lighted room.

How to Make Crystal Remedies

Place stones or crystals in pure leaded glass; fill with distilled water. Place in the morning sun for about three hours. The water will be infused with the vibration of the crystal as well as the color of the stone. Put in dropper bottles and test regarding the amount to take, or use approximately 10 drops several times a day.

Work with the healing affirmations the stones represent. See list of suggested affirmations along with meanings of stones.

Suggested stones for remedies: clear quartz, tourmaline, rose, adventurine and amethyst. Stones can also be used with creams or massage oil to enhance the effect of the massage.

Green stones produce a healing affect, red and orange stones a revitalization affect, pink enhances love and heart opening, blue is calming and violet intensifies the connection with higher consciousness.

Programming Crystals

Thoughts, wishes and blessings can be programmed into crystals. Direct the affirmation or thought into a clear quartz crystal and the crystal will carry the message for you. Crystals will carry out whatever healing intention you might have.

Adventurine Promotes harmony and peace. Calms nerves. Strengthens kidneys, liver, and spleen. Supports Throat, Solar Plexus and Heart Chakras.

Agates Grounding stone. Bestows protection. Tones and strengthens body and mind.

Alexandrite Promotes regeneration. Assists in healing the nervous system, spleen and pancreas. Helps with spiritual transformation.

Amber Brings harmony to endocrine system. Clears electromagnetic field. Promotes healing and is soothing and harmonizing.

Amethyst Works with the Crown Chakra to increase higher consciousness. Good to purify, as in the violet ray. Raises consciousness. Strengthens endocrine and immune systems.

Aquamarine Calms nerves. Strengthens kidney, liver, spleen and thyroid. Purifies physical body. Good for meditation. Supports Throat and Solar Plexus Chakras.

Azurite Enhances flow of energy through nervous system. Heals mental body. Supports Third Eye and Throat Chakras.

Bloodstone Good for bloodstream.

Carnelian Balances and energizes kidneys, lung, liver, gall bladder and pancreas. Vitalizes energy field. Supports Solar Plexus Chakra.

Celestite Reduces stress, brings peace of mind. Good for creative expression.

Clear Quartz Works to amplify any healing or spiritual intention. Good for meditation. Activates pineal and pituitary glands.

Citrine Good for communication. Supports the Solar Plexus and Navel Chakras.

Copper Good for blood purification and detoxification. Enhances, and is a strong conductor of, energy.

Diamond Magnifies all energy, positive or negative. Supports Crown Chakra. Aids in alignment with higher self.

Emerald Tonic for body, mind and spirit. Supports heart, liver, kidneys and the immune system. Aligns energy fields. Enhances emotional body chakra. Supports Heart and Solar Plexus Chakras.

Fluorite Cleanses and refines. Good for healing and meditation.

Garnet Good for grounding. Brings joy and energy to Root, Navel and Solar Plexus Chakras. Heals all body systems. Purifies blood.

Gold Purifies and energizes all systems. Regenerative and restorative. Attracts positive energy into aura. Promotes illumination, love and compassion. Supports Navel, Heart and Crown Chakras.

Hematite Grounding. Disperses negativity. Good for cleansing bloodstream. Energizing and revitalizing.

Herkimer Diamond Good for meditation. Works with Ajna, or Third Eye Chakra. Clears and balances etheric. Cleanses energy field.

Jade Strengthens and supports immune system, heart and kidneys. Brings emotional balance and releases negativity.

Kunzite Opens and supports heart center. Promotes surrender and release. Strengthens cardiovascular system.

Lapis Lazuli Strong support for thyroid. Enhances psychic abilities and communication with higher self. Supports and energizes the Third Eye and Throat Chakras.

Love Stone Good for circulation. Aids in release of stored emotions. Supports Heart Chakra.

Malachite Brings emotional strength.

Moldavite A deep green stone that fell to earth about 15 million years ago. Opens one to higher self and reception to higher dimensional sources.

Moonstone Cleansing for the emotional body. Works with Ajna Chakra. Heals stomach, spleen and pancreas.

Obsidian Clears fears. Grounds and protects. Heals stomach and intestines. Absorbs negativity.

Opal Magnifies energy, positive or negative. Relieves stress. Aids in connecting with higher energies.

Pearl Cleanses and purifies. Brings what is hidden or dark into consciousness.

Peridot Regenerative powers for all systems of the body. Purifies, balances and tones body and mind. Aligns the energy fields. Stimulates personal growth.

Rose Quartz Good for the emotional heart. Promotes nurturing, compassion and forgiveness. Assists in healing the kidneys.

Ruby Grounds and stabilizes. Increases vitality, protects, clears and restores blood and circulation. Supports Root Chakra.

Sapphire Supports Throat Chakra. Good for creative expression. Strengthens heart and kidneys. Activates pituitary gland.

Silver Enhances mental function. Strengthens, purifies and cleanses body systems. Good for grounding and centering.

Smokey Quartz Disperses negativity. Strengthens kidneys and pancreas. Relieves depression. Supports Root Chakra.

Sugalite Good for Third Eye development.

Tiger Eye Grounding and centering. Good for digestive system, spleen, pancreas and colon. Supports Navel, Solar Plexus and Root Chakras.

Topaz Yellow: Good for intellect. Works to increase concentration.

Blue: Good for expression and dreams, for regeneration of the body and for detoxification.

Tourmaline Provides endocrine support. Aligns energy fields. Aids in release of fear and brings protection. Strong healing stone for all areas.

Turquoise Calms nervous system. Good for protection.

Chakra Healing – Balancing the Chakras with Crystals and Gemstones

The seven centers of vital energy receive and transmit energy in the form of color. Their correct functioning depends on both psychological and physical health. Gemstone therapy has a direct action on balancing the subtle energy centers.

To balance the centers with the use of crystals or gems, first detect the center that needs balancing (see energy diagnosis section). Then, when the person is lying down in a relaxed state, apply the stones to the center. (See each chakra chart.)

The Crown Center

Rules the pineal gland, brain and right eye and is balanced by emerald, amethyst, fire agate, labradorite or malachite, diamond, amethyst, clear quartz, crystal, topaz, alexandrite, sapphire and selenite.

The Third Eye Center

Rules the pituitary gland, left eye, ears, nose and nervous system and is balanced by topaz, amethyst, carnelian, emerald, labradorite, malachite, sapphire, lapis, sodalite, quartz and opal.

The Throat Center

Rules the thyroid gland, bronchial and vocal organs, lungs, alimentary canal, and comes into balance through diamond, amber, aquamarine, citrine, emerald, topaz or turquoise, chalcedony, lapis lazuli, agate, celestite, sodalite and sapphire.

The Heart Center

Rules the thymus gland, heart, blood, vagus nerve, and circulatory system and may respond to sapphire, bloodstone, topaz, rose quartz, tourmaline, lapis, amber, tiger-eye, topaz, aventurine, azurite, quartz, malachite, and moonstone.

The Solar Plexus Center

Rules the pancreas, stomach, liver, nervous system, and gall bladder and comes into balance with ruby, amber, aquamarine, citrine, emerald, moonstone, pearl and turquoise, lapis, tiger-eye, topaz, aventurine and quartz.

The Navel Center

Rules the reproductive system and comes into balance by the use of pearl, amber, amethyst, aquamarine, carnelian, coral, fire agate, garnet and labradorite, moonstone, citrine, topaz and tourmaline.

The Root Chakra

Rules the adrenals, spinal column, and kidneys and comes into balance through coral, garnet, turquoise, agate, hematite, blood jasper ruby, bloodstone, smoky quartz, onyx and tiger-eye.

> *Essence is emptiness,*
> *Everything else, accidental.*
> *Emptiness brings peace to loving,*
> *Everything else, disease.*
>
> *In this world of trickery*
> *Emptiness is what your soul wants.*
> *Rumi*

How easily a tranquil pool is disturbed
By the passing winds.
Nay friend,
Seek not thy happiness in the fleeting.
There is but one way:
The path lies in thyself
Through thine own heart.

From Darkenss to Light
J. Krishnamurti

Part Seven
Energy Field
Self-Care Manual
for Body, Mind and Spirit

*Whatever I do, the responsibility is mine
but like one who plants an orchard, what
comes of what I do, the fruit will be for
this. I offer the actions of this life to God
within and wherever I go, the way is
blessed.*

Lalla – Naked Song

By Coleman Barks

Breathing Visualizations

First, always be willing to let go.

Yogic Breath

Inhale though your nose expanding the abdomen, rib cage and chest. Allow the breath to inflate, three-dimensionally, the sides, the front and the back of your body. Exhale slowly, through the nose, allowing the chest to deflate, the rib cage to soften and the abdomen to release back to the spine, in that order. This is the basic yogic breath that is used in these visualizations. Keep your breath full, lengthy and smooth and allow your mind to soften into these visualizations.

Connected Breathing

Begin with the full yogic breath. Connect each breath to the next without a pause in between. Bring your attention into any disturbances in your physical, mental or emotional energy fields. Simply allow yourself to breathe into the discomfort, becoming aware of the sensation. Do this for 10 breaths and then allow your attention to soften into stillness. Notice any changes that might have occurred.

Chakra Cleansing Breath

Begin with the full yogic breath. Inhale and exhale into each chakra beginning with the crown and working your way down. Become aware of which chakras feel over-energized and which chakras feel deficient. Now, begin with the root and visualize a blue, calming energy to reduce the over-energized chakras, or a red, stimulating energy to balance a deficient chakra. Surrender your mind to this healing process. Always give gratitude and seal your intention with an affirmation such as, "I thank the divine healing energy for assisting me to release all disturbed energy from my being."

Breath of Joy

Interlace your fingers and stretch the palms of the hands outward above your head. Inhale, open your chest and arch your back, allowing your head to fall up and back. Exhale; release your arms to your sides. Interlace your fingers behind your back, pull your shoulder blades together, and again arch your back and allow your chest to open. Inhale and exhale using the full yogic breath. While doing this, visualize and feel yourself rooted into the earth. Remember your gratitude for your existence. Feel yourself lengthening up and out of the earth and expanding in all directions into space. Release your arms to your sides and feel the light energy that is present. Repeat this three times saying an affirmation similar to this, "I allow myself to feel the joy that is naturally present within myself and send this joy outward to all."

Daily Chakra Clearing Meditation

Place your hand, palm turned toward the body, at a distance that feels comfortable to you. Start at just a few inches above the body and then move your hand as far away as you can and still feel sensation/energy from the chakra. Hover over each chakra as you speak or think the following affirmations. You can visualize the color of each chakra as you repeat the affirmation.

Affirmations

1st/Root (red) "I am eternally secure. My soul exists through all time."

2nd/Navel (orange) "I am one with the divine mother. I love unconditionally."

3rd/Solar Plexus (yellow) "Power in the center is the core power. I am one with that power and it runs throughout all of my being."

4th/Heart (green or rose) "The river of love flows through my heart and then through my whole body. I am a child of love, present, connected and surrendered to the flow."

5th/Throat (light blue) "My voice is clear and true."

6th/Third Eye (indigo blue) "I see through the illusions to truth."

7th/Crown (pink or violet) "I bring all my learning, gifts and tools from all lifetimes as medicine for the greater good."

(See AuraTouch for an additional method of energy balancing.)

Don't wait any longer. Dive into the ocean, leave and let the sea be you. Silent, absent, walking an empty road, all praise.

Rumi

Self Care Energy Wellness Methods

Grounding Energy

Sit comfortably, spine straight, feet flat on the floor; or lie down, feet uncrossed. Close your eyes and focus on your lower abdomen. Visualize the root center. See it connected to a cord carrying your energy into the earth. This grounding cord is the channel in which energy flows deep below the earth's surface. Allow the breath to assist in deepening your awareness of the moment. Breathe out, releasing all thoughts and emotions. Breathing in, feel a sense of peace and calm. Your sacred cord links you with the source from which you came, the deep silence, the origin of your being. Feel this sacred cord anchor in the earth's core, holding you in the safety of divine light. This cord connects to your foundation, a sense of stability, trust and centering. Use this sacred cord anytime you are in need.

Protection Ceremonies

Breathe deeply and center yourself in your heart. On the inhalation, breathe in a beautiful golden light and surround yourself with this sphere of light as you exhale. Affirm, "I am strong, protected and shielded by divine light."

Shielding Techniques – Use of Energy Shields

Visualize a golden disk, full of light and protection, and mentally place it over the chakras that need protection, especially the solar plexus chakra.

Connecting Heaven and Earth Etheric Energy flow

Begin with awareness at the crown center. Gently breathe and visualize the breath moving down from the crown center to the third eye center, through the throat center, to the heart center, the solar plexus center, the navel center and to the root. With your breath, visualize the colors you need as you bathe in radiant, healing light.

When you feel ready, focus your attention on the foot chakras (soles of feet). Breathe in the energy of Mother Earth through the soles of the feet and up through the chakras to connect the earth and heaven circles of cosmic energy.

The mind turned inward is the Self;
turned outward, it becomes the ego
and all the world.
Sri Ramana Maharshi

Energy Exercises

Cross Crawl

The cross crawl is an excellent exercise to reconnect the energy fields, clearing stagnant electromagnetic energy as well as offering a path to feeling balanced and centered. Use as a daily exercise, before or after a stressful event, to help with learning issues and to help with left and right brain integration. The cross crawl exaggerates normal walking movements, the opposite arm and leg moving together as if marching. Cross crawl can be done standing, sitting or lying down. If unable to exert normal strength, lift the opposite hands and feet, alternately tensing the muscles of the opposing arm and leg pairs, and have someone else lift the opposite arm and leg.

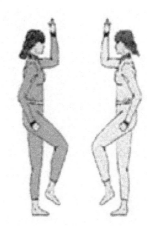

Tibetan 5 Rites

There are seven psychic vortices in the body. Vortex A is located within the forehead. Vortex B is located in the posterior part of the brain. Vortex C is in the region of the neck and Vortex F and G are located one in either knee. These psychic vortices revolve at great speed.

For the First Rite we stand erect with arms outstretched, horizontal with the shoulders. Now spin around until you become slightly dizzy. There is only one caution; you must turn from left to right.

Rite 1

For the Second Rite lie flat on your back on the floor or the bed. Then place the hands, palms down, alongside the hips. Fingers should be kept close together with the fingertips of each hand turned toward one another. The feet are then raised until the legs are straight up. If possible, let the feet extend back a bit over the body, toward the head, but do not let the knees bend. Then slowly lower the feet to the floor and for a moment allow all of the muscles to rela:

Rite 2

Rite 3

For the Third Rite kneel on your mat or prayer rug, place hands on thighs and lean forward as far as possible with the head inclined so that the chin rests on the chest. Now lean backwards as far as possible. At the same time the head should be lifted and tilted back as far as it will go. Then bring the head up along the body, lean forward and start the rite over again.

For the Fourth Rite sit on a mat with legs stretched out in front of you. Place the hands alongside the body with palms flat on the floor. Now raise the body and bend the knees so that the legs, from the knees below, are practically straight up and down. The arms too will be straight up and down while the body, from the shoulders to the knees, will be horizontal. Before pushing the body to a horizontal position the chin should be well down on the chest. Then, as the body is raised, the head should be allowed to drop gently back as far as it will go. Next, return to a sitting position and tense every muscle in the body.

Rite 4

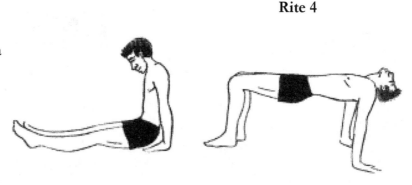

For the Fifth Rite place the hands on the floor about two feet apart. With the legs stretched out to the rear, push the body, and especially the hips, up as far as possible, rising on the toes and hands. At the same time the head should be brought so far down that the chin comes up against the chest. Next, allow the body to come slowly back down to a sagging position, bringing the head up and tilting it as far back as possible.

Rite 5

Chakra Exercises

Root Chakra Exercise

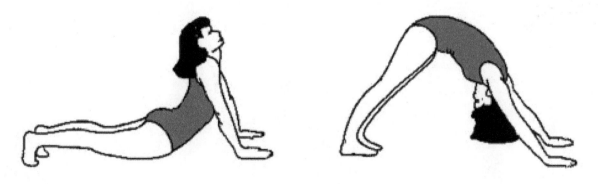

Navel Chakra Exercise

Spleen Chakra Exercise

Solar Plexus Chakra Exercise

Heart Chakra Exercise

Third Eye and Crown Chakra Exercise

Starting Position

End Position for
Right-handed

End Position
for Left-handed

Late, by myself,
in the boat of myself,
no light and no land
anywhere, cloud cover
thick.
I try to stay just about the
surface, yet I'm already
under
and living within
the ocean.

Cook's Hook-ups

A Centering Exercise Created *by Dr. Wayne Cook*

Cook's Hook-ups restore balance to disturbed energy currents. Wonderful for relaxation, concentration and integration of mind and emotions.

1.   Sit comfortably with legs crossed at ankles. Cross the wrists over your chest.
     Turn your hands back towards each other and clasp together.
     Breathe, relax and enjoy.

2.   Hold finger tips together in a "rainbow arch."

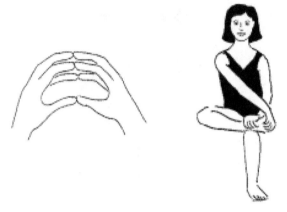

Seek not perfume of a single heart
Nor dwell in its easeful comfort,
For therein abides
The fear of loneliness.
I wept,
For I saw
The loneliness of a single love.
In the dancing shadows
Lay a withered flower.
The worship of many in the one
Leads to sorrow.
But the love of one in the many
Is everlasting bliss.
        From Darkness to Light
        J. Krishnamurti

Energy Tune-up for Daily Self-Care

The energy tune-up can be done in about 10 minutes as a quick pick-me-up for clients or for self-care.

1. Begin the energy tune-up by doing several cross crawls, right leg with left arm, as shown in the Energy Exercises section. You can do this exercise walking or jumping, slow or fast. The cross crawl brings the right and left hemisphere into balance and creates a clear circuit in the energy fields.

2. Run the energy from your pubic bone to the lower lip – Zip-up! This creates a strong protective flow.

3. Thump on the thymus gland, the area of the chest that the fictitious character Tarzan uses as well to increase strength. The thymus gland assists in overall vital energy and increases brain activity. Also good for waking oneself up if feeling sleepy, unfocused and unclear in any way.

4. Rub lymphatic glands in chest area; move hands about 4 inches outside of clavicle and three inches down. Kidney 27 point. This point will assist in bringing energy into the body.

5. Rub kidney points in the back of the body; put hands on waist, fingers pointing toward abdomen and thumbs pointing toward the back. Where the thumbs rest is usually where the kidney point is. If it is tender then it needs releasing. Use bending exercise forward and backward to increase the effectiveness of this point release.

6. Vigorously rub hands along side of outer thighs, from the hip to the knee. These are lymphatic points for the gall bladder and are often very tender. You can use your knuckles for a deeper release.

7. Run the energy from your head down to the feet and back in a sweeping motion, work with appropriate affirmation.

8. Deeply hold the point in the middle of the foot, Kidney 1, known as an emergency revival point. This point helps bring in the vital force and also helps ground displaced energy.

9. Bring energy from earth, scooping it up and bathing the entire energy field, and then release it to the heavens.

10. Zip-up; bring the energy from the pubic bone and from the tail bone to the point below the lower lip, zipping yourself up in a bubble of healing, white, protective light.

Reflections on the Noble Eight-Fold Path

Right Seeing

Live in remembrance of your soul's essence. See the world without illusion; see clearly the facts of life, what *is*. When you live in the moment you are able to view life without the conditioning of the past. See all with an awakened eye allowing the mind to cling to nothing and be born anew each day. Your awakened being will see the beauty of each moment, holding nothing. When you let go of attachment to ideas, concepts, thoughts, images and impressions you find freedom and discover an unconditional relationship to life.

Right Intention

Your intention is to find freedom from personal sorrow. This is your birthright, a life of happiness and goodness. Let go of self-deception and the negative effects of the false identification with the personality. Use your will for the highest good. Learn to live with compassion for this suffering world, offering loving kindness to all sentient beings. Connect your mind with your heart; realize that the highest intelligence can be gained through the blending of love and wisdom. Look at how the search for pleasure brings pain and pain again brings the search for pleasure. Have the intention to stop personal self-inflicted suffering. Live in acceptance of self and others, offering a prayer for happiness for all suffering beings.

Right Speech

Learn to speak the truth and express your true nature. Tell no lies; use words to help or assist learning. Speak kindly and with harmlessness. Speak from your true nature, from the heart of your being. Through prayer you commune with the sacred presence within your heart. A great joy comes through silence.

Right Action

When you practice and honor your intention for freedom, you naturally employ right action. Live in the light of harmlessness with the intention of not hurting any life form. Harmlessness is the teaching that employs right action. You become a gentle being with compassion for others and yourself. Live in the light of service; reach into your heart for a spirit of generosity and goodness.

Right Livelihood

Living in your truth will lead you to do what you love, causing no harm to others and increasing your integrity through your abundant nature. You see that all expressions should be in support of your spirit, honoring and caring for the things most important in life. Await life's call for service.

Right Effort

The intention for freedom of being is the foundation for all practice. Realizing your true nature is the first step in this intention. Living with inspiration from your divine nature and following its guidance will lead you to unconditional happiness and love. Find time for the mind to retreat in silence; commune with the healing force of nature.

Right Mindfulness

Through your awakening process you will learn to let go of the past that was identified with the false nature of the self. Memories of the past based on false identification do not exist; they are records of illusions that need to be released. Relaxing into your true nature of peace, you know that you are, in truth, an untouched being free from all scars of the past. Awareness of your true being leads you to a lasting healing of body, mind and spirit. Releasing the past allows you to be fully present in the now. Stop all activity of the mind that is geared toward memory and allow the meeting of the true self, found in the eternal present.

Right Attention

Surrender all doubt that stems from thought that wanders in and out of consciousness. Train the mind to become focused in the center of being, acquiring stillness and one-pointedness. Forget all that has been acquired through false identification, yet live in remembrance of your true sacred essence. Meditation is simply the surrendering of all holdings, facing the emptiness of being and breathing in your true nature.

Healing Mudras

Mudra means to seal or lock. These sacred hand positions can be used to bring balance to the body, mind and emotions and are to seal in our intention. In yoga philosophy each finger corresponds to one of the five elements. Each position shows the relationship of the chakras and elements in our hands. The thumb represents the fire element corresponding to the solar plexus chakra and the adrenal glands. The index finger represents the air element and corresponds to the heart chakra and the thymus gland. The middle finger represents the ether element and corresponds to the throat chakra and the thyroid gland. The ring finger represents the earth element corresponding to the root chakra and the sexual glands. The little finger represents the water element corresponding to the navel chakra and the pancreas. In all mudras the fire element, or thumb, must be included.

Prana Mudra - Vital Force

Improves energy, circulation, eyesight and general health. Increases vital force, awakens the root chakra. Join the tips of your little finger, ring finger and thumb. Concentrate on your breathing.

Jnana Mudra - Attaining Wisdom

Aids in concentration, meditation, focusing, memory and brain power. Useful for insomnia. Brings a sense of peace and harmony to all aspects of the body and mind. Touch the tip of the thumb with the tip of the index finger. Use for any time relaxation is needed. Fingers are pointing upward, but not fully extended.

Prithvi Mudra - Body Energy and Mental Flexibility

Opens the mind, assists one to experience bliss and balances the nutrients of the body. Helps relieve excess energy in the root and navel chakras. Touch tip of the thumb (fire) to the ring finger (earth). Open the rest of the fingers outward and straight up.

Atmanjali Mudra - Prayer

Namaste or Namaskar, meaning "I salute the divinity within you." A reverence gesture of respectful greeting. Useful in salutations to another, depicting a great respect. Place your hands together, palms facing. You can use this hand position in front of your heart or in front of your third eye for Namaste salutations and prayer positions.

Apana Mudra - Increases Energy

Useful for all water retention problems, helps to remove toxins from the body. It is a wonderful mudra to assist in the realization of the self. Join the tip of the thumb (fire) to the tips of the middle and ring fingers (sky and earth).

Dhyana Mudra - Meditation

Two hands are open and relaxed with the palms up, resting on the folded legs, the right hand atop the left with the tips of the thumbs gently touching.

Abhaya Mudra - Seal of Divine Protection

Dispels fear and promotes protection. Raise your right hand to chest level with palms facing forward. Place your left hand on your left thigh, in your lap or on your heart. Use with mantras, visualizations, prayer, invocation or with a silent mind.

For sixty years I have been forgetful every moment,
but not for one second has this flowing toward me
stopped or slowed. I deserve nothing.
Today I recognize that I am the guest the mystics talk about.
I play this loving music for my Host.
~Rumi

Shanti Mudra - Invocation of Peace Seal

Calms the mind, increases strength and energizes the entire body. Promotes well-being. Sit in a meditative pose. Close your eyes and place your hands on your lap, palms facing up, fingers pointing toward each other. Breathe in, filling your abdomen with air and contracting it. Keep the abdomen contracted and breathe out. Inhale and exhale as deeply as possible.

1   **Concentration**: The root center (muladhara).
    Inhale and fully expand your abdomen. At the same time, raise your hands until they reach your navel again. Coordinate the movement of your hands and abdominal expansion.

2   **Concentration:** The root center to the navel center. Breathe deeply, expanding your chest region by raising your hands to the front of your heart.

3   **Concentration:** The solar plexus chakra and the heart chakra. Breathe in and raise your shoulders, bringing your hands to the front of your throat.

4   **Concentration:** The heart center to the throat center to the third eye center to the crown center. Retaining your breath, spread your arms to the sides, palms facing up. Holding your breath without any strain, stay in this position for a few seconds.

5   **Concentration:** The crown of the head. As you exhale, lower your arms to the sides and place your hands on your lap. At the end of your exhalation, contract your abdomen and relax your body. Relax and repeat this mudra exercise, as you desire. Remember to always do deep breathing along with the movement of your arms.

Healing Prayers and Mantras

NAMASTE, I SALUTE THE DIVINITY WITHIN YOU

Om is the word of creation. In the New Testament (John, 1:1) it is written, "In the beginning was the word and the word was with God and the word was God." The word referred to is *Om.*

The Origin and Nature of Sound

The root chakra is considered the birthplace of sound within our being. Sound travels through the chakras as they are awakened and the highest manifestation of sound occurs in the throat center in the form of *Om.* In the root center it is expressed as a bird chirping; in the navel center it becomes the twinkling of an anklet; in the solar plexus center it becomes the sound of a bell, and then within the heart center it is expressed as the music of a flute.

When the cosmic sound or vibration reaches the throat center it manifests as the cosmic sound, *Om.* The vibration of sound travels along the Sushumna channel, cleansing and reenergizing the karmic patterns of the chakras. Sound evolves from the vibration of the Kundalini Shakti that resides in the base center, into the navel where it is perceived as rumbling. It moves to the heart and is perceived as un-struck. Moving from the heart and through the throat, it produces all sounds. Para is the highest transcendental state, along with pure energy, Shakti – a divine vibration that unites all. Sound is a direct vehicle to access Parashakti, our highest force. Sound meditation, or japa, is the art of using sound to transcend consciousness to the highest level of divine expression. The power of sound is a direct way to self-realization, clearing the mind of the clutter of thoughts, emotions and impressions. When the mind is in its natural, pure state it reflects the pure consciousness of the infinite.

The use of healing sounds that are expressed with the intention of clearing stagnant energy will bring the higher aspect of truth, divine will and the essence of love and peace into our consciousness. When we use our voice to access divine healing energy through mantras and healing sounds we are able to bring all aspects of our being into alignment with these energies. Through the use of healing sounds we learn to hear intuitively and quicken the development of our higher faculties. Healing sounds are nature's medicine to bring our minds into a state of peace, focus, clarity and attention to the sacred in life. By way of the voice we are able to awaken our life force. Our divine consciousness resonates throughout our being and to the beings of the entire world. The awakening of the life force within keeps the mind still and turned inward to the Sacred Heart.

The Vedas state that creation arises from the first sound of the universe. *Aum (Om)* is the primal sound, which emanated with the first of creation. *A* represents the material universe (the waking state), *U* represents the astral plane (the dreaming state), which includes the emotional and mental aspects of our natural plane, and *M* represents the experience that lies above the mind and deep-sleep state. *Aum* signifies the three periods of time, the three states of consciousness and all of existence. The *OM* sound is represented by these symbols: The three is the material world. The dot or bindu is the absolute consciousness, encased by the veiling power of mind and body. The crescent sign is the deep sleep subconscious where one holds the knowledge and impressions received from previous incarnations. The *OM* sound has three aspects representing Brahma, Vishnu and Shiva. The three aspects also represent the trinity of the God head. These three aspects are embedded in the letters of *A, U, M.* The sound *A* arises in the throat, the *U* arises from the tongue and *M* arises from the lips. When they join they become *OM* which arises from the navel. It covers the whole field of the vocal organs. Thus *OM* represents all languages and the world. The navel is compared to the lotus and is the place where the life force resides. When *OM* is pronounced it should appear as if a plane is coming from a distance, then drawing closer and closer to us and eventually flying from us. Saying the mantra *OM*, will rejuvenate the nervous system, and bring peace and balance to the body, mind and emotions.

Healing Prayers, Sacred Chants

Our prayers are our direct communications with the creator. It is the action or our pure hearts and mind to surrender to divine will and receive guidance.

The Great Invocation

From the point of light within the mind of God,
let light stream forth into the minds of men. Let light descend on earth.
From the point of love within the heart of God,
let love stream forth into the hearts of men. May Christ return to Earth.
From the center where the will of God is know,
let purpose guide the little wills of people, the purpose which the masters know and serve.
From the center, which we call the race of men,
let the plan of love and light work out and may it seal the door where dwells.

Let light and love and power restore the plan on earth.

Prayer of Saint Francis

Where there is hatred let me sow love,
Where there is injury, pardon
Where there is despair, let me sow hope
Where there is darkness, let me sow light.
For behold, the kingdom of heaven is within you.

The Lord's Prayer

The Lord's Prayer is useful to all healing and is a great benefit to the alignment of the chakras with the soul.

Our Father, which art in heaven *(the Crown Chakra)*,
hallowed by Thy name *(the Third Eye Chakra)*.
Thy kingdom come
(The Crown & Head Chakras as well as the Spiritual Chakras above the head).
Thy will be done *(the Throat Chakra)*
in earth *(the Root Chakra)*
as it is in heaven *(the Crown Chakra)*.
Give us this day our daily bread *(Root, Navel and Solar Plexus Chakras)*
and forgive us our trespasses *(the lower three chakras)*
as we forgive those who trespass against us
*(bringing the energy of the earth through the lower chakras transforming it to light and
moving the energies through the upper chakras)*.
And lead us not into temptation *(the Solar Plexus Chakra)*
but deliver us from evil *(the resurrection of the Heart Center)*
for Thine is the kingdom *(the Throat Chakra)*
and the power *(the Third Eye Chakra)*
and the glory, forever.
Amen *(the Crown Center)*.

Divine Invocations

Ask and it will be given to you; seek and you will find; knock, and it will be opened to you. For everyone who asks, receives; and he who seeks, finds; and to him who knocks it will be opened.
Matthew 7:7-8

Invocations to the Archangels

Michael, Angel of protection, is a protective force we can call upon to clear the obstacles of darkness and ignorance and remove the veil from our true identities as beings of light. Gabriel, Angel of strength, death and resurrection. Uriel, Angel of communication, messenger of God. Raphael, Angel of healing.

*May Michael be on my right hand, Gabriel on my left, before me Uriel, behind me Raphael
and above me the all-pervading Divine Presence.*

Divine Affirmations for the Body, Mind and Spirit

When working with divine affirmations, it is important to find one that supports the evolving nature of the soul. Divine affirmations help us release old programming by seeing consciousness in its perfection. Below are some ideas for divine affirmations.

Divine Affirmations for the Body

- I am whole, well and in complete balance with the perfection of nature.

- I am radiant, free and full of vitality.

- I completely let go of all imbalances in my system, allowing my body, mind and spirit to be in perfect balance.

- I let go of all memory held in my body, breathing in the present moment, free from the past. I see now that my body, mind and spirit are in perfect harmony.

- As I inhale, I focus bringing healing light to my pain and discomfort. As I exhale, I let go of all disharmony. I see myself free from pain and imbalance.

- I am not this physical body; I am not my emotions or thought. I am eternal and not bound to these conditions.

- I bring space, awareness and light to my life, knowing my nature is infinite, unbounded consciousness.

Divine Affirmations for the Emotional and Mental Energy Fields

- I transcend all emotions from my ego nature into the pure emotions of love, light and joy that are expressions of my true self residing in my heart.

- I observe all thoughts that come into my pure consciousness while remaining firmly planted in my heart of purity and stillness.

- My compassion understands that my thoughts and emotions are scars left from identification with my ego self. I now turn my attention to my heart of sacred wisdom and rest.

- I allow nothing to obscure the vision and oneness of my true nature; all that is temporary simply flows through me and out again. I am a sieve of discernment and goodness, loving the divine above all.

- I embody the beauty of the universe, completely letting go of all tendencies to create suffering or pain. I offer my life in service to the divine.

- I let go of all feelings of separation as I merge with my divine consciousness of love and truth.

- I hold my true self dear. I have found a precious rare jewel and will keep it safe, polished and radiant at all times.

Divine Affirmations for the Spirit

- I am one with the divine, offering my life to service and truth.

- I offer all of my being to the divine, all that is hidden, all that is revealed. I remain open to divine will, surrendering all personal desires.

- I give my life as a garland of roses, each rose being a lesson learned, each rose with the fragrance of purity and the eternal beauty of my soul.

- I surrender all to the divine, allowing space and emptiness to meet life's calling. I humbly await the opportunity to serve.

- The past is completely forgiven for I am born anew in the infinite possibilities of my freedom, as pure and divine consciousness.

- I let go of all sorrow and memories knowing that my true reality is found in the timelessness of life, where I remain.

Healing Chants, Mantras and Sounds

In a spiritual context, the throat center is best used for liberation of the personality self. Through repeating mantras, saying prayers and singing sacred chants we are able to achieve the peace, love and God-consciousness that we yearn for. Mantras are powerful invocations to the divine. They work through the vibration of sound and the intention behind them. Through the practice of turning inward into the stillness of our heart, we begin using a mantra, or divine affirmation, in support of our soul. When identification shifts from ego self to true divine nature, a mantra simply assists the focusing of our mind. Through the use of a mantra, or divine affirmation, we are able to direct attention to our ever-present eternal nature, dissolving any sense of separation, opening to the infinite. The mantra, or statement of choice, is our vital energy (Shakti) expressed as sound, invoking the divine consciousness within our being.

Many of the mantras suggested in this chapter are derived from the Sanskrit alphabet, the language of the divine. The power of a mantra, when applied to a situation, will transform the energy, bringing about a change in reality. The correct sound is like an invocation or divine command that sets the vibrations of the cosmos into motion, attracting to us the requested result.

The Throat Chakra is considered the chakra of miracles because the voice is able to transcend outer reality through a simple command. The Throat Chakra is the center where the voice, when used in relationship to the highest good, can create miracles through commands, prayers and affirmations.

As mantras are very powerful invocations to the divine, they are used for the intent to change and transform energy. The vibrations from a mantra will move energy for whatever purpose or intention. To infuse a mantra with power is to activate vibrational channels that produce altered states of consciousness, which aid us in remembering our true nature.

The Gayatri Mantra

The Gayatri is the Mother of the Universe, the supreme Shakti, and there is nothing she cannot do. Her mantra purifies the mind; destroys pain, sin and ignorance; brings liberation and bestows health, strength, vitality, power, intelligence and magnetic aura. This mantra is the essence of Vedanta that sharpens the intellect. It has three parts: praise, meditation and prayer.

First, the divine is praised and then meditated upon in reverence and then, lastly, the appeal is made to the divine to awaken and strengthen the intellect, the discriminating faculty of man. The Gayatri is the most essential mantra ever known. It is important to recite it at least three times a day, morning, noon and evening. The Gayatri dispels the darkness of ignorance and promotes knowledge, wisdom and discrimination. This is a treasure you must guard all your life. It will protect you from harm, wherever you are. The presence of Brahma will descend upon you, illuminating your intellect and lighting your path as this mantra is chanted. Gayatri is the Shakti that animates all life.

Gayatri Ancient Meaning and Pronunciation

Om (Aum) Symbol of the Para Brahman, the basis of creation.

Bhur (Bhoor) Bhu-Loka (physical plane), the earth.

Bhuvah (Bhoo-vah) Antariksha-Loka (astral), atmosphere.

Swah (Sva-ha) Swarga-Loka (celestial plane), absolute substratum of creation. Heaven, beyond the causal.

Tat (Taht) Transcendent Para-atman, that ultimate reality. Savitur-Ishwara or creator, equated with divine power, contained in the sun.

Varenyam Fit to be worshiped or adored. With adoration we worship the glorious power of the pervading sun.

Bargo Remover of sins and ignorance. Glory, radiance.

Devasya Resplendent, shining from whom all things proceed. Divine radiance, grace of God.

Dhemahi We meditate.

Dhiyo-Yo-Nat Pracho-dayatt May the prayer direct our intellect towards ultimate reality.

Dhiyo Buddhic intellect, understanding. May he enlighten our intellects.

Yo Which, who

Nah Our

Prachodayat Enlighten, guide, impel.

Mantras for Your Life Path

Om Gum Ganapatayei Namaha

Om and salutations to the remover of obstacles (Ganapathi) for which Gum is the seed.
Ganapathi or Ganesha, the elephant-headed deity. Remover of obstacles.

Om Shrim Maha Lakshimiyei Swaha

Om, I invoke the great power of abundance.

Om Ram Ramaya Swaha

A mantra to correct actions on the physical plane.

Om Namo Bhagavate Vasudevaya

Om, the indwelling source within all of life, kindly reveal the truth to me.
The indweller is Vasudeva, the soul, which resides in the heart center. This mantra helps you to
call on that power within your soul to further your spiritual growth.

Om Shanti, Om Shanti, Om Shanti Om, Om Shanti, Om Shanti, Om

The Great Peace Mantra

Om, Mane Padme Hum (Aa-Oo-M Mah-Nee-Pad-May Hoom)

Om, jewel in the lotus, Hum – Harmonizes nerve tissues, clears subtle impurities from the
nadis and nerves, empowers all actions on the subtle level, infusing the cosmic life force into
the healing process. Male and female energies come into balance.

Om Namah Shivaya, Om Namah Shivaya, Om Namah Shivaya, Shivayah Namah Om

Shiva, lord of ascetics and recluses, is part of the Hindu trinity. Brahma and Vishnu, the other
two parts, are associated with creation and preservation. Shiva, the cosmic dancer, presides over
the destructive energies, which break up the universe at the end of each age. This is the process
of the old making way for the new; in a more personal sense, "I honor the divine within."

Hare Om, Hare Om, Hare Hare Om, Hare Om, Hare Om, Hare Hare, Om

Hare is another name for Vishnu. The aspect which forgives the past actions of those who take
refuge in him and destroys their negative deeds. Hare is a redeemer and a guide to personal
salvation as well as the world preserver.

Hare Rama, Hare Rama, Rama Rama, Hare Hare, Hare Rama, Hare Rama, Hare Hare, Hare Krishna, Hare Krishna, Krishna Krishna, Hare Hare

Hare is the glorified form of address for calling upon God. Rama and Krishna were two of the
best-known and most beloved incarnations of Vishnu. They took human birth on this earth to

lead mankind to eternal salvation. This is the maha mantra, the easiest and surest way for attaining God realization in this present age.

Om Sri Ram Jai Ram, Jai Jai Ram Om Sri Ram Jai Ram, Jai Jai Ram

Victory to Rama (Jaya means victory).

Gate Gate, Paragate Parasamgate, Bodhisvaha

Meaning "Gone, gone, beyond all illusions of the physical plane, on the breath."

Om Tara, Tu Tare, Ture Svaha

Homage to you, Tara, Divine, Radiant Mother of Compassion and Great Protector.

Healing Sounds, Mantras, Invocations and Prayers

Sound / Pronunciation / Meaning and Benefits

Aum / Om (rhymes with home) The divine word serving to energize or empower all things. Good for the spine and restores and energizes the entire body and mind. Awakens Prana, opens channels. All mantras begin and end with Om. Clears the mind and increases the strength of our immune system. Awakens prana of positive energy and healing.

Ram (rhymes with calm) Brings in divine protection giving strength, calm, rest and peace. Good for mental disorders such as insomnia, bad dreams, nervousness, anxiety, excessive fear, and fright. Helps build the immune system.

Hum (rhymes with room) Wards off negative influence, which manifests as diseases and negative emotions. Awakens the Agni, and increases digestive fire.

Aym Improves mental concentration, reasoning powers. Mental and nervous disorders and speech. Awakens and increases intelligence. Restores speech communication, control of the senses and the mind, and is the sacred sound of the Goddess of wisdom, Saraswati.

Shrim (rhymes with seem) Promotes general health, beauty, creativity and prosperity. Strengthens overall health and harmony.

Krim (rhymes with seem) Gives capacity for work and actions. Adds power and efficacy, good for chanting while making preparations.

Hrim (rhymes with seem) Cleanses and purifies, giving energy, joy and ecstasy.

Hraim (rhymes with time) Very good for kidney support.

Hra (sounds like hurray) Continuous long a. Strengthens the rib cage, purifies the alimentary canal.

Hram (hraaammm as in calm) Clairifies lungs, relieves asthma. Restorative.

Hrum (rhymes with Room) Stimulates liver, spleen and stomach and reduces abdomen.

Sham Mantra of Peace. Create calmness, detachment, contentment. Alleviates mental and nervous disorders, stress, anxiety, disturbed emotions, tremors, shaking and nervous system disorders.

Shum (sounds like shoe but shorter vowel sound) Increases vitality, energy, fertility.

Som (rhymes with home) Increases energy, vitality, joy, delight, creativity. Strengthens mind, heart and nerves. Good for rejuvenation.

Chakra Sounds

Root Chakra	LAM
Navel Chakra	VAM
Solar Plexus Chakra	RAM
Heart Chakra	YAM
Throat Chakra	HAM
Third Eye Chakra	KSHAM
Crown Chakra	OM

The following mantra is for the recovery of illness, or to invoke divine healing light.

The Mritunjaya Mantra for Healing

OM TRAYAMBAKAM YAJAMAHE
(Om-Tri-Yam-Bu-Kam)

SUGANDIM PUSHTI VARDHANAM
(Su-Gan-Dim-Pushti-Vard-Han-Am)

URWARUKAMIVA BANDANART
(Ur-Waru-Kam-Iva-Banda-Nart)

MRITYOR MUKSHIA MAMRITAT
(Mrit-Yor-Muk-Shia-Mam-Ri-Tat)

Forgiveness Journal Process

Our ultimate path of well being, self-love and self-care is through releasing the past. We can let go of painful disturbances in our energy field through conscious awareness of who we are *now*. We can be in this moment and experience our true reality as brand new and untouched by the past. Our past is only held in thought, which is the source of all our suffering. This thought is not true, for all things change. We have the opportunity to live our life free from the suffering of the past. To be well, we must take the steps in our lives of letting go of the past along with releasing judgment of ourselves and others.

This is a journaling practice that will assist you to let go and experience yourself as fresh, renewed and available for life's opportunities, without holding the pain of the past.

Begin by breathing deeply. On each inhalation allow the breath to guide you inward. On each exhalation consciously let go of disturbances caused by thought forms, worry and other disturbances. Allow your breath to guide you into your Sacred Heart space. Gently allow the breath to deepen and your attention to move to your heart. Place your hand over your heart, and ask the sacred presence within your heart to assist you in this forgiveness process. State your intention to return to your true nature of peace, joy, compassion and love.

1.   Write down any issues in your relationships that you wish to heal, to forgive others, or areas in which you seek forgiveness.

2.   Identify the feelings in relationship to the forgiveness you are seeking such as fear, abandonment, misunderstood, fear, betrayal, anger, abused, let down, sad, resentment, confused, victim-hood, revenge or what your true feelings are about the relationship.

3.   Identify the thoughts and beliefs around the feelings. Example: "I have thoughts of fear when I think of seeing _____ again," or, "I think about ways to get back to _____." Write these thoughts down.

4.   Accept these feelings, but be willing to go deeply into their root cause. Use statements such as, "I am willing to look at my victim consciousness." Write about the ways you have played the role of victim. Reflect on what lessons the relationship has brought you.

5.   Ask your loving guide, within your heart, how you can learn to see the soul gift of your experience. How has it made you feel stronger, more courageous? Look at what you have needed from the situation, what was attained and how your expectations were met or not met. Note what needs did not get fulfilled from the situation.

6.   See how the life test has helped you become aware of areas of your being that need to be healed. See how being upset, or feeling anger and resentment, point to some desire or want in you that has not been filled by another person. Identify and note what you want from another person or persons.

7.   When you feel upset, what areas of your inner self need to be healed? Look for the gift of the soul, the unrealized power, how you can turn within to find the love you are seeking.

8.   Write what you have denied in yourself, how you can reclaim your lost sense of self through self-love. Also, how you can offer yourself the joys, the attention and the beauty that you have sought outwardly.

9.   Observe any feelings of lack and observe how you can extend forgiveness to yourself and to others through the new awareness that life has brought you a great blessing, teaching you to love yourself first.

10.   See that your life is always mirroring the inside, the misperceptions, the seeking of lost love that has been abandoned in the heart. Look within the heart to find the love you seek.

11.   Within your wholeness you have never been separated from your source. Forgive the pain of fragmented emotions such as guilt, anger, shame or judgment. Examine these emotions and write down how you can reframe them through the hidden blessing of gratitude. Example: *"I am grateful to my father for teaching me, through shame, the lessons of my soul, and I receive the gift of worthiness, self-love and dignity by forgiving him and myself."*

12.   Write down ways in which you can increase the flow of love throughout your life, looking for areas of blockage and applying your light and love to them.

13.   Release any areas of blame or victim-hood in your life. List your soul affirmations.

14.   Letting go, surrender to the presence of perfection. Within you is the source of all healing, the perfect blueprint of your soul. Turning within, allow yourself to surrender into the presence of light, drink from the Sacred Chalice of your Heart and take to your chalice all the pain of separation. Let go of all tendencies, patterns and habits of the mind that have caused you suffering. List all areas of your life you wish to surrender, and reaffirm what gifts you will take with you from the chalice of your heart.

15.   Record your changes of perception, the transformation of your thoughts and beliefs about your life. Write about the miracle of your life, as experienced from this change of perception.

Kinesiology Self-Testing Method

Self Test – One

Hold thumb and index finger of one hand 2-3 inches apart, depending on the size of your hand. Place the thumb of the other hand under the thumb of the first hand and place two or three fingers of the second hand on the top of the index finger of the first hand. The testing is to attempt to bring the thumb and index finger together using slow, even pressure.

Yes – Thumb and index stay apart.

No – Thumb and index come together.

Self Test – Two

Bring thumb and index finger together, forming a circle. Place the thumb and index finger of the opposite hand together and slip them into a circle created by the first hand. The movement is to spread the thumb and index finger of the second hand apart in the attempt to open the circle created by the position of the first hand. Apply slow, even pressure.

Yes – Thumb and index come apart.

No – Thumb and index stay together.

Self Test – Three

Place the middle finger of your hand of choice on the index finger of the same hand. The action is to use the middle finger to attempt push the index finger down.

Yes – Middle finger strong.

No – Middle finger weak.

Everything I do is for the Host
~Rumi~

Muscle Testing for *Yes* or *No* Answers

Testing for Products

Put the substance on, or in front of the solar plexus.

Ask: "Is this product for my highest good?" Test.

If the muscle tests strong the answer is yes.

If the muscle tests weak the answer is no.

Repeat the procedure asking: "Is this product harmful to me?"

Testing for Lifestyle Questions

Refer to the Lifestyle Questions List

Ask: "Is there a lifestyle change on this page that I should investigate?" Test.

If the muscle tests strong the answer is yes.

If the muscle tests weak the answer is no.

Testing for Nutrition and Supplements

Start with a clear indicator muscle.

Ask: "Do we have permission to test for this?"

Go down the list, testing each item. A weak muscle indicates the item is not needed, a strong muscle indicates it is needed.

When looking at vitamins and other supplements use the Priority Testing Method. Hold thumb and index finger together.

Ask: "We would now like to check for priority, which supplement is the best?" Go down the list, testing each item.

Optional Testing Method

To test for those who are not present, distance-test using a surrogate (such as another person's arm), as follows.

1.   Ask permission to use a surrogate. Make sure the person is clear about what they are doing and are ready to be tested.

2.   Ask the surrogate: "Can I use your body to test for _____ at this time?"

3.   Ask the questions needed to clarify what supplements, nutrition or life questions need answering.

Pendulum Testing

Pendulum testing can be used to find an answer to all questions in the same manner as kinesiology testing. To review see the pendulum instructions in Part Three.

For All Testing Methods and Questions

End with a prayer of gratitude and remember to add, as appropriate:

"This person is (or I am) 100% willing to receive the gift of this balancing."

"This person is (or I am) 100% willing to release all obstacles to this balancing."

Testing Charts for Energy Health

The Tissue Salts

Wilhelm Heinrich Schuessler originated the twelve tissue salts, also called cell salts. He found that there are certain important inorganic substances that need to be present in order for cells to work effectively and that the deficiency of these substances is often responsible for physical disorders. Tissue salts are the principal inorganic substances found in the cells of the human body and are essential to cellular metabolism. They allow the cells to be properly nourished, to cleanse and regenerate themselves. The salts are prepared and administered in homeopathic potencies of about 6X, which makes them readily assimilated by the body.

The practitioner is helped by knowing how the tissue salts work individually; he then has a lead on applying them to the symptoms of any given case. With use of the pendulum you can confirm the choice of salts for treatment. Where two remedies are equally indicated, they should be taken alternately. In acute cases, the doses may be taken every half hour; in less acute cases, every two hours is recommended; and in chronic cases, three or four times daily.

Calcium Fluoride (Calc. Fluor.)

Gives elasticity to the tissues. It is found in the walls of blood vessels, connective tissue, and in muscular tissue. When it is absent, tissue develops a relaxed condition. Calcium Fluoride preserves the contractile power of elastic tissue. Symptoms of relaxed tissue include piles, sluggish circulation and fissures in the palms of the hands and between the toes. This salt is used to treat diseases which attack the surface of the bones and joints, and loose and decaying teeth. Muscular weakness is also treated with Calcium Fluoride.

Calcium Phosphate (Calc. Phos.)

Assists the coagulator for blood. It helps to form hair and teeth and restores tone to weakened organs and tissues. It is concerned with nutrition and is important to growing children, where it is specific for rickets. It helps speed recuperation, improves the blood where anemic conditions prevail, assists digestion and, coincidentally, promotes good circulation.

Calcium Sulphate (Calc. Sulph.)

A blood purifier. It promotes the removal of waste material in the liver and has a general cleansing influence on the whole system, helping tissues to throw off toxic substances. It is often recommended for purifying the blood for acne and for clearing up abscesses before they become septic. It can offset the early stages of a sore throat or an infection.

Iron Phosphate (Ferr. Phos.)

Helps the blood carry oxygen, by building up the red blood cells. It is often used as a supplementary remedy with other cell salts. Symptoms of oxygen deficiency include quickened pulse, congestion, inflammatory pain and high temperature. It is used where there are hemorrhages and in cases of anemia.

Potassium Chloride (Kali. Mur.)

A cure for sluggish conditions, symptomized by thick white discharges, creating catarrhs that affect the skin and mucous membrane. Both potassium chloride and calcium sulphate are involved with purifying the blood. In cases requiring potassium chloride, the blood tends to thicken and clot. Symptoms include: white-coated tongue, light colored stools, slow liver action, frequent coughs and colds and bronchitis.

Potassium Phosphate (Kali. Phos.)

A nerve nutrient, good for nervous disorders. It may be useful in cases of fretfulness, ill humor, bashfulness, laziness and timidity, or what are called "tantrums" among children. Other conditions which may be alleviated by this substance are nervous headaches, nervous indigestion, sleeplessness, tiredness and low vitality, depression, irritability and general listlessness.

Potassium Sulphate (Kali. Sulph.)

Helps in the oxygen exchange from blood to cell tissues, and is helpful in respiratory problems. Wherever there are sticky, yellowish discharges from the skin or mucous membrane, this tissue salt is recommended. Skin eruptions are helped by potassium sulphate, as are intestinal disorders and stomach cramps.

Magnesium Phosphate (Mag. Phos.)

This is the antispasmodic tissue salt and supplements the action of potassium phosphate. Deficiency of this tissue salt causes the white nerve fibers to contract, producing spasms and cramps. This salt is a fast pain reliever in such cases, and also in cases of neuralgia, neuritis, sciatica and stabbing headaches. It helps in cases of muscular twitching, hiccups, convulsive coughing, and cramps, especially such of the foregoing as are accompanied by sharp spasmodic pains.

Sodium Chloride (Nat. Mur.)

This is the water distributing salt, part of every fluid and solid in the body, where it maintains proper moisture distribution. It is related to nutrition, glandular activity and internal secretions. Excessive dryness or moisture is a symptom indicating a need for this tissue salt. Some of the following symptoms are also indicators: low spirits with a feeling of hopelessness; headaches with constipation; thin blood; pallor of the skin, sometimes with a greasy appearance; difficult stools, with rawness and soreness of the anus; colds with discharge of watery mucus and sneezing; dry, painful nose and throat; heartburn due to gastric fermentation with slow digestion; great thirst; toothache and facial neuralgia with flow of tears and saliva; weak, sensitive eyes; hay fever; drowsiness with muscular weakness; chafing of the skin; hang-nails; un-refreshing sleep; after-effects of alcoholic stimulants; loss of taste and smell; craving for salt and salty foods.

Food Allergy and Nutritional Testing

To find out if a food or supplement is lacking or if there is too much: after a balance, hold the substance on the Solar Plexus Chakra. Test. If it tests strong then that food is good for you; if weak, you could consider not using that particular food or substance for a while.

Minerals

____ Calcium Fluoride

____ Calcium Phosphate

____ Calcium Sulphate

____ Iron Phosphate

____ Potassium Chloride

____ Potassium Phosphate

____ Potassium Sulphate

____ Magnesium Phosphate

____ Sodium Chloride

Food Supplements

____ Acidophilus

____ Alfalfa

____ Aloe Vera

____ Barley Grass

____ Bee Pollen

____ Betaine

____ Blue-Green Algae

____ Bromelain

____ Brewers Yeast

____ Chlorophyll

____ Cod Liver Oil

____ Coenzyme Q10

____ Liver Support

____ Fiber

____ GLA EFA

____ Lecithin

____ Garlic

____ Ginseng

____ Kelp

____ Omega 3 Flaxseed

____ Royal Jelly

____ Wheat Germ

____ Spirulina

Digestive Enzymes

____ Pancreatin

____ Papain

Foods

____ Berries

____ Beverages

____ Carbohydrates

____ Chocolate

____ Fats and Oils

____ Flours

____ Fowl

____ Fruits

____ Grains

____ Herbs

____ Juice

____ Legume

____ Meat

____ Beef

____ Chicken

____ Fish

____ Lamb

____ Pork

____ Nuts

____ Seeds

____ Shellfish

____ Sprouts

____ Sugars

____ Vegetables

____ Water

Amino Acids

___ Arginine
___ Aspartic Acid
___ Branch Chain
___ Cysteine
___ Carnitine
___ Glutamine

___ Di-Methyl Glycine
___ DLPA-DL Phenaladarine
___ Gaba
___ Ornithine

___ Gluthathione
___ Glycine
___ Hystine
___ Inosine
___ Lysine
___ Methionine

___ Phenalalarine
___ Taurine
___ Theonine
___ Tyrosine

Essential and Trace Minerals

___ Boron
___ Calcium
___ Chlorine
___ Chromium
___ Cobalt
___ Copper

___ Flourine
___ Germanium
___ Gold
___ Iodine
___ Iron
___ Lithium

___ Magnesium
___ Manganese
___ Molyodenum
___ Phosphorous
___ Potassium
___ Selenium

___ Silicon
___ Sodium
___ Sulphur
___ Zinc

Vitamins

___ A
___ Beta Carotene
___ B7 Biotin
___ B1 Thiamine
___ B2 Riboflavin
___ B3 Niacin

___ B8 Inositol
___ B5 Pantothenic Acid
___ B6 Pyridoxine
___ Bioflavonoids
___ B12 Cobalamin

___ B Complex
___ B9 Folic Acid
___ B4 Choline
___ B15 Pangamic Acid
___ C Ascorbic Acid

___ D Viosterol
___ Ergosterol
___ E Tocopherol
___ K Menadione
___ Paba
___ Unsaturated Fatty Acids

Metals

___ Aluminum
___ Arsenic
___ Copper
___ Gold

___ Hematite
___ Iron
___ Lead
___ Mercury

___ Meteorite
___ Platinum
___ Pyrite
___ Silver

___ Titanium
___ Zinc

Endocrine System

___ Adrenal
___ Liver
___ Lymph
___ Ovaries

___ Pancreas
___ Parotid
___ Pineal
___ Pituitary

___ Prostate
___ Mammary
___ Spleen
___ Testes

___ Thymus
___ Thyroid

Systems

___ Cells & Tissue
___ Chakra
___ Circulatory
___ Digestive
___ Endocrine

___ Genital
___ Immune
___ Lymphatic
___ Musculature
___ Para Sympathetic

___ Psychological
___ Respiratory
___ Sensory
___ Skeletal
___ Spinal

___ Sympathetic
___ Urinary

Nutrition / Allergy Chart

Miscellaneous

Aspirin
Baking powder
Baking soda
Bancha green tea
Black tea
Carob
Chamomile
Chewing gum

Chocolate
Coffee
Coffee, Swiss, H$_2$o process,
  decaffeinated
Coffee, Sanka decaf
Gelatin
Kuzu
Licorice root

MSG
Nondairy creamer
Nutrisweet
Splenda
Sweet & Low sweetener
Tapioca
Tobacco

Grains

Amaranth
Barley
Buckwheat
Cornmeal, blue
Cornmeal, white
Cornmeal, yellow

Cornstarch
Millet
Oat
Quinoa
Rice, brown

Rice, white
Rice, wild
Rye
Wheat
Wheat bran

Oils

Butter, cow milk (everclear)
Corn
Crisco

Margarine (everclear)
Olive
Safflower

Sesame
Soy

Milk & Cheese

Blue
Brie
Cheddar (raw milk)
Cottage
Hokkaido

Monterey Jack
Muenster
Parmesan
Romano
Swiss

Cow milk, lowfat D
Goat milk
Sheep milk cheese
Lactose
Yogurt (cow milk)

Meat – Organic

Beef
Chicken
Lamb

Pork
Coconut

Meat – Nonorganic

Beef
Beef liver
Chicken

Lamb
Pork
Turkey

Seafood

Codfish – scrod
Haddock
Halibut
Mackerel
Octopus
Salmon
Crab
Swordfish
Tuna

Fruit – Non-organic

Apple - Rome, Yellow
    Delicious
Blueberry
Cantaloupe
Cherry, Bing
Currant
Date
Grapes
Kiwi
Lemon
Lemon rind
Lime
Lime rind
Mango
Papaya
Pineapple
Raspberry
Strawberry
Tangerine
Watermelon

Fruit – Organic

Apple - Granny, Red
    Delicious
Banana
Grapefruit
Orange
Orange peel
Peach
Plum
Rhubarb

Spices

Allspice
Anise
Arrowroot
Basil
Bay leaf
Cayenne powder
Chicory root
Chili powder
Cinnamon
Cloves
Curry
Dill seed
Ginger
Horseradish
Hops
Marjoram
Mustard
Nutmeg
Oregano
Paprika
Pepper, black
Sage
Salt, mineral (Spike)
Salt, miramoto
Salt, sea
Thyme
Vanilla bean

Eggs

White
Yolk

Nuts

Almonds
Brazil Nut
Cashew
Filbert
Peanut
Pecan
Pinenut
Macadamia
Walnut

Sea Vegetables

Agar agar
Arame
Dulse
Kelp
Kombu

Ferments – Liquor

Beer
Brandy
Gin

Vodka
Wine, red
Wine, white

Whiskey

Ferments – Liquid

Tamari
Tamari, wheatless

Vinegar, apple cider
Vinegar, balsamic

Vinegar, brown rice
Vinegar, umeboshi

Ferments – Solid

Miso, barley
Miso, brown rice

Yeast, baker's
Yeast, nutritional

Sweetners

Barley
Beet sugar
Cane sugar

Fructose
Honey
Maple syrup

Rice bran syrup
Turbinado

Vegetables – Nonorganic

Artichoke
Asparagus
Avocado
Bamboo shoots
Broccoli
Brussels sprout
Cabbage
Carrots
Cauliflower
Celery

Chard
Collard green
Cucumber
Eggplant
Green beans
Leek
Lettuce – romaine, iceberg
Lotus root
Mushroom
Okra

Potato
Radish
Snow peas
Squash, acorn
Squash, winter
Squash, summer
Turnip
Watercress

Vegetables – Organic

Beets
Broccoli
Carrots
Cabbage, green
Cucumber
Daikon root

Kale
Lettuce, leaf, butter, romaine
Potato, white
Potato, red
Pumpkin
Spinach

Squash, zucchini
Sweet Potato
Swiss Chard
Tomato

Life-style Questions

Test *Yes* or *No* if any of the below need attention.

1. Addictions
2. Allergies
3. Behavior
4. Career
5. Cell Salts
6. Change of Job
7. Change of Partner
8. Change of Residence
9. Children's Issues
10. Choice of Products
11. Codependence
12. Daily Emotions
13. Daily Thoughts
14. Devotion
15. Diet
16. Energy Drain
17. Environmental Toxins
18. Exercise
19. Family Ties
20. Fitness
21. Follow Joy
22. Geopathic Stress
23. Health Questions
24. Integrity
25. Life-style Testing Charts
26. Manipulation
27. Medication
28. Minerals
29. Money
30. Music
31. Nature
32. Need for Clear Intention
33. Need for Meditation
34. Need for Prayer
35. Need for Quiet
36. Need to be alone
37. Nutrition
38. Over-caring Issues
39. Parent Issues
40. Personal Products
41. Radio
42. Reading Material
43. Relationship to Higher Power
44. Relationships
45. School
46. Services
47. Sleep
48. Spiritual Growth
49. Spiritual Practice
50. Supplements
51. Television
52. Therapist Choice
53. Vitamins

Study Questions

1. List the vibrational remedies for the energy toolbox and explain how they are offered in a session.

2. When offering a *LEAP* session, list some of the energy field self-care methods to give your clients for support.

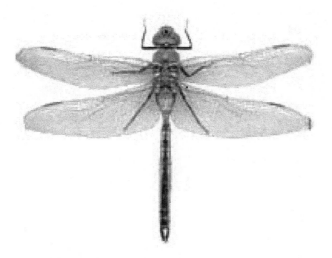

In quietness all things are answered,
and is every problem quietly resolved.

T,533
A Course In Miracles

Part Eight
Living Meditations

*Release all and open
to your highest
good. Wait and
watch as the miracle
unfolds.*

Jaya Sarada

Return to Joy

Return to your true nature of abiding joy, which is free from all outer things. This is a place of unconditional love, the core of your real being.

Return to joy, a place where you feel no limitations and your spirit soars to infinite possibilities.

Return to joy, where you are energized with light, beauty and the harmony of unity.

Return to joy, where you know you are not separate from the source and your energies are aligned with the light of Atma, the energy of God.

Return to joy, where you tap your inner creative spirit and co-create with the maker.

Return to joy, where you release all discordant thoughts and emotions and you are reborn in your divine essence.

Return to joy, where you delight in witnessing the essence of perfection in all of life.

Return to joy, and dance with the mystery of nature, unfolding, blossoming, resting and bursting out once more.

The path of joy comes when you are aligned with your true purpose, and you are an instrument of a higher will, the will of your inner knowing. Release all to open to your highest good. Wait and watch the miracle unfold.

Accept the Calling

Lifetimes have been focused on the preservation of the false. Very few people have seen through this endless suffering and loss. Because of deep conditioning most of us do not know our true essence, believing that our separate individual identities make up who we really are. Our misidentification creates a deep soul weariness, propelling our tired souls to repeatedly search for truth and meaning in this impermanent life. There is the endless search for the self, either in the material world or the spiritual world.

The revelation is this: all searching must end! When you surrender to the inevitable, you will meet the true self that has been present all along. When this transformation occurs, through the recognition that you are, in reality, an eternal being, you will hear the sacred calling of your life. To accept the calling is to listen to the voice of the silence within, surrendering to the divine guidance of truth and wisdom. Accept the calling - let go of all personal holdings, and see through this temporary reality. Dive into the river of grace, trusting in the divine current. In this most sacred river, you are cleansed from all separation, allowing the refreshing waters to renew your being.

Acceptance

Unconditional acceptance is the embracing of pain and sorrow with calm equanimity, knowing from the wisdom of your heart that all is subject to change. Unconditional acceptance is living your life in the deepest compassion of your heart, accepting all, even the most painful or most pleasurable of circumstances. In this acceptance you neither contract because of the pain nor project the desires of pleasure. Each moment is honored as the truth within. Here you refer back to the unchanging nature of stillness.

Unconditional acceptance allows your feelings of sadness, pain, desire, uncertainty and passion to arise completely. The body feels all, and lets all flow through you without leaving an impression on your being. Unconditional acceptance fully embraces the results of all actions created by the mistaken identification with the temporal self. You accept fully that you are truly a divine being, untouched by the past and forgiven by the divine witnessing of your true nature. This witnessing sets you free.

Living with Divine Intelligence

In each human being there is an innate divine intelligence that is rarely touched. This divine intelligence is the supreme intelligence, untainted by thought, memory or time. It stems from the universal source of the infinite. The mind, when silent, is unbound and free to discover this pure consciousness of the heavenly realm. When expressed, this awareness has the ability to soar to the edges of eternity to infinite understanding. Intelligence that is unconditioned, free to act according to the truth of being, is one with divine wisdom - the source of life. The awakening process begins when there is an elegant release of all identification with that which binds you to thought, belief, or memory, seeing that your true nature is, in fact, freedom. When the mind is liberated from the habits of identification, it touches the eternal path of wisdom.

The return to your natural resting place of silence leads you to surrender all things of a personal nature. The mind is a reflective pool that has the ability to discriminate between thoughts that are geared toward validating the personal self and thoughts that reflect the light of the inner truth. The awakened being is intelligence in action, observing all that enters consciousness, while remaining detached and compassionate.

The awakened being turns to the divine source of silence to express the highest aspect of knowledge and divine will. In the silence of the mind and heart, you will realize the spaciousness and emptiness of your true nature. As you deepen your understanding of your sacred nature, all conditions that stem from the impermanent nature of life will be released to the eternal and unchanging.

The awakened being sees the nature of the will and how it is directed either to self-pleasure or to the highest good. Through awareness of your true self, you can see how the will is used for self-gain; it plants the seeds of suffering on a personal or global level. Awareness is the art of the true self; opening the inner eye of wisdom, seeing all and remaining in emptiness.

Awareness lies in the skill of quieting your personal inclination to entertain thoughts, emotions and desires geared for temporary self-gain. Awareness is the supreme understanding of desire and the fruits of desire. The awakened being seeks to stop the roller coaster of pleasure and pain, thereby ending the involvement and belief in a personal story. The awakened being always turns towards its source - the heart of wisdom, the everlasting source of your strength.

The awakened being quietly listens, trusting in the source of its being and the sacred movement of life. There is a continual awareness of life, seeing that life is not about the fulfillment of the personal seeker. It is, rather, the recognition that you are a free and whole human being. The awakened mind is completely aware of the personal self and how it reappears for recognition and survival. It never fails to offer its rest within the source of silence.

The awakened being ends the habit of identification with the body/mind and returns to the source of consciousness. In the depths of stillness there remains only the recognition of what is true and eternal within the soul. The most powerful tool that you have as a spiritual being is the ability to see with an awakened, intelligent mind. Use this seeing as a sword to cut through the false nature of existence. The mind that is silent has space for the perception of the direct stream of pure consciousness, the consciousness of real love.

The awakened being is guided to the sacred and clears all illusions, conditions and patterns that have obscured right viewing. The awakened one turns within to the sacred path of the divine, trusting the journey as the ever-deepening awareness of the infinite. Your eternal home is the silence of your infinite being, your sacred resting place. It is a place of peace and communion with that which is eternal, vast and unbound.

The awakened being knows, deeply, the nature of its source, residing in the sanctuary of the spiritual heart. As the doorway opens to the divine within, there is an immense amount of energy that floods the soul, washing out any residues of misidentification. Return often to the ever-abiding silence within, trusting in your eternal divinity found deep within your spiritual heart.

Awareness: Seeing from the Heart, Feeling from the Mind

When there is no discernment between the real and the unreal, the self is carried away into a web of illusion. It is through the integrated awareness of the heart and mind that you can begin the transformation of the self. The root cause of the loss of self can always be traced back to the belief in separation. From separation thought is born. Integrated awareness is seeing that your happiness is found by bringing the attention back to silence - the nature of the true self.

On the path of wisdom, it is possible to develop integrated awareness, seeing with the eyes of love and feeling from the wisdom of truth. It is through the blending of the heart and the mind that the full circle of truth is created. Your true nature is this blending, this integration of love and wisdom. Integrated seeing is engaging the love of your being at all times, accessing the wisdom of your true nature.

The separate self, who claims to believe in the thoughts and emotions that come and go, is caught in the web of illusion. Your true nature, the divine witness to all, is actually the master of this separate self. It is your inner truth that has the duty of mastering the belief in a separate ego-self. Integrated awareness is using the love of your true nature and the wisdom of your higher mind in healing any separation. A great humbling occurs when you can admit you are not the "doer" of your life. The compassionate heart sees clearly that all must be brought to silence and in this silence all separation becomes whole.

The most useful tool when you are caught in the illusion of thoughts and emotions is being steadfast in self-inquiry. The inquiring mind is a mind that is devoted and steadfast in finding the truth, leading you to freedom. Integrated awareness is seeing with the totality of being, with the wisdom of the heart. This compassionate heart is the heart of witness consciousness, where all is seen unconditionally. What is observed is brought to silence. The wisdom of your true nature sees clearly without the interference of the ego-self and all is seen in the light of divine witnessing.

Living in Balance

Life is an interaction between the divine energies within and the outward personality (the body, mind and emotions). Your true reality is that you are not your body, mind or emotions. You are divine energy inhabiting the body, with all its accompanying processes. Your true nature is not subject to duality, the process of birth and death, or time. It is always present in silence and is infused by the sacred energy of life. Living in balance is to return to your true self, experiencing your divine and eternal nature, not obscured by the chatter of the ego-self. In the quiet of your spiritual heart, you meet your innermost teacher who will assist you in uncovering the truth of your being. The understanding of your truth comes from knowing what you are not; you are not your body, your emotions, or your thoughts. This revelation takes you deeper and deeper within until you meet the emptiness of the self, which is pure peace. Upon recognition that you are this peace, the false layers of identification begin to fall away.

Living in balance is to walk in the outer world of manifestation while all along being firmly planted on the inner path to the infinite. This state of equilibrium is found within through effortless being, steadfastly knowing that your true reality is not found in this temporary manifestation. The ease of being that comes from the letting go of personal effort occurs when you flow with the natural unfolding of life.

Living in balance lies in understanding the root cause of duality, seeing that where there is pleasure there will be pain. This is the cycle most humans suffer from, and so true happiness and joy are rarely found. When you investigate the nature of the personal self, awareness develops of the root cause of suffering. You see clearly that a life in pursuit of self-gain is laced with personal suffering. When you make the radical choice to get off the wheel of cause and effect there is a profound life change. This change leads you to let go of the personal quest for self-pleasure, seeing that it is a never ending road. The life of the body requires a great integrity of being to function in the world. Upon turning within, you come into a healthy balance between living life on behalf of physical survival and living for inner survival of the sacred.

The nature of life is always moving through the cycles of polarities that have to do with the impermanent nature of things. Walking the middle path is to stay centered in your divinity, keenly aware of the polarities in life. When you remain in your truth, pure awareness, you will keep the channel of your being clear. In this way the love of your being flows purely and there is not a personal self who is swinging through the cycles of desire. Your divine center within is ever-present, the place within you where you touch the creative spring of life.

When you experience the stillness of your true nature, holding the energy within as deeply sacred, you will live your life from the center of your being. Living in balance is to return to the quiet of your being, where there is no personal effort and striving, where all expressions come from the emptiness and silence of being.

Deep compassion for this walk is required, as the nature of manifestation is imperfection and we are profoundly subject to this condition. You must be humbled to the degree that you just accept whatever happens and move back into the center of your being, your natural state of quiet. Within the silence of your being you are able to find complete rest and equanimity of being. When retreating to this place of rest one can see that all of life springs from it. Living in balance is to see the oneness of life, treating all as sacred, giving it your complete love and attention in the moment.

Seek within your heart the guidelines for your life. Know that all wisdom is found in your spiritual heart. Upon living the truth of your heart, all expressions of life will be in honor of that. In your true reality you are pure goodness and wisdom; this is revealed when the personal nature of the self is laid to rest. Your true reality is peace itself, found when one finds the inner balance between the divine and outward reality.

Beauty

Sacred living from wholeness, beauty and deep gratitude is seeing, with God's eyes, the incredible holiness of life. When you touch into the sacred, a deep communion with life begins, creating a sense of unity and oneness in daily life and in the appreciation for beauty.

Beauty is living in grace, fully appreciating and seeing goodness in this manifested world. Beauty within is like being bathed in the brilliance of God's creation, expanding into the infinite consciousness of being. Opening like a flower, allowing your nectar to be touched and felt by all, is sharing in beauty.

You are beauty itself when your identification and attention shift from what is subject to time, to the timelessness of your inner true nature. All of the beauty of life is found within; as you live from your wholeness, you are one with the magnificent oceans, the splendid array of nature, the grandness of this earth's unfathomable beauty.

The celestial song of the divine creates melodies unheard by most ears, melodies that portray the beauty and grace of life. The song of life teaches us to just observe, to trust that we are in the hands of something larger, more magnificent than our small selves could ever fathom.

Listen to the celestial song of the divine, found in the stillness of the heart. This song will inspire you to live life according to your innermost truth, and will teach you about the joy of the divine and the beauty of surrender. Living in beauty is to know beauty as your true nature, honoring it in your daily life.

You are the bouquet of flowers given to the Holy Spirit within; the beauty of the sea, where the wave knows its source is the ocean itself. You are the grandeur of the mountain, knowing that the first step up the mountain is the same as the arrival. You are the love in a child's heart, knowing wonder and innocence as your true nature. You are the beauty of your daily life, where each moment is precious when lived to the tune of your Celestial Song.

Compassion

Compassionate seeing is viewing all that appears with an unconditional heart and an open mind, accepting all in the flow of consciousness. In this way of seeing, there is total honesty, total acceptance of "what is," and a possibility of transformation. Allowing all thoughts and their accompanying desires to surface, without running away from or holding onto them, keeps your channel clear, remaining in pure consciousness.

Surrendering to your spiritual heart is the way of the compassionate spirit, your path of divine love. When you learn to observe with eyes of compassion, what is seen is brought into the light of truth. Compassionate seeing is to live in complete acceptance that all aspects of life are changing. When compassion is applied, one is able to see the suffering of others with a heart of service.

In seeing with the wisdom eye, the doorway to your inner truth opens, touching upon the mystery of life. This brings about an understanding of, and the ability to disengage from, identification of what is appearing in the moment. This seeing without identification is the real act of love applied, allowing the ever-evolving truth to reveal itself.

Compassionate seeing is deeply surrendering all attachments and desires of the personal self. Living in compassion is to see yourself and others as the embodiment of peace itself. Seeing with compassion is to view all of your personal motives and tendencies for self-gratification and accept them fully, surrendering them to the fire of compassion. Observe that your true essence is love of a much higher nature and your true happiness is found when you are living in service to your truth.

Compassion lies in understanding the suffering process in oneself and in others. The love within you, when accessed, has the ability to heal the deepest afflictions of spirit. This love fills the empty cup of all searching souls. We spend most of our lives looking through eyes of desire and want, veiled in the ignorance of the personal self. These eyes, when deluded by our personal nature, have a great mist blinding us to "what is." This mist is the sum total of our accumulated desires and wants. The veil of deception clouds our seeing with images, thoughts and projections of the false self.

Compassionate seeing observes the tendencies of the personal self, mastering it with the fuel of the wisdom of the heart. When the force of the observer lifts the veil, a great freedom of being is revealed. A profound commitment to seeing the truth develops, preventing the veils of the false self from ever developing again.

Witnessing from inner truth and compassion affects your daily life by bringing beauty and transformation to all you touch. You learn to see yourself, and others, with unconditional love. Love applied unconditionally is the supreme balance of love and wisdom, resulting in responses that stem from your divine intelligence. Each moment is a new opportunity to apply the love and compassion needed for what life is presenting. Living in the moment with compassion requires letting go of the past, its images, memories and impressions.

Compassionate seeing is to look at your family and friends as they are, without denial, to see their calling and their yearning, and to see beyond their fragmented souls. Compassionate seeing is to see the roots of suffering with great understanding and love. The act of compassionate seeing is to look dearly, carefully, and with a heart that accepts and loves unconditionally, seeing the core of truth in all.

In seeing with the wisdom eye, there is a deep understanding that life's passing events are just a part of the play in the drama of life. The roles we take on in the drama of life will never define our true eternal nature. We begin to feel a sense of joy and lightness when we know that we are not these roles. A compassionate heart is your inner guide to the pathway within, where you find all nurturing need for your journey. Voyage within to the deep wisdom of the heart where your true self dwells. Upon entering into this ever-deepening vastness, you will meet the eternal presence who will be your companion, guide and master throughout all expressions of life. Trust in your inner true self, the light of your being and the light of the world.

Courage

To live in a world where there is great suffering and negativity requires great courage. Living with courage is holding the intention to be free from needless personal sorrow and to no longer contribute to the sorrow of humanity. Each moment is a new opportunity to reflect upon your life, accessing the courage needed from your inner truth. The courage to see requires observing - with honesty and integrity - the workings of the personal self. The courageous soul sees the impermanent nature of things, turning within to rest in the eternal source of life.

Returning to the light of your being will nurture and reveal the truth of your self, giving you more and more strength to live in your light. Retreating to that place of stillness within requires courage and trust in yourself, knowing that this is your true home. Courage to see the false must be there in order to see the real, lasting, and unchanging nature of life.

Most people spend their lives chasing after a desire and reject that which is no longer wanted. It is like being locked up in a maze, going around in circles, never finding the center. The divine center within cannot be found in the pursuit of self-gratification. It is only found in the spiritual heart, free from the personal self.

To live for the truth of the moment takes great courage. The tendency is to have a reference point from memory. When living in each eternal moment, you must have the courage to allow the new to transpire by releasing the past. To live with courage is to be a warrior of the true self. This requires you to observe the workings of thought and desire in life. Courage and love go hand in hand as these qualities assist you in remaining ever mindful and compassionate to the workings of the ego-self. Observing the nature of the mind to identify with the outward stream of life takes great courage. In this observation, you return to the silence of being, where all separation is immersed in the light of oneness.

It is important to remember to have courage when it comes to really looking at the false. Conditioning, past experiences, and misguided ways can be frightful when they come up for view. The more fear, the greater identification is with a personal self, believing in a personal experience that is rooted in time and memory. Until the true self is realized there is often an unquestionable belief in the life of the individual, with all its memories and stories. The bravery of the soul comes from being clear that you are not your past, your body, or your memories. Your participation in life's drama comes from the mistaken identity that you have taken yourself to be.

Compassionate and loving attention to self, and surrender to what is true, will transition you from the temporary to the eternal. Observation is the act of being courageous. Letting go of all that is false will bring about a freedom, a breath of fresh air, to your being. This observation of yourself should be a gentle one of non-judgment and should elicit total acceptance to what is seen. Courage is seeing things the way they are, discerning the real from the unreal, and uncovering the essence of your true nature.

Devotion

Great is the love force within all souls, a love that is deep and unlimited, found in your sacred being. Love is the essence of pure consciousness, deepening as you unfold into the light of pure being. To love yourself is to love the eternal sacred force that is your true self; from this love comes the love of the divine. To love yourself is to recognize the living divinity within, seeing that there is only oneness in truth. This love of one's true self kindles a great devotion to the beloved within all beings, knowing that we all come from one source.

When there is a turning away from outer reality (the body, senses and emotions of the separate self) you turn inward to the source of love, wisdom and divinity. This turning away from worldly identification stems from a deep realization that true happiness is found in the kingdom within, resulting in a deep yearning for the divine. Suffering of a personal nature is no longer a reality as you become a devotee of the divine. Your separate identity drowns in divine love. Life becomes a living prayer and communion with that which is sacred.

Devotion is deepened in the recognition of the divine within and all is held in silence. Living in devotion is to listen within to the wisdom of the divine in all walks of life. Devotion to the sacred source behind life is to return to the joy of pure being. This reservoir of joy sustains all.

A yearning for the beloved, a devotion to God, is all that is required to let go and let the river of grace carry you home. Leave behind worldly identification with a separate self. Surrender to the beloved. Know that realizing your true self will unravel the knot of involvement in the world as you approach eternal freedom.

Living in devotion is to see all as one being, to have a great compassion for yourself and for all beings, with an awareness of the suffering of this world. When you touch upon your own divinity there is a deep realization of the root cause of suffering; separation, and identification with that which is temporary. Turning within, where you meet the eternal, you find complete rest, knowing this to be your true home.

Living with Discernment

To discern is to see the real from the unreal in this powerful illusory stage we are acting upon. Living in discernment is to be firmly planted in witness consciousness, seeing and observing the nature of your temporary thoughts and emotions. The nature of thought is one of traveling energies, floating in and out of consciousness. It is the silent mind that refers back to emptiness, no matter what is appearing. Upon the realization of the true self, the skill of discernment becomes stronger, seeing all as flowing through consciousness, while staying firmly planted in witness consciousness. The nature of witness consciousness is divine; all displays in this consciousness are flooded in silence, the truth of your being.

Insight into inner truth, the wisdom of your soul, becomes accessible as you retreat in silence. The mind, when quiet, is a reflection of the source of the true self - pure consciousness. All things that come into your life can be viewed in the calmness and peace of the true self. This quiet mind is the inner door of wisdom, allowing you to live in the complete harmony of your true nature.

Discernment comes from your inner wisdom, with the strong intention to live according to the voice of your true nature. The mind, in its conditioned state, will continue to spiral down the road of personal suffering. When freed from the conditions of a separate individual, the mind will serve the intention of truth. Living in discernment requires a great strength of being, to see what is real and what is false in the display of consciousness. When the mind identifies with itself and the external world, the veil of illusion is created. One must be vigilant in tearing down this illusory veil. Freedom awaits as the veil falls away.

Forgiveness

Forgiveness of yourself and others is having the compassion to understand that mistakes are made from the illusory self, and there is never any harm meant. All comes from ignorance when you walk in the mistaken identity of the self. All is forgiven when you turn to the light of your true nature.

Many separate individual selves, in pursuit of self-gain and self-gratification, do not have the slightest idea of the inner reality of life. When you see the violence, brutality and deep cause of suffering that your ego-centric behavior causes, a natural inquiry develops. Asking yourself who you are is the most essential question in finding out the cause of suffering in your personal life and the world. Going within to the source of all wisdom is easy when the attention is turned from outer answers to inward contemplation. In contemplation, one can clearly see how individual selves, in the pursuit of self-gain, have caused untold harm to themselves and to fellow beings. The question leads one to uncover the nature of violence and harm in a world graced with so many blessings.

The nature of the mistaken identity is often hurtful, stemming from the deep conditioning of its separateness, and needing to hold on to some position. When that is dropped, there is only love; all of the past is gone and forgiven.

Forgiveness allows you to start over, both in yourself and in relationship to others. See how your liberation from the past quickly comes into play when you practice the art of forgiveness. Processing forgiveness in your life requires you to not only have deep compassion for yourself, but also for the relationships you have had throughout your life. When there is compassion and an understanding that, in fact, all beings are one, there can only be forgiveness.

Forgiveness leads you to the light of the true self that is ever-abiding in each sacred moment. This moment that has its foundation in eternity can only bring perfection, if you let go of the past and live from truth, here and now.

Your true nature has an immense capacity for understanding and compassion, when there is no more personal need to change anything, or make anything different. You are free to see things exactly as they are, which is the freeing of intelligence. A new way of viewing life takes place when there is no longer a need to have it a certain way, or have a personal motive that clouds the fact of the moment. You are able to see clearly where the error in identification lies and where the mistaken beliefs are. You are then able to see the display of emotional states that come and go, and simply watch and remain detached.

Having compassion is to understand your heart, and that of others, knowing that the suffering lies in not knowing the true nature of the self. All sorrow stems from this ignorance. You can only have compassion for what is not seen, not recognized. All mistakes are born from this ignorance of truth. Compassion is to see the conditioning of the false self, understanding the only way out of suffering is to realize the self in its true reality. Once you see this you can quickly forgive yourself and others, and begin to experience your compassionate heart, the truth of your being.

Look at passing feelings such as fear, doubt, hatred, and jealously, and see when you participate in these passing emotions and feelings how it creates a traumatic energy in the moment. Learn to see these passing feelings and states as temporary; avoid giving yourself completely over to them. With a compassionate heart you can observe that your personality consciousness is entertaining these passing emotions and thoughts, but your true nature is firmly secured in witnessing. In this way you will allow these temporary states to pass and your true self will remain strong, untouched - the true master of any situation.

Each moment is an opportunity to observe from your true self and to act according to the dictates of that true self. When that does not happen lovingly and with compassion, look within and heal the separation that is created from the split of the personality consciousness and the divine consciousness. In the compassionate heart you are able to see what is to be learned from the situation. Learning comes from detachment of the self, a willingness to honor the truth of life. Each moment is the opportunity to return to the wholeness and truth of your true being, expressing your thoughts and emotions from this true state.

In the compassionate heart you find humility, knowing that you always have the opportunity to learn, and to start "anew" in any given situation. Forgiveness of yourself and others is a powerful tool, bringing all of yourself to the current moment. Allow the flow of life's grace to deepen your understanding of yourself, therefore deepening the understanding of all beings. This sacred flow of life raises you to the light of pure consciousness, freeing all past impressions.

True service is finding your divine nature and sharing your essential being with the world. Your being is one with the divine consciousness of life, guiding you to your sacred destiny. In this way it is essential for you to know and trust yourself.

Compassion sees all with deep, understanding eyes, and knows that despite the appearance of things, we are all one. Compassion is the expression of deep, unconditional love, a love that sees only the eternal divine reality, recognizing that all beings are this truth. Compassion is the utmost respect for divine energy, seeing the everlasting self in all beings.

Allow your heart to open to its true flowering, the heart of wisdom, light and compassion, seeing that the suffering world is a result of separation from oneness. Compassion leads you to deeper oneness with your true essence, and to the essence of all living beings. Let go and surrender all areas in your life that are not in harmony with the nature of pure consciousness. You are the very essence of goodness, beauty, and timelessness.

Attachments, Bondage and Desire (Seeds of Suffering)

Please inquire as to the nature of suffering. What is it that truly suffers and what remains quiet, calm and in a state of peace? What is suffering other than a state of separation and misidentification?

Suffering of the personal self is a result of the 'I' consciousness not fulfilling the planted seeds of desire. What comes will never quench the thirst of the empty personal self. In reality there is not a separate individual achieving desires, being satisfied and forever being contented. There is, in truth, no separate individual who achieves anything at all. It is all a product of thought which is projected onto life.

Desires that stem from the mind are a product of thought, never manifesting what the restless mind projects. Desire is the great revealer of the content of your consciousness, leading to the awareness of what you truly want from life. Observation of the desiring self is honestly looking at your patterns and tendencies, from past impressions. The inner work for the person seeking freedom from illusion is to observe subtle tendencies that keep you from truth. Allow them to surface while remaining in silent witness consciousness. Past, present and future become one, healed and transformed by divine observation.

The human condition is to spend life devoted to temporary accumulation and to the satisfaction of desire, very rarely glimpsing the eternal. It is only through inquiry into the truth of life that one begins to turn within to find everlasting happiness and peace. When thoughts and emotions are stilled in the light of pure being, peace becomes the foundation for your life. The invitation from the eternal nature within is to retreat into the light of your pure and divine consciousness where all is immersed, leaving no residue of suffering.

By ceasing unnecessary suffering, we have the strength to face the innate suffering of the life and death process. It is urgent for you to see the suffering of the world, and look within the heart to be of service. This requires the study of the self in relationship to desire, seeing that all desire has its roots in the separate ego-self.

The strong will of the personal self is convinced it has a life of its own, never reaching the end of its projected needs, never tiring when it is fed by worldly gain. Suffering ends when your plate is full of disillusionment, and you see clearly that all effort to fulfill your desires usually results in great loss and disappointment. When your life ends the course of self-gratification, there is a natural turning within, to your own divinity. A great yearning and devotion develops to the living truth within, where fulfillment is found.

In the quietude of our hearts and minds we fall deep into our sacred home of emptiness, where personal wants and desires are no longer in power. We see that, in truth, our essence is one of emptiness; our personality is actually temporary in nature and can be used for service in this lifetime. Identified with eternal nature, full and alive, we are one with the universe in totality and truth. Knowing the truth of life is the greatest service we can offer mankind.

The search for your true nature leads you to let go of all desires and attachments that keep you from finding freedom. In reality your true nature is always free, but the veil of the personal self prevents you from fully experiencing the vastness of your being. When the veil is removed there is oneness of being, complete wholeness, and the vitality to live in truth.

Desires of a self-centered nature, when acted upon, bring a deep sense of loss, because our sacred energy goes to that which is nonexistent in nature. The personal self is an empty well and will never be filled by the fulfillment of desire. When you turn within, the divine replenishes what is lacking; all seeking ends. The life of desire is to live generally regretting what we don't have and looking for something better to fill our empty wells. We seek power and security in a powerless and insecure world, never finding an ounce of security as all attainments turn to ashes in the end. Our true stable ground is to dive into the eternal within, letting go of all identification with the search for security. Know that your essence is one with divine consciousness, lacking nothing.

Life is change, and all outward manifestation is subject to the laws of nature. If we see that nothing in manifestation is permanent, we naturally move to that which is eternal, the unknown force of our life. Suffering and pain come and go, as do joy and happiness. These are the conditions of this birth. Remain in constant center throughout the changes and see your unchanging eternal nature.

In truth and ultimate reality, you are a whole human being, unaffected by all outward changes. The awakened mind has inquired into the nature of existence and has discovered that suffering is the result of separation. This lifetime is an opportunity to discover what you are not, by turning your attention inward to the source of life. Know thyself and you will enter the kingdom of heaven where your eternal nature rests.

Your essential nature of goodness is like a sieve, allowing all to go through and holding only that which is in service to your divine nature. Strengthen this sieve as you develop the jewel of discernment. Your true nature is one of love, goodness, and peace itself. By expressing these gifts of your soul you tend to the garden within, nurturing and creating beauty and everlasting goodness. Your eternal nature is the pathway to the infinite where you realize the vastness of being, bringing everlasting joy and peace.

Knowing your true essential nature, and trusting in that, is recognizing that your home is the emptiness of your pure consciousness. Each moment that goes by in personal suffering contributes to the suffering of the world. Each moment spent on behalf of freedom and love of the divine will radiate out to the world.

Understanding your true nature, pure consciousness, is essential to the peace of this world. The work of freedom is to no longer allow our human temporary nature to taint this sacred life with its self-centered conditioning. The whole person within is complete unto itself, not dependent on the belief in a separate self who lives for self-gain and self-pleasure. Turning away from this deep conditioning will change the world, for each of us is a part of the whole. The responsibility lies within.

Know that your essential nature is one of great wisdom and you can be at peace with yourself. When you realize the true nature of your being, you will embark upon a journey of transformation where the outer becomes the inner, the dark becomes the light and the self becomes the one. There is a deep rhythm where all turns, and in the center you remain in pure awareness - the bliss of being.

Peace is absolute trust in your divine self, turning within to rest in the sanctuary of your silence. Open your wings, surrender to the winds of grace; you will be guided to freedom and peace of being.

The Sacred River of Grace

Grace is the sacred river behind all of life. It flows, in its mysterious way, through your lifetime, guiding you and assisting in the revelation of true reality. All of life's difficulties are disguised in grace, each painful experience leading you closer to your eternal stillness of truth and wisdom, healing the cause of sorrow.

Pain and suffering are the result of great grace, showing you where your life needs more love, more attention. Grace is seeing yourself with total honesty, having the humility to take what is seen, knowing that the veil of ignorance that covers your true essence does not exist in reality. Grace is seeing that life is a continuous pointer to your true reality, timeless and eternal, and that all errors are born in separation from it.

Humility and grace are born from knowing that your true essence is divine and eternal, seeing that expressions from your personality are not always in the light of your divine nature. Grace is the clear observation of that which is false, seeing that truth is found in turning away from a separate identity. It is a deep letting-go of all that is not of your true self, opening to the light of pure consciousness.

Grace is allowing all the accumulated memories from the past to dissolve in the sacredness of your true self. Grace is your inner guide that leads you to look beyond the personal and see your true essential nature. Grace comes in the form of gentle reminders, and grace is the fearless force for cutting off the false.

Whether grace shows itself as the gentleness of a divine mother, or the fierceness of the divine father, all should be welcomed in assisting you in removing the veils to your real self. Grace may come when least expected, when you are blessed with unseen guidance to assist you in remaining true to yourself.

See all as grace, even the most humbling situations and the darkest and emptiest moments. Life always has its divine hand in the one who has taken the fork in the path of the personal self. All that occurs is by the sacred force of Grace.

The Sacred River of Grace flows in the lives of all beings, and is accessible by simply turning within and letting go of personal striving. Grace is the blessing of life itself, your very breath, the beat of your heart. All is given from the generous nature of grace and all are miracles in the light of grace: the smile of a child, the love of an elder, the touch of a friend, the truth that is shared amongst souls of God. Grace is the miracle of life. When there is a letting go of all of one's personal identification, exposing all in the sacred river, the swift current of grace takes you home. This mysterious force is the grace behind everything. Grace is always moving in our lives, guiding, protecting and providing for us.

Grace has a direct relationship with faith, allowing that which is unseen and sacred to take care of our souls. Trusting in that which is eternal and surrendering to the quiet voice within will lead us to the sacred resting place where complete peace abides.

Grace is the sacred force that guides us home to our inner truth, the core of our being. Life continues on, time moves on, experiences come and go, but the true essence within is eternal, beyond all conditions of time. Grace is the everlasting awareness of your true nature, living in the peace and love of its blessing.

Your natural state is wholeness, one with the source of life. As a spark of this oneness, your expression from your individual identity is merely a reflection of your eternal being, deep within your heart. Grace is the force that calls all souls home to rest in divinity. Listen to the voice of grace and see what part of you is yearning for the beloved within, your ever-abiding Christ light. The very yearning for what is real, sacred and eternal is the work of grace. When your mistaken identity no longer dictates your daily life, grace reveals your true nature, free from all states, all experiences, and conditions in time. Lifetimes have been spent in the familiar territory of the body, mind, and senses, which can be viewed as the rocks, the forks, the individual objects of the river. Now it is time to see the essence of the river itself, not just the parts. In seeing this essence, you are propelled to dive into its current, which is beyond the personal will of separation. The River of Grace is the current of life, the very current of your being, dissolving all seeds of sorrow in its mightiness.

The Sacred River of Grace asks only that you trust the current that is the sacred force behind the manifestation of life. This trust is to turn your life over to the real abiding force that is eternal and true, regardless of all appearances.

Gratitude

Gratitude is a natural blossoming of your understanding of your true nature. Life becomes a daily blessing, pointing to the true source of your being. Painful experiences and joyful experiences, all become part of the great play of divinity; life's experiences all contain the miracle of truth. Gratitude is the force that reveals the truth in your personal suffering, the force that strips the self down to the core of its divine nature.

Gratitude is being deeply thankful for the opportunity to see the sacred consciousness of life, in all beings and in oneself. Living in gratitude is to experience the sacred in life, honoring and expressing it throughout all changes. Gratitude is seeing that we have been blessed with time to realize the reason for this birth. To look within and discover the sacredness of being, seeing all as sacred, is to walk in reverence of the divine force behind all of manifestation.

Living in gratitude of life's holy teaching we give up a self-centered way of being and turn inward in great humility. We are blessed beyond comprehension to know this birth as a revelation of the divine. In gratitude, we discover how suffering and sorrow play a part in revealing the divine in life. All suffering contains a message that guides you to your true nature of strength and wisdom. Living in gratitude is to see that no matter how painful life is you are able to see the divine blessing that is being revealed. Gratitude is accepting blessings in whatever form they appear, seeing life's guidance as a message of the divine.

Gratitude deepens your heart as you appreciate all of life's blessings, seeing them as unfolding miracles. Knowing deep gratitude within is honoring each precious moment, seeing each moment as a wonderful opportunity to be one with truth. Gratitude is an acknowledgment of grace in your daily life, seeing the outer manifestation as an opportunity to live in the grace of being.

Life is a miracle. Gratitude deepens as we see the miraculous nature of life and recognize the divine energy behind manifestation. The foundation of gratitude is deep humility, reverence for life and trust in the sacred behind life. Humility is a vigilant awareness of the separate sense of self, with a constant return to emptiness, the nature of reality. Life becomes a deepening gratitude knowing that as you turn to the emptiness within, the divine miracle appears.

Looking at the vastness of this, how can we not be humbled by this great force that is behind it all? When we acknowledge that we are nothing in the eyes of the world, we let go of the self the way we have known it to be, and experience our true essence, which is simply spacious awareness. Letting go allows you to dive into your sacred force and to experience a deep communion with the eternal.

Happiness and Joy, Delighting in Spirit

The journey of a being in this physical body often creates a pattern for outward searching to find meaning and happiness. You can spend a whole lifetime seeking happiness in many different ways and never finding fulfillment. When the seeking turns to exhaustion from worldly effort and striving you have the opportunity to turn within - to the grace of being. Turning within to your true nature, which is always present, will lead you to the happiness that you seek.

Happiness is a simple state of pure being, the state before thought and before waking, a place where there is no effort. You are the very essence of happiness and joy, for what is behind all of your thoughts, emotions and physical sensations is the flow of life itself, which is pure happiness.

In your truest being, you are a song of joy to the divine, rejoicing in the simplest display of life, the beauty that is before you. There are no conditions that you must have in order to be happy. In fact, all conditions must be dropped; you just need to turn inward and witness the bliss of your true nature. Happiness is found in the song of your heart, when the burden of worldly identification is left behind. Happiness is your wholeness, your holiness, untouched by the world. Your true nature is pure witness consciousness that sees peace in all, remaining in a state of equanimity amongst the winds of change.

Letting Go, the Generosity of Being

Letting go of all things that are not in direct reality with your true nature of divinity is the most sacred process in uncovering what is vital and eternal. The art of letting go is seeing clearly that your true nature is revealed only in freedom where you no longer hold on to the past. Letting go and dying to the past, you learn to truly live in the moment, giving yourself to life instead of demanding something from it.

Your inner work is to remain current, always new in relationship to life's movement. The moment is full of life's teaching, opening and unfolding to the truth of being. Letting go is the art of giving to life, the supreme generosity of being, where you live in the opportunity to commune with the sacred. Letting go releases personal holdings that prevent you from living in your true nature. In generosity of being, you live in gratitude, asking how you can give back to incredible blessings that are given day after day. Letting go, you find yourself floating in the current of life, feeling amazingly natural and honoring the moment with no resistance.

In letting go, you must see clearly how your moments are spent in conditioned responses from the past. This is the very root of why the new can never be experienced. The love of your being is yearning to *just be* without any contamination from past experiences, and generosity of being is to give of yourself to the moment, giving up all that keeps the self from fully living *now*.

Letting go is dying to your patterns, your habit of believing in your separate, individual self. It is to see clearly, without a doubt, that your true nature is beyond any limitation of self-identity and that you are a spark of greatness. This greatness is not from the light of a small self; it is in the light of the infinite of which you are a part. All your small, individual thinking is blown away by the wind of the most powerful force of the infinite, leaving the silence of the self. In this silence nothing can be found but the sound of the universe, the sound of your innermost heart.

If you were to truly look now, in this moment, for the self without memories, it would be nowhere to be found. When there is a letting-go of thought about the self, grace will surprise you and the sacred self emerges out of the quiet and silence of being. Letting go and living in the moment frees you from the past tendencies and conditioning that have bound you, your family, and your ancestors to the illusion of separation. To be truly free, you must be ever-present, letting go and allowing for the new and eternal possibilities of life. In order to dance with the new, you must die to the old, releasing memories that veil the true self. Through this unveiling, there is a revealing of your sacred nature.

The Light of the Soul

Through lifetimes of mistaken identity, our true essence is veiled in ignorance of the personal ego-self. When we cease to identify with the ego-self, we open the channel for the light of the soul to come through, and the unfolding to the core of our being takes place. In life, there is a great deal of sorrow, unhappiness and suffering. Viewing life from the true inner self is to see how sorrow plays an important part in the lessons of the individual. When we are enmeshed in our ego-self, we live a life according to pleasure and pain. Sorrow from this level is never-ending, for you can never be free from cause and effect as long as you are rooted in identification with the separate individual. Sorrow of a personal nature subsides when you discover that the true self is found by a simple turning-away from the outer to the inner.

When we live life in identification with our body and mind, we experience limitation, constriction, and a lack of understanding. We live our life in service to physical, emotional and mental expressions, and our true nature that is whole, undivided within, is seldom met. When the meeting with our true nature occurs, identification with the outer reality is seen through the light of our soul. Upon meeting your true essence within, a deep yearning to remain in your pure nature becomes a daily call. The familiar pulls such as fear, attachment and worry, continue to bring you back into the limitations of a separate self. Remember your true nature, and seek within to have the vigilance required to slay the illusion of the ego-self with all its expressions rooted in fear. Keep the light burning by believing in nothing other than your own inner light, nurturing it, keeping it bright through devotion to truth.

Harmlessness becomes an important act of consciousness, as you see the importance of true caring in the world of thoughts, words and deeds. When awakened, life becomes much more of a quest to live in service to this suffering world, going beyond self-needs, helping others along the way. A great compassion develops deep within the heart, understanding the imperfections of this temporary manifestation, knowing that all is truly perfect in the light of pure sacred consciousness. The qualities of patience are employed knowing that we are truly eternal even though we live in time.

We conquer the nature of fear by seeing clearly that fear comes from believing in the illusion that we are our thoughts, our emotions or our physical body. Fear is based on separation. When there is a realization that there is no separation, fear is dropped, leaving only love. Life brings us to the deep feeling of gratitude, seeing all as God's will, being grateful for what is true, eternal and sacred. Gratitude leads us to the love of our true selves, where we live in the energy of thankfulness every day.

The mastery process requires an inner strength that is generated by your truth. You learn the art of looking inward, gradually increasing steadfastness in looking and in observation, until there is no looking or observing, there is just *being*. This is when you drop all effort to observe; the observer and the observed are a unified whole. When the light of the soul is brightest there is no thought of the self. The self is neither free nor bound, neither separate nor whole, and you live in absolute stillness as an open channel to the light of the soul.

Love, the Sacred Chalice of Life

Love is seeing the truth in yourself and in others, understanding all is one. Love is inclusive without judgment, accepting and embracing all. In embracing all, we learn to live without judgment, with total acceptance, loving all that appears, loving this mysterious changing reality. For in loving "what is" there is an immense freedom to be of service.

Most beings hold in their hearts hidden hurts, fears and identification with the past. In this way, we are never free to live in the moment, free from wounds of separation. To apply the sacred force of love within is to deeply witness where the memories and painful scars are held. In this divine witnessing, the transformation of your separate identity occurs and merges with truth.

Your consciousness is pure love, a witness to all things; where there is silence within, all is seen without attachment. Knowing deeply that misidentification is the root cause of all human suffering, you can observe in the light of service, surrendering all to your eternal energy. In silence the conditioning from the past surfaces. Here, healing takes place in the light of your pure consciousness.

Where there is personal sorrow, love is hidden by the veils of the illusion of suffering. Suffering calls attention to areas in life where love is lacking, requiring you to reach into the spiritual heart of truth, applying love where needed. In loving yourself, as well as others, you gain the ability to uncover all that is false, living in conscious union with wisdom and truth.

True love in the light of pure consciousness is remaining in your divine center, free from the pull of opposites, seeing that real love is not the opposite of hate. Love that is free and pure is love where you have no personal investment. It is love when there is no separation, only seeing all as divine and serving the purpose of divinity and truth.

Love that is free from the personal self radiates the force and the clear energy of truth. Love is looking at whatever is appearing, from a place of witness consciousness, knowing that the silent mind, when applied to each moment, is the most profound act of love that can be given. The silent mind expresses the impersonal force of love, where there is no activity of the personal self trying to attain, change, or reject. Love applied from the silent mind is attentive to the fact of the moment. Attention comes from the silent mind that is completely free from the past and alive in the moment.

Love is the attention given to any moment. When attention is lacking, love is also lacking. This attention, in which the ego-self is not invested, will result in right action, right speech and the fruits of the pure energy of love.

Love, in the deepest sense, is to give up all caring from the personal point of view. Always in personal love, there is a motive, a need, a becoming of the self in relationship to love. Love is the internal organic response to life, the action of bringing your life into the light of pure consciousness, where there is freedom.

Love is the absence of projection into the future; instead, it is living in the moment and honoring the sacredness of what *is*. Love is asking yourself, "What do I want?" This question unravels the deep patterns of desire and personal motives, and uncovers any obstacles to the meeting of your true essence, love itself.

Love is understanding that at the root of desire you usually find the quest for peace and happiness. Love is turning your attention from outer-looking, to looking within where you tap the unlimited love of your being. In this profound understanding, the desiring for anything stops; going within, you find complete contentment and joy. The source of peace and happiness is within you.

Mistaken Identity

The moment there is a meeting with your eternal true nature, there is an end to worldly identification, and the realization comes that you are one with the cosmic flow of life. All sense of separation dissolves in this oneness; the spark of your divinity now shines. There is then the transition from identification with the outer, temporary reality to the inner, eternal reality. A great light is revealed that assists your return to your true nature. The divine presence within appears and there is a feeling that you no longer walk this path alone.

When the identity shifts from the separate ego-self to the true self, all of your being comes into holiness, or wholeness. When you stop the identification with the "doer" of your life a miracle of life occurs. Life then works through your being and there is not the illusion of a separate individual in control.

Life is an expression of the divine, where all things stem from silence, where you surrender control. Observe how your life unfolds when you are not directing it. Action stems from the truth of the moment, originating from the awareness of your true nature. At this point the seeds of the personal self are no longer being planted in the garden of illusion. The result is an end to unnecessary suffering.

In the light of pure consciousness, all is an expression of the universal source of sacred energy, happening beyond personal effort or control. In this way, all expressions reflect the love and truth of your being. Your true destiny is to know yourself as an embodiment of pure love and pure wisdom. The love and wisdom of your true nature provides immense freedom when there is no longer the identification with a separate individual. Freedom is your true nature, discovered when there is no longer the belief in personal nature as your reality. Freedom is found in the unbounded consciousness that you are.

Peace

Your nature is pure bliss and innate happiness, covered by the veil of misidentification, which occurs when one believes reality is found in this manifestation. The outward reality of life changes constantly bringing an array of experiences, from pleasure to pain. During all these changes, the eternal aspect of consciousness remains in peace and awareness, embedded in divine love.

Understanding your true nature offers great comfort from the changing scenery of life. Notice that throughout time there is always the part of you that remains unchanged. See how this part is deeply untouched and joyous.

Sorrow occurs when life's difficulties are taken seriously, believing that this temporary existence is our only reality. All of your sacred energy is given to suffering and the belief in the temporary story of life. Turn your sacred energy within and retreat to the wellspring of your being where you receive the nurturing needed from the eternal. Peacefulness, which is your true abiding nature, is always present within for your renewal of spirit.

Life is a complicated journey with many conditions and requirements for happiness and contentment. This often leaves little room for peace. You must stop the projection of the self and turn the attention inward to the source of fulfillment. You see clearly that chasing after desires for personal happiness is never a means to an end. There is no cessation of desire because nothing can satisfy the empty nature of the personal self.

There is only peace and bliss in your true nature after all ideas of separation end. When you turn within a great fire ignites, burning away any veils that keep you from recognizing your true nature, leaving only peace and bliss.

In knowing your true nature, you can return home at any time to experience the nurturing of the peace and quiet within you. The beauty of life is that in each new moment there is a new opportunity for this return.

The Essential Question

Who am I? What do I want? The question, "Who am I?" is the most essential question for the purpose of self-inquiry. It is essential not only to begin with the question, "Who am I?" but, "What do I want?" looking into the heart of your truth for the answers. When the investigation of your true nature is tainted with strong personal desires for self-gratification, there can never be a sincere answer to this vital question. It may be more productive to start with an inquiry of *what you want from life*, and proceed then to the question of *who you are in life*.

This question will reveal the workings of the desiring mind, which is obscuring the vision of your true nature. In life, we have the delusion of an apparent reality, that which is seen and felt, and the strong illusion of the 'I' consciousness. The great mystery is behind all appearances.

There is a stream of consciousness that is not dependent on anything. You are, in truth, this reality, a flowing consciousness untouched by the temporary nature of life.

The nature of desire is the deep conditioning that most humans suffer. We spend a lifetime seeking to fulfill desires that are created by our self-centered programming. This programming is held deep in the conditioning of humanity, and must be questioned to begin the inquiry into the essential nature of life.

The simple truth is: self-seeking has poisoned your life long enough, creating untold suffering in humanity. When you turn the attention from seeking outward gratification to the inner wealth of spirit, all desires are satisfied. Peace and happiness are found in abundance when you recognize your true nature.

The truth within all beings is one of radiance and beauty, not found in any outer circumstance. Touching upon your radiance, you will soon develop a passion to merge with your God-self. This is the fuel for your inquiry into the nature of your existence. The thirst for the eternal becomes a daily exercise in uncovering the veils that prevent you from this merging. Unifying with your sacred nature is the most precious endeavor of your life.

The inquiry into the nature of your life will lead you to uncover all that has been hidden in the recesses of your being. On behalf of freedom, you will see that nothing is real except eternal nature and the eternal nature of all beings. Once the nature of existence is realized, all will be surrendered in the light of truth, liberating you from any residue of the past.

When one lives in investigation into the nature of the self, the veils are lifted that obstruct your true vision. What is revealed must be embraced and then submerged in the light of your true radiant being. You will see the root cause of suffering and compassionately look for ways to serve all beings.

The revelation of your 'true self' is the simple return to the source of your being, which is your sacred and divine nature. This revelation is silence itself, which calms and brings peace to the process of thoughts and emotions.

Living the question, "Who am I?" leads you to turn within, where the living sage resides. The silence of your true self is where emptiness becomes fullness and silence is the voice of wisdom. Live this vital question moment to moment, discovering all that you are not, unfolding the mystery of your being.

Insight into the vastness of your being will be your gift to yourself as you journey into the deep cavern of your heart. Inquiry is the tool that clears away the mistaken identity embedded by your conditioning. Look into the nature of your true self and all that you are not will fall away, revealing the immense light of your true nature. As you meet yourself completely, dance in the light and love of your being. This dance of your life will become a daily sacred celebration.

Your inquiry into the truth of yourself will reveal all that is not true. A simple letting go is all that is needed to release the false identity that has been created through time and memory. The intention in finding out who you are is, in truth, a great yearning for the God force within you. This yearning is a call from your true self, your divine nature. The sacred fire within transcends all behaviors, patterns, and destructive thoughts that are not aligned with your true nature. This sacred fire will create the path that leads you from the unreal to the real.

Look into what you are seeking from this life. If it is happiness and peace you seek, then know that it is found within the stillness of your true nature. When you investigate the question of who you are and what you want from life, you will uncover your true wish. All seeking and desire stems from the search for happiness. Discovering what you are not will lead you to uncover your inner truth, which is the ever-unfolding mystery of your being.

The moment where the true self lives is untainted by past impressions, whether they are pleasurable or painful. The moment is capable of great peace and love. From this place all is created. The moment is free from desires that are a product of time. It is unlimited happiness and bliss of being.

The personal self, along with its accompanying deep conditioning, has the habit of years and years of outwardly chasing thoughts and desires. If you look deeply you will see that these desires and thoughts are never satisfied, leaving a lingering feeling of emptiness. There is no end to this seeking, no fulfillment of any desire. For the personal self is a bundle of thoughts and reactions, based on memory, nonexistent in truth. How can the personal self, which doesn't, in reality, exist, ever find fulfillment in seeking?

Live the questions of life that reveal the secrets to your eternal being; these questions are vital to uncovering the truth of your life. The personal self will continually carry the reactions, attractions and repulsions of its self-centered conditioning, resulting in pain and suffering. Most human beings spend their life in this way. Waking up to this programming is to open the heart of compassion and question the reason for this birth. Through realization of the eternal self, you begin turning away from outward gratification of the personal self, to turning within and nourishing your inner, true self.

Inquiry into the truth of your being is the groundwork for letting go and opening the path to your true nature. To begin, one observes the self-centered programming; the pursuit of self-gratification, resulting in satisfaction, then repulsion, a cycle that will be repeated throughout your lifetime. See how the endless search for the self in pleasure results in pain and the wheel of cause and effect continues on for a lifetime. When you see that this is the way most humans spend their lifetime, it ignites the fuel for self-inquiry. The illusion that there is a personal self attaining something is deeply embedded in our thinking. We rarely turn within and experience our ever-present fullness. Discernment is seeing the pattern of desire, while turning the attention within to stillness and observation. This eagle vision will lead you to a greater intelligence in your life, seeing clearly and acting from the awareness of your true nature.

The realization that the personal self is not your true nature opens the channel for the light of your truth and wisdom to shine. When the personal self is seen as the functioning self, in service to the truth within, there will be a unity with your true, abiding, sacred nature.

The heart which is pure and free is the heart that is free from the past, creating a spaciousness of being and passion for life. The deep feeling of your heart is that it feels the pain and the joy of the world, while understanding the temporary nature of this passing time on earth. The deep feeling of the heart is a most sacred and profound guide, offering a map to your life's path. When you listen to your spiritual heart, you hear the wisdom of your own divinity. The true song of the heart is a song of great devotion to the eternal God force within you.

In all walks of life, whatever position you hold, taking time to nurture your true nature is the greatest gift of self-love. Your life and the roles you take on can be played out with more compassion, detachment, and understanding when you know that you are not these roles or conditioning. Within you is a sacred being worthy of attention, respect, and honor. Know yourself as this sacred being.

The veils that cover your true nature are the many layers of belief in a separate individual. When you realize the self, the veils are lifted. As long as there is a belief in a separate person who lives life for the gratification of desire, the veils of separation will exist. When you return to the silence of being, separation ceases and the radiant light of your being is revealed.

Trust in this mysterious life of miracles and know that you are a part of the sacred energy of life. By deep understanding of your real nature, the wants and desires become a divine play in your life, but are not seen as essential ingredients to bringing you the peace and happiness you seek. Your true nature is peace and happiness, regardless of what has been attained.

Clarity of being is to live life with good intentions and to serve the purpose of the divine self within you. The divine self is your true and ever-abiding nature, whose expression is pure love. The intention to live in your truth is to bring about a great love for yourself, the divine yearning to end your personal suffering and end the suffering of all of humanity. If the intention is to truly meet the sacred, then you must end identification with the ego-self and return to your true nature of pure being and peace. Silence, your sacred resting place, stills the emotions, the thoughts and the activity of the personal self. In the silence of your being, the wisdom of your heart opens to itself bringing to you a vital force.

The illusory aspect of ourself is formed by following thoughts and desires rooted in self-gain. This way of being has its roots in separation and fear, where your true nature is veiled by the ego's willful, self-centered program. This creates an individual who lives a life of striving, thinking only about personal survival. Inquiry must be an ongoing process; an investigation of what lives behind the activity of the personal self. This may take you to a ruthless observation of the self and to the programming that goes along with it. When the true self is realized, love needed to bring your life back to wholeness becomes accessible. Separation and fear are dissolved in the love of your sacred self, the source of truth.

What you have gathered through thought and experience are just bundles of memory. The real "you" has never been defined by thought or memory, it is pure consciousness. The inquiry into your true nature leads you to uncover what is hidden by false identification. What is uncovered is the real essence of your being. No longer defined as separate, you fall deep into your eternal presence of infinite beauty.

The personal self engages in life and receives the consequences for all involvement. This involvement can be understood as your karma. If you observe the personal self clearly, ending its self-centered program, there is a possibility that this cycle can be broken. The work of your being is to surrender to the truth of life; grace will take you the rest of the way. Grace is the great force that assists you in returning to your divine home, the stillness of your being. The heart, when set free from worldly identification, has a great space to open into the deep peace and silence of its true nature.

The art of observance is living in union with your true self, radiantly aware and present in the moment. This is the most beautiful expression of your being that you can ever know. When self-consciousness is dropped, you enter into true meditation and communion with the divine, touching great beauty. Your true essence, in its simplest form, is pure witness consciousness, partner of the divine.

The divine witness is your guardian angel within, clothed in great discernment, beauty and truth, on the throne of great love. Look within and see what is sacred, full of song, joy, wonder and divine inspiration. Release the burden of worldly identification. Live in the world but not of it. You are, in reality, a free being regardless of the entanglements of the world. Let the inquiry into your true nature become a living, breathing question, moment to moment, revealing your true self.

Life is a drama in which we play many roles. When there is a deep realization that you are not the roles you play, your path to freedom opens. You see clearly that it is only identification with the drama and with the parts you play that is the cause of sorrow. We suffer immensely when we invest in these roles with our *life essence*, rarely glimpsing our eternal nature. We are caught in the web of time, with the process of becoming, and the effort of the personal will toward self-gain. Is this the most useful way for us to live?

You see that by shifting attention toward inner security, you can stop the endless cycle of personal suffering. Death becomes a great reminder that your time in this body is so very precious. Inquiring as to the nature of life, we see that most of life is spent believing in our external roles, rarely meeting our eternal nature. Investing in the eternal aspects of life is a rare opportunity, offering us a security that is everlasting.

We hold the key to awareness that can end needless suffering for ourselves and for others, assisting the holy within to do its work without impediment. Abide in the true reality; allow your true self to emerge. This is a simple shift of attention from known reality, to the unknown sacred force that is the river of life.

When the attention has shifted from what is your known identification to the eternal consciousness within, years of accumulated memory and sense of 'I' begin to crumble. As the grace of your true self emerges, all that you take yourself to be - your roles in life, your relationships, and your past - will be seen as expressions in time. In your deepest knowing, you rest in the light of your eternal nature, touching into the infinite energy of the divine.

Beyond Thoughts, Emotions and Conditioning

Within the realm of the personality live conditioned thoughts and emotions that display in consciousness. Thoughts and emotions have a life of their own and will continue to appear and then disappear; this is their inevitable nature. Thoughts that relate to your functioning life are used as tools of your intelligence, to employ right action.

The nature of consciousness is observation. All is seen as passing clouds in the sky. Knowing that you are an eternal being, free from identification, will allow all to pass freely in your consciousness. Following thoughts and emotions outward and getting lost in their illusive nature, is the cause of the loss of self. The self that remains quiet, in observation, remains untouched by what is seen. This is the key to happiness, remaining free from the changing nature of life.

The work of the true self is to discriminate and discern between what is appearing and disappearing in consciousness. Upon observing the nature of thoughts and emotions, you can see that all thoughts and emotions come and go, but somehow there is always a part of you that does not change, that remains in witness consciousness.

Within your being is the unchanging nature of pure consciousness. The meeting with your true self, directly, without the interference of the activity of thought, is the answer to all personal suffering. This meeting, which is always present, is recognized when there is pure being, when all activities of the personal self are in silence.

A simple way of being is to know all passing states are temporary and to remain watchful, neither trying to run away nor trying to hold on to these passing states.

It is often past scars and experiences that create deep tendencies of desire and repulsion. These tendencies, with their associated habits, will lead you to believe in your wounded self, seeking ways to correct this self. A greater awareness is necessary to observe the tendencies of your thinking and to see the source of these thoughts clearly. When the observer clearly sees that a "little self" has been created from thought and memory, you begin to question the reality of this individual. Seeing your true nature facilitates liberation from the past, bringing forth the love needed to meet any fear that arises from the separate, fearful self.

If you see that you are essentially a divine being, you can easily let go of the identification with the story of your life. When the reality of your true self comes you are completely free from the past, the story and the possibility of the story continuing. The most courageous action you can take is to realize the sacred eternal self that resides within your spiritual heart. By turning the attention from identification with the personal self to the truth of your sacred being, you are able to let go of your individual suffering. Letting go of individual suffering is the result of the love of your true nature drowning the fear and separation caused by believing in a personal identity. It is the false personality, with years of memory, that has created your false identity. When your attention turns away from the belief in who you think you are, based on memory, to your sacred pure being that lives within, you will find freedom.

Fear is the holding of your identity in separation, finding comfort in the old familiar ways of belief in thoughts and emotions. Look inside to silence, perceiving the deep peace that awaits you in your spiritual heart. Your true nature (pure love) will dissolve all sense of fear and separation when you trust in that. Letting go of the personal nature of your life, surrender to the ocean of your pure consciousness. Any self-consciousness or little wave beating upon the rocks will be dissolved in this process.

Your inner divinity will wash away all scars, all identity of the wounded, fearful self. In letting go, all conditioning is dissolved and purified by the fullness of your true nature. The consciousness of your life is your true nature, the sacred river of your being. This sacred divine energy is the vital force of life, pure in being, free from content. Nothing that encompasses your worldly life can take away, touch upon, or change this divine energy river of your being.

Life's experiences lead you ultimately to the truth, for suffering has its place in pointing you back to the cause of suffering. The root cause of suffering is revealed in the complete understanding of separation and misidentification. Finally, all suffering can be seen as a great grace leading you to true being and ultimate freedom.

In reality, your true nature is awareness and the embodiment of love and wisdom. Awareness is pure seeing with the love and compassion of the spiritual heart. Awareness and love make up the filter system for all thoughts and emotions. This creates a deep wisdom in the life of the self. This wisdom is your true and ever-present consciousness and, when activated, it transforms your life and completely heals the past, creating a holy relationship to each moment.

Service, Response-Ability

Service is acting according to the dictates of your heart and responding in the moment, free of personal motive. Being in the moment, free from entanglements of the past, is holding the intention for service. Awareness is born from the love of your true nature; service is applying this love to whatever life presents. Service is simply living in your truth, shining the light of your true nature.

Early in life we are guided to live by the conditioning of our personal self. We are deeply conditioned to live according to the values of a broken world that is ill from seeking personal gratification. Service begins with the compassionate heart, seeing the truth of life and acting with integrity, honoring the sacred in life. Service is removing the illness of separation in our life, bringing ourselves back to the wholeness of our true nature. Service is having unlimited compassion for this journey while loving our inner being, and seeing through the veils accumulated through our selfhood.

True service lies in an understanding of wholeness, knowing that each fragment is essential to the whole. In this understanding you see a deep responsibility to find wholeness within, to assist the healing of all of humanity.

Response-ability is the action of responding in the moment to the teaching of life. When responding in the moment, you are free from the past. In this freedom it is possible to serve and apply love to whatever is presenting itself. You are graced to have the ability to live a life in service to pure consciousness, to live according to the dictates of your true self. The true grace of divinity is when you see the cause of suffering, turning your life inward to what is everlasting and eternal. The radical change in consciousness is when your attention turns away from the personal nature of life toward the sacred. This change deepens your compassion and love for the sacred in life, leading you to live a life beyond the personal.

That is the greatest work of life, to become free from personal bondage and suffering, knowing that in this freedom you are truly assisting the healing process of the human condition. Your true destiny is to know yourself as an embodiment of pure love, reflecting this love in all areas of your life. Love is attention to all things lacking in the moment. You are holding a golden chalice of love, ready to give to all. This is the true meaning of service. Knowledge of your true self, love of yourself and love of others, is the pathway to becoming a whole human being.

Service of Divine Love

One of the greatest services you can give to others is that of seeing others as your true self. As you see yourself in the light of pure consciousness, you will also see others in the same light. Seeing the good in people and knowing they are pure God consciousness is a way of assisting them in knowing their true selves. This seeing is the very act of love. In seeing the truth in yourself and in all beings, a letting-go of the false occurs. What remains is the pure beauty of the Divine. Life has blessed each and every human with a span of time to practice the truth of "know thyself."

This time is so very precious and it's a beautiful moment when a soul sees the true meaning of this birth. Life with the purpose of uncovering the veils to truth is a life that goes beyond personal suffering. Suffering is a fact of life, but when viewed in the light of your true nature, you are able to live with less attachment to the impermanent nature of life. There is an ever-deepening understanding of life, and the nature of the self who is the creator of sorrow. Suffering is viewed in a much different light when there is the radical understanding that the self who creates sorrows doesn't truly exist. Through turning inward to meet your sacred eternal being, the personal self will no longer have a voice that stands by itself. You will undeniably know who you truly are and the outer life will be changed forever more.

Divine service is living in devotion to your everlasting true nature. Sit at the feet of your own inner master in great devotion to the sacred within your being. This is your path to joy and peace. Service to the Divine is an act of selflessness, a time of remembrance, and a great humility that opens you to the communion with your own Christ light. Service is opening your inner lotus in love and devotion to the source of all life. A great service to all is to trust in yourself, where you see you are the light of the world. As the light of each being grows stronger, the world becomes brighter.

Silence, the Fertile Ground of Being

Listen quietly within where it is possible to perceive the emptiness of this vast universe, knowing that all of creation appears from immaculate stillness. Behind all that lives is the quiet pulse of the sacred, mysterious life force. So still is our true nature, we only need to go to the quiet to hear its divine melody. The divine music that assists the waves, creating the wind, opening the bud of a rose - all of this comes from the sacred force of the quiet.

In the quiet temple within, we are pure *being-ness*, free to expand into the vast eternal emptiness from which we come. Silence is a great force that assists in healing our bodies, our minds and emotions, for it is within the silence that all things come into order. Silence is a great expression of order, bringing things into rest, allowing the natural process of balance to take place.

Silence is the storehouse for miracles, as miracles are the blossoms of silence. Looking through the eyes of gratitude, you will begin to observe the truth of life, which is miraculous beyond our comprehension. All gifts of the spirit are discovered in silent observation. The gifts of gratitude, beauty, love, peace, generosity, and service are found in your inner self, born of silence.

Listening to the will of the quiet is truly listening to your innermost heart, the sacred chalice of love. The silent mind is a mind that is free to perceive the most profound truth. In this perception, the mind is quiet, and reflects the eternal consciousness of humanity.

Action from the past viewed from the perspective of silence will be transformed, washing away the painful memories held in the heart. It is the deep tranquillity found in silence that assists in healing all scars. We hold onto the past because there is an ego-self, with memories in time, seeking to recreate the past or project into the future. Understanding your true nature is to see that all things from the past and all things in the future are absorbed in the sacredness of true being. In truth there is only one being, eternal and untouched by all experience. In silence, all activity of searching comes to an end, for deep in this ocean of infinite truth the true being that you are is pure consciousness, unbounded and undeniable.

Your life is full of challenges, bringing constant opportunities to remember that the temporal world is always changing, bringing an array of pleasure and pain, in new ways and new settings. The life of the disciple of truth is to turn away from believing in either the pleasure or the pain that is occurring in the moment, and to turn your attention to the truth of being. Being in the world, functioning and living according to your truth, is the very essence of this being that lives in the luminosity of your heart.

From the fertile ground of silence springs forth the nature of the divine, with incredible beauty, joy, untold happiness and peace of mind. All things from truth come from silence. In this way there is unlimited potential in divine creation. You can observe nature, the immense, breathtaking beauty and magnificent display of creation, all stemming from the silence of the universe.

Living in Surrender

Recognizing that there is only pure consciousness is to surrender to the peace, light and silence of your pure consciousness. Upon letting go of all false identification, impressions and accumulated memories are immersed in the light of your true nature. The gateway to this unbounded consciousness is the door to your soul, always open and assisting you in your return. All that is required in divine law is surrender to that which is always present within, your true eternal self.

Seeing the reality of your identification with the world and the suffering it brings will propel you to shift from your personal nature to your impersonal, timeless nature. In this shift, you see the futility of holding on to the memories of life's occurrences as being the ultimate reality. Memories, good and bad, are the changing scenery of life, but the background is your true reality. Knowing that the scenery is in constant change, you begin to relate to the vital force of life itself behind all the changing scenery.

Surrendering into your true nature is letting go of the willful self, meeting the sage within, honoring and cherishing this ancient soul. This sage, who is the dweller within all hearts, is a sacred being with great wisdom and knowing. This vital force is the return of truth, leaving layers of false identity behind.

Surrendering to your true nature, which is in reality the Christ consciousness of all hearts, brings a new life of peace, harmlessness, and a great love for truth. All personal effort is put aside as the divine will within reveals itself and sets the course home to the sacred.

Surrendering is a great and profound turning within, merging your self with divine consciousness. It brings a renewal of being and a new vitality for life, seeing that all parts of your life, which has been devoted to personal self, have been a mirage. There is an eternal sense of knowing and freedom from all conditioning as you surrender to the light of pure consciousness. This surrender brings about a great lightness and bliss, revealing the peace of your true nature.

A momentous revelation is meeting the true self within. All personal striving is thrown into the sacred fire of truth. Surrendering to your eternal nature brings a safety never known before, a security everlasting and protected by infinite grace.

Attention in Relationship to Silence

Daily life presents the most extraordinary opportunity to live your life from the silence within, the foundation for all action. The nature of silence itself is the background of all activity, thoughts, emotions and actions, where all is displayed. Silence, being the background, is the foundation for truth; what is displayed is the temporary nature of life. Turning to the foundation of silence will assist you in remaining steady in witness consciousness throughout any display.

Attention is vital to *being-ness*, for when you are not fully in the moment, attention based on truth is impossible. When the personal nature of life is no longer believed to be your true reality, all memory and conditions of separation fall away. What is left is pure *being-ness*, where attention is pure vitality. Silence is the foundation for being. It is your sacred resting place, where your radiance shines. The silence of your being is your true nature, immediately accessible by turning your attention away from outer identification. When attention is turned from outer identification to inner truth, a great strength is applied to all areas of life.

Because attention is no longer focused on what is not true, your separate identity, you have immense vitality to uncover what is true. You live your life from a different point of view, one of seeing without a personal hold onto what is seen. All actions stem from the quiet of your true self, reflecting integrity of being. Integrity of being is to live from the wholeness of your true nature, fully engaged in life with your truth. When you live from your truth, the expression of your sacred being, all action is correct and based on universal wisdom. Action that is based on the sacred is action that makes all one, taking responsibility for the whole and living according to this truth.

When attention is applied to the truth of being, a most profound realization occurs: that of the light of being, the everlasting source. Attention is the fuel for the truth, for in applying attention in the investigation of your true nature, the false is burned by the light of this attention. Attention is the giving back to life, the generosity of being that is called for from the divine. It is the tool to clear away what is false, and the courage to walk ahead in truth, conviction and steadfastness. A life lived that is alive with attention is a life that prevents the cobwebs from the personal from creating any obstructions to truthful being. Living in attention is to fully embrace all in the light of truth, knowing that attention is the flame that burns away the unreal.

Living a life of clear attention is to be in constant communion with the eternal fire of truth, throwing all that is untrue into this fire. Attention to the moment is the instrument of awareness, based on truth, where personal reactions have no voice. The fire of attention is born from complete freedom from the past, applying the sacred energy of the moment fully, and without impediment.

The silence within has an immense intelligence when it is free from the conditions of the personal self. You must learn to yield, to bend and to heed this silence, by constantly surrendering your personal investment in each new moment. The sacred silence of your true nature is the voice of attention; there is no distraction of a personal nature. It is having the freedom to attend to life in whatever way life calls for. This is the true meaning of service.

Living in attention is to live in the center of being where you can access the vital energy needed to attend to the moment. Remaining in equanimity toward life is to live in the center of all manifestation, not being led astray by one side of polarity or the other. This point between duality is where the sacred is found, the eternal wellspring of joy and the source of unlimited vital force.

When you touch into the radical freedom of your being, all of the past is wiped away. You have no reference as to who you are as an individual separate identity. The personal nature of the self with a story drowns in the flood of divine pure consciousness. Instead there is no longer a separate individual who identifies with the outer cycles of life. There is a constant awareness of change. Embracing the wind of change, you move with the ebb and flow of this mysterious reality.

Action, when you are free from personal conditioning and memory, has the force of attention needed to uphold your truth throughout all of life's challenges. This is action that is pure and free from the content of the past. Attention from the silence of being is when there is a complete giving of yourself to the fact of life, the highest love that is accessible to your being.

Know deeply that you are free from all outer conditions, from things of the past. In reality, that which lives within cannot be touched by any outer circumstance, or be affected by time. Through knowing your true self, deeply letting go all coverings of your inner being, you are able to access immense energy for life.

The immense energy that flows through your being allows for the mind to go to the depth of understanding. When the mind is free from ego-self distractions, it has the fire of attention, being able to discern the real from the unreal. This freedom allows you to live in the point between duality, out of time and free from the effects of birth and death. Your true nature is freedom itself, inviting you to partake of the flight of your soul, to flow in the current of your life, peaceful, blissful and one with eternity.

The Timeless Flow of Life

The illusion of life, that you are bound by any condition, is based on the thought of who you think you are. All human beings are graced with wisdom and the ability to contemplate the real meaning of life, seeing that, in truth, you are a free being, flowing down the timeless river of life. With the intention for freedom to discover the root cause of sorrow, there is vigilance in uncovering the truth.

You realize that happiness cannot be found when you are caught in conditions bound by time. Real happiness is found by turning within to your timeless nature. Happiness is found when there is a complete letting-go to the timeless flow of life, where you are not bound by any conditions at all. When you surrender to the timeless flow of life, energies are used on behalf of the eternal presence, and life is lived in devotion to everlasting divinity. When you learn that your true nature is the essence of the eternal, untouched by anything, naked and alone, you are no longer interested in the temporary gain of the world. A life lived in the world with a strong sense of self-realization is knowing that at any time you can retreat into the silence of your being, where you unite with the timeless flow of life. Know deeply the truth of your being. Use this life as the most precious opportunity to surrender any sense of separation to the timeless flow of life, realizing that, in unity, you will be whole.

Your Intention in Truth

The intention to live in your truth comes from the recognition of your true nature that is always present, found in the silence of your spiritual heart. As you practice the art of return, you will naturally turn your attention within, realizing that all comes from the emptiness and silence of being. The light of intention is to be deeply devoted to the source of your true self. The habit is to be untrue to your source, and follow the outward stream of life into all its entanglements and suffering. The intention to live in your truth will guide you from looking outward, to looking within, to the wisdom of your eternal nature.

The intention to live in the truth of your being must be steadfast among the changes of your visible reality. It then becomes a daily prayer, living in the art of return to the silence of being. You will soon become more familiar with your sacred resting place, deepening your communion and understanding of your true nature. Your true self is a beautiful and radiant being who abides in the sacred and quiet of the Divine. Know that in daily life you are not separated from your true self. Your daily prayer and meditation can be one of bringing back your wandering consciousness to its source, resting in the silence of the heart.

Each new moment is a new opportunity to live in love of your true nature. As each new moment arises, surrender all to the healing light of the Divine. In each new moment, there is a new breath that brings the awareness back to your true nature of silence. As the art of return becomes your dance of life, you will be continually called back to deepen your rest in the light of your being. This light is the source of all activity, thoughts and actions.

Hold the light of your being in great reverence, knowing that this light is the light of the world. Live in constant recognition that you are this light, the light that makes us one. The ebb and flow of consciousness is to go out of your silence into expression, returning to your eternal pure light of being. This is the foundation for all action that is aligned with your divinity. Holding the light within is to live in the love of your true self, the love of the Divine. Remain in this love no matter what appears.

Wisdom

In each human being there is an innate, divine intelligence that is rarely touched. This divine intelligence is the supreme intelligence, untainted by thought, memory, and time, stemming from the universal source of the infinite. The mind, when silent, is unbound and free to discover the pure consciousness of your being that reflects the divine consciousness of the heavenly world.

The intelligence of your being, when expressed, has the ability to soar to the edges of eternity and to infinite understanding. Intelligence that is unconditioned, free to act according to the truth of being, is one with divine wisdom - the source of life. The awakening process begins when there is a letting go of all identification with anything that binds you to thoughts, belief, or memory, seeing that your true nature is freedom. When the mind is liberated from the habits of identification, you are free to travel the eternal path of wisdom.

The return to your natural resting place of silence leads you to surrender all things of a personal nature, into the light of your divine intelligence. The mind is a reflecting pool that has the ability to discriminate between thoughts that are geared toward validating the personal self and thoughts that reflect the light of the inner truth. The awakened being is intelligence in action, observing all that enters in your consciousness, remaining detached and whole in nature.

The awakened being turns to the divine source of silence to express the highest aspect of knowledge and divine will. In the silence of the mind and heart, you can now realize the spaciousness and emptiness of your true nature. As you deepen your understanding of your sacred nature, all conditions that stem from the impermanent nature of life will be released to that which is eternal.

The awakened being sees the nature of the will and how it is directed either to self-pleasure or surrendered to higher good. Through awareness of your true self, you can see how the will, used for self-gain, plants the seeds of suffering, personally and globally. Awareness becomes vital to seeing this will and to discerning the personal and the impersonal desires and thought patterns. Awareness is the art of the true self, opening the inner eye of wisdom, seeing all, and remaining in emptiness.

Awareness is the skill of quieting your personal inclination to entertain thoughts, emotions, and desires that are geared to temporary self-gain. Awareness is the supreme understanding of desire and the fruits of desire. The awakened being seeks to stop the roller coaster of pleasure and pain, ending the involvement and belief in a personal story. The awakened being always turns toward its source: the heart of wisdom, the everlasting source of your strength.

The awakened being quietly listens, trusting in the source of its being and the sacred movement of life. There is a continual awareness of life, seeing that it is not about fulfillment of the personal seeker; rather it is the recognition that you are a free and whole human being. The awakened mind is completely aware of the personal self and how it reappears for recognition and survival, always laying it back to rest in its source of silence.

The awakened being ends the habit of identification with this body and mind, and returns to the source of consciousness. In the depths of stillness, there is only recognition of what is true and eternal within the soul. The most powerful tool that you have as spiritual beings is the ability to see with an awakened, intelligent mind and to use this seeing as a sword to cut through the false nature of existence. The mind that is silent has the space for great perception of the direct stream of pure consciousness. Pure consciousness is the essence of real love; this is the source of all being.

The awakened being takes the fork that leads to the sacred, clearing any illusions, conditions and patterns that have obscured clear seeing. The awakened one turns within, to the sacred path of the divine, trusting the journey as one's eternal home, ever-deepening the awareness of the infinite. One's eternal home is the silence of your infinite being, your sacred resting place. It is a place of peace and communion with that which is eternal, vast and unbound.

The awakened being knows deeply the nature of its source, residing in the sanctuary of the spiritual heart. As the doorway opens to the divine within, there is an immense amount of energy that floods the soul, washing out any residues of misidentification. Return often to the ever-abiding silence within, trusting in your eternal divinity found deep within your spiritual heart.

1.   How do meditation and the quiet mind play a part in your journey? Share your feelings about your connection with the source of life itself.

2.   Summarize your understanding of the meaning of the *Life Essence Awakening* Living Meditations.

Glossary

Abhaya - fearlessness, one of the most important virtues, the fruit of knowing one's true nature.

Abhaya mudra - hand position to dispel fear, fingers on the right hand raised, palms facing forward, gesture of protection.

Absolute - ultimate reality

Acupuncture point - specific points of energy along acupuncture meridians.

Advaita - non-dual

Advidya - ignorance

Agni - the fire god

Ahamkara - personal ego

Ahimsa - nonviolent path, harmlessness

Ajna - the sixth chakra or third eye, located between the eyebrows.

Akasha - space

Akashic records - the records held within the causal body of the soul.

Alarm point - specific acupuncture points used for the detection of over-energy in meridians.

Anahata - fourth chakra, meaning unstruck, located in the heart center.

Ananda - bliss

Anandamaya - the subtlest bliss-formed sheath of the causal body. The sphere of all transcendent, blissful consciousness.

Ananta - endless

Antahkarana - the building of the ego instrument or bridge between lower manas (mind) and higher manas. "That path which lies between thy spirit and thy self."

Apana - the prana, which carries away the waste products from the human body.

Arupa - literally, without form; that is, a form from the standpoint of the physical plane.

Asmita - egoism (I am that)

Astral body - body containing prana, mind, intellect and emotions.

Atman - the self; the divine aspect in the seven-fold constitution of man; his highest principle.

Aum - the sacred three-syllable word of mantric significance, it is at once an invocation, a benediction, an affirmation and a promise.

Aura - literally, means breeze; the vital force surrounding the body.

Awareness - individual consciousness, knowing, witness, perception.

Being - pure consciousness, essential divine nature; changeless, formless, existence.

Bhagavad Gita - the divine song.

Bhajans - singing of religious songs.

Bhakti - devotion

Bhava - becoming

Blessings - the unseen grace of life, not conditioned upon good or bad but on events to open one up to divine reality.

Brahma - the creator

Bridge of light - antahkarana

Buddha - the enlightened one

Buddhi - intellect

Causal body - the subtlest of the three bodies, also known as the seed body. Contains the karmic imprint that determines who you are.

Causal plane - the highest plane of manifestation.

Celestial - heavenly region of divine beings.

Chakra - the astral force centers or spiritual center located in the Sushumna, literally meaning disk or wheel.

Chin mudra - hand position of joined thumb and index finger.

Circuit locate - To access nerve or energy circuits in the body by finger touch and then muscle testing to see if the circuit is 'active' or 'involved'.

Circuit retaining mode - Technique used in kinesiology to hold something, usually an imbalance of some kind, in the body's nervous system or circuit. 'Circuit Retaining' is like selecting a file on a computer and having it stay on the screen so that it can be worked on.

Clairvoyance - clear seeing

Compassion - the art of seeing the truth in complete acceptance of what is, awareness leading to unconditional love.

Conscience - inner state of right or wrong, the knowing voice of the soul.

Consciousness - waking-memory, thought, desires, cognition, all things in manifestation.

Consciousness thread - the bridge of light or Antahkarana, the thread that is located in the pineal gland. Union of life and substance.

Creative thread - the cord that links up with the center at the base of the spine. The creative thread is responsible for the development of the personality, anchored in the throat center.

Daiva - divine

Desire body - the pull of opposites.

Deva - a celestial being, shining one

Dharma - righteous conduct, life purpose or life path, God-given talent.

Dhyana - fixed god realization, meditation.

Discrimination - viveka, the ability to distinguish between the real and unreal, eternal and transient, as in the upanishad maxim, "It is not this, it is not that."

Duality - the phenomenal world, where each thing exists along with its opposite; joy and sorrow, etc.

Ego - individual identity

Emotional body - moving field of energy eighteen to forty-eight inches into the aura; colors, shapes and reflections of feelings.

Endurance - tolerance

Energy being - physical, etheric, emotional, mental, intuitional and divine planes of consciousness, held together by the vital force.

Equanimity - the state of remaining calm and centered, despite changes.

Essence - the ultimate, unchanging nature of things.

Etheric body - electromagnetic field surrounding the physical, circulating prana, or life energy, throughout the system. The protective web.

Five elements - The Law of the Five Elements from Chinese Healing Philosophy. Explains that everything in the Universe belongs to one of the Five Elements of Fire, Earth, Metal, Water and Wood. These elements are not so much physical ideas but 'qualities' of things. The Five Elements are a widely used concept in kinesiology.

Food sensitivity - In kinesiology food allergies are usually termed food sensitivities. However, food sensitivities can be much more. Medically, allergies are sympathetic rashes, etc., caused by food, chemicals, etc. Food (or chemical) sensitivities include any substance that imbalances or stresses the body in any way, whether or not rashes are present.

Ganesha - the elephant god that removes obstacles.

Gayatri - one of the most sacred vedic chants; goddess.

God realization - the direct and personal experience of the divine within oneself.

Grace - beloved, giving, revelation, awakening to one's true nature.

Heart Chakra - the center for direct perception.

Ida - the nadi or energy channel that is left of the sushumna: intuitive, holistic, inner-directed, emotional, subjective, feminine, cool.

Impressions - see Samskaras or Skandas

Indicator muscle - the muscle chosen for the test one wishes to perform, i.e. in food sensitivity testing one chooses an indicator muscle that, when tested, will 'indicate' an imbalance, stress or sensitivity to the food.

Instinctive mind - the lower mind, which controls thought and emotion based on survival and protection.

Integration - the working together and communication between the left & right hemispheres of the brain.

Intellectual mind - the source of discernment and higher perception.

Intuitional body - the vibration of our truest essence; the vehicle of the self to express love, wisdom and truth. The holding place of Akashic Records, the records of the soul.

Invocation - using prayer, mantras and sound to invoke the assistance of a higher nature. The skillful knowledge of the use of energies to guide, protect and heal.

Jai - victory

Jiva - the principle of life, the individual.

Jnana - knowledge or wisdom

Jnana mudra - wisdom and preference hand gesture.

Jyoti - light

Kala - a ray, digit of manifestation, the transcendental wave.

Kama - desire

Kama-manasic - the web of mind and emotions.

Karana - the prime cause.

Karma - action, the law of action and reaction, death and rebirth. We are actors in the world and reap the fruits of action. Actions leave impressions, give rise to thoughts, affect our decisions, leading to further actions and impressions. The wheel of cause and effect and suffering.

Karma yoga - literally, the yoga of action.

Krishna - the name of one of the greatest teachers of India, an avatara.

Kundalini - meaning to coil, the energy that is dormant located in the Root or base Chakra. The home of Shakti, our pure energetic potential as human beings.

Kyan Yin - the Chinese goddess of mercy, called the divine voice.

Laksmi - prosperity, success, goddess of fortune and beauty.

Lam - the seed mantra of the muladhara chakra.

Laya - absorption, whose goal is merging the individual consciousness with the divine consciousness.

Life thread - located in the heart, links the subtle bodies with a sacred grounding cord, unifying all energies. The path in which the personality unites with its divine reality. The channel for the path of return through the form, upward.

Light - clear white light, permeating all of existence. Glowing, radiant, healing force of love.

Lotus petals - the Sanskrit letters inscribed on their specified number of petals indicate sound vibrations representing the varying intensities of the energies working in the different chakras.

Maha - great.

Mahatma - literally the great self, a great soul.

Mala - a string of 108 beads, it is a powerful tool to help focus the mind for meditation.

Manas - mind.

Manasic - the mental principle.

Manipura Chakra - the third chakra, located in the navel.

Mantra - a prayer, poetic hymn, incantation, sacred sound that has the power of Shakti, reflection of the ultimate; provides protection for the transmigratory life.

Maya - that which may be measured; that which is subject to change, illusion.

Mental body - <u>Higher</u>: the plane of intuition, intellect, perception, emotional intelligence, witness consciousness. <u>Lower</u>: The plane of reason, logic, thought, desire, amkara, the "I" self.

Meridian - The energy pathways or channels discovered by the Chinese almost 3,000 years ago that are still used by acupuncturists to this day.

Mind - <u>Lower mind</u>: the container of impressions that have resulted in past experiences, habits, tendencies, beliefs and memories. <u>Higher mind</u>: the reflection of pure consciousness, discernment, will-power, discrimination. Peace of mind is the release of scars and the habits of scarring, through returning to the source from which it came. <u>Conscious mind</u>: wakeful, thinking state. <u>Subconscious mind</u>: beneath the surface, the storehouse of impressions. <u>Super-conscious mind</u>: the mind of light, the all-knowing intelligence of the soul.

Moksha - freedom, liberation

Mudra - a mystic sign or symbol, hand gestures to seal the union of prana-apana.

Muladhara - the Root Chakra.

Muladhara Chakra - the first or lowest center of spiritual energy located at the base of the spine.

Muscle test - The act of testing a muscle to find out something about the state of the body/mind. The fundamental and key technique that has made kinesiology famous and popular today.

Nada - mystical sound or energy wave.

Nadi - astral nerve or conduit. There are over 72,000 nadis in the body.

Nadis - the channels of the subtle body through which the vital, pranic and astral currents flow.

Namaskara - palms together at the heart or head area in reverence of blessings

Namaste - "I salute the divinity within you."

Negative spiral - the soul plummets downward into negative entanglement through identification with wrong impressions.

Nirvana - the state of absolute consciousness.

Neuro-lymphatics - Correction point in kinesiology where one gently massages the point to stimulate lymphatic flow/drainage around a particular part of the body.

Neurovascular - Correction point in kinesiology where one gently touches the point with one's fingertips to stimulate vascular flow to a particular part of the body.

Om - Sanskrit, aum

Om Mane Padme Hum - the jewel in the lotus.

Over-energy - Where there is too much energy flowing through a meridian or energy pathway.

Padma - lotus

Para - highest, unmanifested sound, the highest stage of consciousness.

Paramita - a virtue, or perfection.

Parashakti - the highest energy, the supreme goddess. The great force, primal source, all-pervasive light, pure consciousness, all-knowing, merging identification.

Path - a way, the way to ultimate realization; all paths lead to the same destination, uniting with the source from which we have all come. Truth is one, paths are many.

Pingala - the right side of the sushumna channel. Its nature is aggressive, logical, analytical, outer-directed, rational, objective, hot, masculine, mathematical and verbal.

Plane - a stage of existence.

Positive Spiral - soul ascends upward through remembering its origin.

Prana - the vital force; the seat of prana is in the heart.

Pranayama - control of prana.

Purusha - the supreme being, the spirit who dwells within the body, the transcendent self.

Pretests - Simple tests, performed before any kinesiology work, for determining if the body is ready for efficient and accurate muscle testing. Pretests may include a dehydration test, test for switching, test for Central Meridian reversal or a test for ionization.

Raja yoga - literally, union with one's higher self, increasing power of discernment, selecting positive impressions which lead to higher emotions, clear and peaceful thoughts. Living in harmlessness, no sorrow for self or others.

Ram - the seed symbol of the manipura chakra.

Reincarnation - the results of karma, the birth into a physical body for the purpose of evolving love.

Repose - to rest in your true nature, resting peacefully in just *being*.

Rudra knot - psychic blockage in the ajna chakra, cleared by attaining the non-dual state.

Rupa - form.

Sabda - sound.

Sadhana - spiritual practice.

Sahasrara - seventh or highest chakra, thousand-petaled lotus. Highest psychic center, wherein the yogi attains union between the individual soul and the universal soul.

Samadhi - the super conscious state.

Samsara - continuous round, or wheel of births and deaths, a succession of states.

Samskaras - subtle impressions of past lives, accumulations, karmic consequences.

Sat - the one ever-present reality in the infinite world.

Satchidananda - existence, absolute knowledge, bliss. Chi - knowledge; ananda - bliss.

Sattva - the quality of lightness and purity.

Satyam - truthfulness.

Self-realization - realization of soul's actions and reactions.

Shakti - power.

Shakti chalini - exercise for raising Kundalini.

Shamballa - attainment of happiness.

Shiva - the third aspect of the trinity, destroyer of evil, regenerator.

Silver cord - this sacred cord unifies the subtle bodies and is anchored in the heart center. Through the silver cord we remain in contact with our soul.

Skandas - attributes, consciousness, form, sensation, perception, mental impressions and tendencies.

Soma - divine nectar.

Soma Chakra - between Third Eye and Crown Chakras.

Sorrow or suffering - self-abuse.

Soul - the real being of man, the relationship between spirit and matter, pure consciousness. The link between God and form, integration between spirit and matter. Christ principle, in-dwelling life, conscious response to matter, light between opposites.

Soul gates - knots of un-transformed consciousness, clockwise upward pull, counter-clockwise gravitational pull.

Spirit - illumination, enfolding, uplifting beauty.

Sristi - creation.

Stress release points -The use of the Forehead Neurovascular Points to stimulate blood flow to the frontal part of the brain for clear, calm thinking and processing.

Subconscious mind - part of the mind that is beneath the conscious mind, the impression mind. The subconscious mind is the recorder of all experiences, holder of past impressions, reactions, desires, unconscious emotions.

Subtle body - energies which surround the physical, that extend out to higher and higher frequencies.

Suksma - the subtle body in which the different psychic centers are located.

Super consciousness - mind of light. Intelligence or soul, causal mind being the cause not the effect. Universal: non-dual. Turiya: fourth state - intuitive, benevolence, universal truth.

Sushumna - the central nadi, or astral nerve, which runs through the spinal cord. The father or will aspect of our being, channels the soul energy. The spiral nerve, which connects the heart with the crown center.

Sutra - the thread on which jewels are strung.

Sutratma - the thread of the self, the immortal principle of man, which incarnates from lifetime to lifetime. Individuality in which countless personalities are strung. The central channel along the spine in which the free flow of energies travel on the path of return.

Swadhisthana Chakra - second, or navel energy center.

Switched on/off - In a muscle test the muscle can be switched on or off. The term is also used to describe the state where one's nervous system is switched on or switched off to an activity, i.e. reading, walking, concentrating etc.

Tat - "that"; boundless, para brahman.

The path - the movement in consciousness to the realization of our true nature of divinity. The path takes us from identification with dense form to the formlessness of our infinite potential of beauty and freedom.

The self - the source in which "I" has sprung.

Thought forms - they arise from the deep impressions of the soul, creating disharmony or peacefulness depending on the actions or experiences from the past. Thoughts are seeds of actions and experience. Pure experiences plant seeds of goodness, which is nurtured by the desire for peace, knowledge, contentment, love, power and joy, creating a foundation for peaceful thoughts.

Transcendental - the quality of being that transcends the limitations of the mind.

Turiya - the state wherein the yogi sees God everywhere. The state of super-consciousness. The fourth state transcending the waking dreaming and deep-sleep states.

Upanishad - esoteric doctrine of the Vedas.

Vam - the seed mantra of the svadhisthana chakra.

Vasanas - subconscious inclinations, habits, patterns. Impressions that are the driving force behind actions.

Vedanta - the end of all knowledge. Sri Sankaracharya is regarded as the founder of Vedanta.

Vedas - the most ancient and sacred of the Sanskrit works.

Vichar - right inquiry, the second state of jnana (knowledge).

Vidhya - knowledge

Vishnu - the second person of the Hindu trilogy, the sustaining force of the universe, the presence.

Vishnu knot - the psychic block associated with the fourth chakra, anahata

Visuddha - fifth chakra or throat energy center.

Viveka - discrimination between what is permanent and impermanent.

Vyana - the vital air or breath that governs the circulation of the body.

Will - putting into practice, ideals for well-being. Activity that is harmless, not affected by past scars.

Yam - seed mantra for the anahata chakra.

Yoga - union, to join or unite.

Bibliography and Recommended Reading

Anodea, Judith. *Wheels of Life*, 1987. Llewellyn Publications, St. Paul, MN.

Bailey, A. A. *Esoteric Psychology*, vol. 1, 1936. Reprint, Lucis Publishing Company, New York, 1975.

Bailey, A. A. *Esoteric Psychology*, vol. 2, 1942. Reprint, Lucis Publishing Company, New York, 1975.

Bailey, A. A. *A Treatise on Cosmic Fire*, 1925. Reprint, Lucis Publishing Company, New York, 1974.

Bailey, A. A. *A Treatise on White Magic*, 1934. Reprint, Lucis Publishing Company, New York, 1974.

Bailey, A. A. *Esoteric Healing*, 1953. Reprint, Lucis Publishing Company, New York, 1977.

Blavastsky, H.P. *The Secret Doctrine*, 1988. Reprint, Theosophical University Press, Pasadena CA, 1977.

Brennon, Barbara Ann. *Hands of Light: A Guide to Healing Through the Human Energy Field*, 1993. Bantam, New York, New York.

Bruyere, Rosalyn L. *Wheels of Light - A Study of the Chakras*, 1994. Fireside, Simon and Shuster.

Choa Kok Sui. *Miracles through Pranic Healing*, 1996. Sterling Publishers, Ltd. New Delhi, India.

Choa Kok Sui. *Pranic Psychotherapy*, 1989. Sterling Publishers Ltd, New Delhi.

Clifford, Terry. *Tibetan Buddhist Medicine*, 1984. Samuel Weiser.

Davis, Patricia. *Subtle Aromatherapy*, 1991. The DW Daniel Company Ltd, Great Britain.

Dossey, Larry. *Healing Words*, 1993. Harper Collins, San Francisco.

Eden, Donna. *Energy Medicine*, 1998. Tarcher/Putnam, New York.

Epstein, Gerald. *Healing Visualizations: Creating Health Through Imagery*, 1989. Bantam Books, New York.

Gerber, Richard MD. *Vibrational Medicine*, 1988. Bear & Company, Santa Fe, NM.

Gerber, Richard MD. *Vibrational Medicine for the 21st Century*, 2002. Harper Collins, New York, New York.

Hodson, G. *The Seven Human Temperaments*, 1952. Reprint, Theosophical Publishing House, Adyar, India, 1981.

Hunt, Roland. *The Seven Keys to Color Healing*, 1971. Harper and Row, New York, New York.

Jagadish. *Natures Way, A complete guide to health through yoga and herbal remedies*, 1999. Times Book International, Singapore.

Jurriannse, Aart. *Bridges*, 1985. Sun Center, Cape South Africa.

Kilner, Walter. *The Human Aura*, 1965. University Books, Inc.

Krishnamurti, J. *The Book of Life*. Daily meditations with Krishnamurti, 1995. Harper Collins, New York, New York.

Lama Surya Das. *Awakening the Buddha Within*, 1997. Broadway Books, New York, NY.

Lansdowne, Z. *The Rays and Esoteric Psychology*, 1989. Samuel Weiser, Inc., Box 612, York Beach, ME 03910.

Leadbeater, C. W. *The Chakras*, 1987. Reprint, Theosophical Publishing House, Wheaton, IL 60187.

Leadbeater, C. W. *Man Visible and Invisible*. Quest Books.

Lewis, Den. *The Tao of Natural Breathing*, 1998. Full Circle Publishers, Delhi, India.

Mookerjari, Ajit. *Kundalini Arousal of Inner Energy*, 1982. Thames and Hudson, Ltd, London.

Motoyama, Hiroshi. *Theories of the Chakras*, 1981. Quest Books.

Myss, Caroline. *Anatomy of the Spirit*, 1996. Crown Publishers.

Natarajan, A.R. *A Practical Guide to Know Yourself, Conversations with Ramana Maharshi*, 1993. The Ramana Maharshi Center, Bangelore, India.

Nisargaddatta Maharaj. *Consciousness and the Absolute - The final talks of Sri Nisargadatta Maharaj*, Edited by Jean Dunn, 1994. The Acorn Press, PO Box 3279 Durham, NC 27715-3279.

Pandit, M.P. *Kundalini Yoga*, Lotus Light Productions, Twin Lakes, WI.

Powell, A.E. *The Causal Body*, 1972. Reprint, The Theosophical Publishing House, Ltd, 68 Great Russell Street, London, WClB3B.

Powell, A.E. *The Etheric Double*, 1983. Reprint, Theosophical Publishing House Ltd., London.

Powell, A.E. *The Mental Body*, 1986. Whitefriars Press, Ltd., London.

Powell, A.E. *The Astral Body*, 1987. Reprint, Theosophical Publishing House, Ltd., Wheaton, IL 60187.

Pundit, M. P. *Kundalini Yoga*, 1993. All India Press, Pondicherry, India.

Sarada, Jaya. *Trust in Yourself - Messages from the Divine*, 1988. Grace Publishing, WA.

Sarada, Jaya. *The Path of Return - The Light of Parashakti*, 2001. Grace Publishing, WA.

Saraydarian, T. *The Psyche and Psychism*. Vol. 1 & 2, 1981. The Aquarian Educational Group, P.O. Box 267 Sedona AZ.

Simpson, Liz. *The Book of Chakra Healing*, 1999. Sterling Publishing Company, New York.

Sree Chakravarti. *A Healers Journey*, 1993. Rudra Press, Portland, OR.

Steindl-Rast, Brother David. *Gratefulness, the heart of prayer - an approach to life in fullness*, 1984. Paulist Press, Ramsey, NJ.

Swami Rama. Rudolf Balantine, Alan Hymes, MD *The Science of Breath*, 1979. The Himalayan International Institute, Honesdale, PA.

Swami Sada Shiva Tirtha. *The Ayurveda Encyclopedia*, 1998. Sri Satguru Publications.

Swami Sivananda Radha. *Mantras, Words of Power*, 1980. Sterling Publishers, PVT., Ltd.

Swami Sivananda Radha. *The Science of Pranayama*, Divine Life Society, Himalayas, India.

Swami Venkatesananda. *The Concise Yoga Vasistha*, 1984. State University of New York Press, Albany, New York.

Tansley, D. *Chakras - Rays and Radionics*, 1984. The C.W. Daniel Company Limited, Essex, England.

Tansley, David. *Radionics and the Subtle Anatomy of Man*, 1971. Great Britain, Whitstable Litho LTD, Whitstable, Kent, England.

Tansley, David. *Subtle Bodies, Essence and Shadow*, 1985. Thames and Hudson, Great Britain.

Tansley, David. *The Raiment of Light, A Study of the Human Aura*, 1984.

Thich Nhat Hanh. *The Heart of the Buddhas Teaching*, 1988. Parallax Press, Berkeley, California.

Willis, Pauline. *Color Therapy*, 1993. Element Books Limited, Shaftesbury, Dorset, England, SP78BP.

Wood, E. *The Seven Rays*, 1985. Reprint, Theosophical Publishing House, Wheaton, IL 1984.

Worwood, Valerie Ann. *The Fragrant Mind-Aromatherapy for Personality, Mind, Mood and Emotions*, 1996. New World Library, Novato, CA.

Zinn, Jon Kabat. *Wherever you go there you are, mindfulness meditations in everyday life*, 1994. Hyperion, 114 Fifth Avenue, New York, New York 10001.

"Spiritual growth may be measured by a decrease of afflictive emotions and an increase of love and compassion for others."

Chagdud Tulku

Come without memory or premonition
Come blindly into it
Sit without resistance
Let your rampant vibrancy exchange with the abstract and incomprehensible
Feel the sweet death of being out of control.
There is no ending point
Your surrender is the infinite language
You are the co-creator of this uncommon existence
Dance within the rolling waves
Fill the sky with your magenta dreams –
Put the world to bed under the crystal night sky.
The fairy-tale is yours

– Mahima

RESOURCES

From the unreal, lead me to the real

From the darkness, lead me to the light

From death, lead me to immortality

Om Shanti, Om Shanti, Om Shanti

Vibrational Remedies Suppliers

Nelson Bach USA, Ltd.
100 Research Drive
Wilmington, MA 01887
1-800-319-9151
http://www.nelsonbach.com/usa.html

Flower Essence Services
PO Box 1769
Nevada City, CA 95959
1-800-548-0075
www.floweressence.com

Alaskan Flower Essence Project
PO Box 1329
Homer, AL 99603
907-235-2188

Australian Bush Flower Essences
Box 531
Spit Junction, NSW
2088 Australia
www.ausflowers.com.au

Ellon, USA, Inc
644 Merrick Road
Lynbrook, NY, 11563
516-593-2206

Perelandra, Ltd.
P.O. Box 3603
Warrenton, VA 20188
1-800-960-8806
www.perelandra-ltd.com

Pegasus Products, Inc
PO Box 228
Boulder, CO 80306
1-800-527-6104
www.pegasusproducts.com

Living Essences of Australia
P.O. Box 355
Scarborough W.A. 6019
Australia
Tel#:+61 8 94435600
http://www.livingessences.com.au

Desert Alchemy Essences
PO Box 44189
Tucson, AZ 85733
1-800-736-3382
www.desert-alchemy.com

3 Flowers Healing
Aromatherapy, Columbia River Gorge
Flower Essences and Gaia Lotion
541-387-3528
www.3flowershealing.com

Tara Mandala's Herbs
www.taramandala.com
Wise Woman Herbals
541-895-5152
www.medherb.com

Sound Healing Resources
www.healingsounds.com

Edmund Scientific Company
101 Gloucester Pike
Barrington, NJ 08007
609-573-6250

Dinshah Health Society
100 Dinshah Drive
Malaga, NJ, 08328
609-692-4686

Tools for Exploration
Independence Avenue
Chatsworth, CA 91311-4318
818-885-9090
www.toolsforexploration.com
Source for light and sound therapy
instruments
www.doorwaypublications.com
Good pendulum source

The L.I.F.E. System
Jennifer Walton 520-297-0336
A unique and highly effective biofeedback
program that can provide direction and
focus in vibrational assessment and
treatment

Sanjeevani Remedies & Remedy Cards
G-Jo Institute
PO Box 848060
Hollywood, Fl. 33084-9755

Based on the teachings of Sathya Sai Baba,
this prayer system of healing is free. Using
prayer along with radionic symbols, healing
codes are sent through the scalor wave to the
recipient.

Spiritual & Energy Healing Centers, Schools & Resources

Dynapro International, Inc.
PO Box 3002, Ogden, UT 84409
Order- 1-800-877-1413

Omega Institute for Holistic Studies
www.eomega.org

Esalen Institute
Highway 1
Big Sur, CA 93920-9616
831-667-3000
http://www.esalen.org

Institute of Noetic Sciences
101 San Antonio Road
Petaluma, CA 94952
707.775.3500
www.noetic.org

Institute of Transpersonal Psychology
1069 East Meadow Circle
Palo Alto CA, 94303
650-493-4430
www.itp.edu

Natural Therapies/Schools Directory
www.naturalhealers.com

International Society for the Study of Subtle
Energies and Energy Medicine
11005 Ralston Road, Suite 100D
Arvada, CO 80004
Voice: 303-425-4625
www.issseem.org

Intuition Network
http://www.intuition.org

Barbara Brennan School of Natural Healing
PO Box 2005
East Hampton, NY 11937
1-800-924-2564

Colorado Center for Healing Touch
& Healing Touch International
www.healingtouch.net

The Chopra Center
www.chopra.com
Depak Chopra's Wellness Center
www.hollyhock.bc.ca

Conference and Retreat Center
IM School of Healing Arts
www.imschool.com

Brietenbush Hot Springs
www.brietenbush.com

Conference and Retreat Center
Mt. Madonna Spiritual Center
http://www.mountmadonna.org

Conference and Retreat Center
Kairos Institute of Sound Healing
157 Pacheco Rd., Box 8
Llano de San Juan, NM 87543
Phone: 505-587-2689
www.acutonics.com

Touch For Health®Kinesiology Association
PO Box 392
New Carlisle, OH 45344-0392
800-466-8342
www.tfhka.org

Quantum Touch
P.O. Box 458
Kapaa, HI 96746
888-424-0041
www.quantumtouch.com

Dr. Eric Pearl
Reconnective Healing
www.thereconnection.com

Findhorn Foundation
www.findhorn.org

Wholistic Educational Center and
Community
Theosophical Society of America
www.theosophical.org
Classes, workshops and retreats.

Amachi
www.amma.org
Spiritual Teacher

Sri Satya Sai Baba
www.sathyasai.org
Spiritual Teacher

Lorian Association
P.O. Box 1368
Issaquah, WA. 98027
435-427-9071
http://www.lorian.org

Spiritual Education in the Findhorn
Community Tradition.
Emotional Freedom Technique
www.emofree.com

Classes, videos, and practitioners of Tapping
Treatment.
The Energy Medicine Institute
www.energymed.org

Holfield Institute
5275 S. April Dr.
Langley, WA 98260
360-321-7226
http://www.holfieldinstitute.org

Training in Field Dynamics for practitioners
in service professions.
Circles of Life - Solutions
www.circlesoflife.com

Products to enhance well-being and quality
of life. "The strength of one can empower
the many."

Energy Medicine Resources, Research, Information & Websites

Alternative Medicine Home Page
http://www.pitt.edu/~cbw/mailing.html

National Center for Complementary and
Alternative Medicine
http://nccam.nih.gov

Better Health Campaign
www.betterhealthcampaign.org

Center for Health and Healing
www.healthandhealingny.org

Consumer Health Organization of Canada
www.consumerhealth.org

Larry Dossey, MD
Author and educator in alternative health
therapies.
www.dosseydossey.com

Wholistic Healing Research
www.wholistichealingresearch.com
Cutting edge research on energy, medicine,
consciousness.

Bruce Lipton Ph.D.
Uncovering the Biology of Belief.
www.brucelipton.com
Biomedical sciences research proving how
holistic therapies work.

Dr. David Hawkins M.D., Ph.D.
The Institute for Advanced Spiritual
Research
P.O. Box 3516 W. Sedona, AZ 86340
928-282-8722
www.sedonacreativelife.com
www.veritaspub.com
Research on kinesiology testing as a tool for
assessing value, motive, truth and path of
consciousness as a race and as individuals.

Kinesiologists United
P.O. Box 48957
Coon Rapids, MN 55448-0957
1-877-581-1678
www.kinesiologycentral.com

Dr. Caroline Myss
www.myss.com
Online resource directory.

Recommended Practitioners

Dr. Lotus Linton
http://lotusfinton.byregion.net
206-675-0495
Sound Healer, Counselor
Author - *Seeking Self in the Waters of the World*

Andreanna Vaughan
Teacher of holistic and alternative health therapies
www.andreannavaughan.com

Jennifer Walton, M.A
Executive Director, Living Well
520-297-0338
"Life System" and biofeedback practitioner

Dr. Judith Orloff
http://www.drjudithorloff.com
Intuition for Health and Healing

Dr. Roger Callahan
www.tftrx.com
Callahan Techniques
Thought Field Therapy

Fred Gallo Energy Psychology
www.energypsych.com

Jaya Sarada
www.wellbeingfoundation.org
Well Being Facilitator
Life Essence Awakening Process
1-800-282-5292

Judyth Reichenberg-Ullman, ND, LCSW and Robert Ullman, ND
Licensed naturopathic physicians, board-certified homeopathic medicine. Authors-
Mystics, Masters, Saints, and Sages: Stories of Enlightenment and other books on homeopathic medicine.
www.healthyhomeopathy.com
www.mysticsmasters.com.

Annapourne Colangelo
BlossumNow
360-579-3735
Intuitive readings, guidance, counseling, hands-on healing and mentoring on our journey home

Leah Green, M.Ed.
Re-patterning; trauma recovery; psychotherapy
P.O. Box 583
Langley, WA 98260

Judith Gorman, DCSW
Biofield Healing Arts
360-321-7226
http://www.blofieldhealingarts.com
Health & well-being consultant, Licensed Clinical Social Worker, Biofield Therapist & Counselor, BioShen Energyfield Practitioner, Teacher & Mentor

Suzanne Fageol, M.Div., S.D.
360-321-2501
spirit@whidbey.com
Spiritual Director, Life Coach from Falling Awake, Craniosacral Therapist, Lorian Association faculty member. Codirector, Holfield Institute.

J. Insul Glehl
206-533-6373
insul@earthhnk.net
Life transformation coaching, health for body, mind, emotions, spirit. BioShen Energywork

Laurie Keith
Licensed Massage Therapist
Deer Lake Healing Arts
360-221-4010
Life Essence Awakening Process, Archetypal Healing & Bodywork

Recommended Books

Emoto, Masaru:
Hidden Messages in Water.
Beyond Words Publishing, 2004 (www.hado.net)

Hunt, Valerie V.:
Infinite Mind: Science of the Vibrations of Human Consciousness.
Malibu Publishing, 1998

Brennan, Barbara Ann:
Hands of Light: A Guide to Healing Through the Human Energy Field.
1988.

Oschmann, James L. Ph.D., Pert, Candace Ph.D.:
Energy Medicine: The Scientific Basis of Bioenergy Therapies.
Churchil Livingstone, 1st ed., 2000

Benor, Daniel:
Spiritual Healing-Scientific Validation of a Healing Revolution.
Vision Publications, 2001

Benor, Daniel:
Consciousness Bioenergy and Healing.
Wholistic Healing Publications. 2004

McGarey, M.D, William A.:
The Edgar Cayce Remedies.
1983

Karp, Reba Ann:
Edgar Cayce: Encyclopedia of Healing.
1986

Gerber, Richard:
A Practical Guide to Vibrational Medicine: Energy Healing and Spiritual Transformation.
Quill, 2001

Sarada, Jaya:
The Path of Return - The Light of Parashaleti.
Grace Publishing, Freeland, WA, 2001

Trust in Yourself - Messages from the Divine.
Grace Publishing, Freeland, WA, 1998

Living Meditations.
Grace Publishing, Freeland, WA, 2005

Well-Being in Body, Mind, and Spirit.
Grace Publishing, Freeland, WA, 200.

Index

Jaya Sarada brings to her work years of experience and education in the field of Energy Medicine and Spiritual Awakening. Traveling to India many times, Jaya took a spiritual name, Jaya Sarada meaning 'Goddess of Victory'. ***Divine Light Gifts*** is the culmination of the work of Jaya Sarada.

With the understanding that the soul has many facets, like a diamond, Jaya assists her readers and students to awaken to the gifts of their being. These gifts act as guideposts to remember your soul's origin and they are felt and understood by accessing the higher frequencies of love, light and truth.

We are on the forefront of a new humanity. It is a time in our soul's development where each individual is being called to bring forth what is true and real inside. We are guided to listen to our inner calling and match the miracle of life that we feel inside through the expression of deep gratitude, joy, love and service.

Jaya offers guidance on how to tap into the magnificent being that you are, how to feel awake, alive and full of vitality, how to reconnect with your sacred source, and how to discover your unique soul's purpose. During this time of evolutionary awakening we are guided to take a step into our divine potential. Jaya invites you to take this step and enter the temple of your inner light, where you are simply asked to let go of all that is prohibiting you from experiencing your radiant being.

Jaya is an ordained Priestess, Energy Therapist, Intuitive Counselor and Teacher.
She offers sessions in Sacred Alignment, Crystalline Energy Healing,
Soul and Akashic Readings, and the Life Essence Awakening Process™.
She is available for seminars, retreats, book signings,
lectures and guest speaking engagements.

Please call for more information or to make an appointment.
Divine Light Gifts 1.855.505.3935
For private sessions and classes with Jaya visit
JayaSarada.com

Divine Light Publishing
is a series of books, audio, video, trainings, events and services.

For more information please visit:
DivineLightGifts.com
Or call toll free: 1.855.505.3935

A Sampling of the *LEAP* Training Program Offerings

Level One: Etheric Field Kinesiology

Etheric Field Kinesiology teaches procedures such as: overall vital force testing, meridian testing, chakra testing, life force grounding, nutritional testing, food testing, allergy testing, surrogate testing and testing for other health questions. Some sample healing treatments and testing methods are: vibrational remedies, Bach Flowers™, essential oils, gem stones, color and sound therapy. Level one also teaches energy tune-ups and the Etheric Revitalization Therapy™ as well as many techniques for energy wellness self-care.

Level Two: Emotional Field and Mental Field Kinesiology

Emotional Field Kinesiology teaches students to identify emotions that may be the root of energy imbalance and the cause of physical symptoms. EFK can pinpoint which therapeutic technique will best unlock the emotional patterns and restore balance to the system. Some of the techniques used include EFT (emotional freedom technique), meridian healing, tapping, affirmations, goal setting and The Forgiveness Process. Since the emotional field is closely related to the etheric field, bodywork may be offered along with emotional release work. Energy field and soul kinesiology sessions are greatly enhanced by vibrational remedies. *LEAP* offers education and training in kinesiology testing methods to determine which vibrational remedy will best support the individual's healing process. A complete list of remedies and guidelines for their use may be found in the Energy Toolbox section of the book.

Mental Field Kinesiology teaches students to identify belief systems that may be the root cause of energy imbalance and how these belief systems contribute to physical and emotional imbalances. Corrections are then offered to release unwanted conditioning and negative belief systems. Some of the techniques offered are: meridian tapping, reframing and reaffirming the positive in life through new decisions and Conscious Choice Therapy. The mental field greatly affects the emotional field.

Level Three: Intuitive Field Kinesiology

Intuitive Field Kinesiology offers students ways in which to access the intuitive field, the field of knowing. The essence of this energy field brings a greater light, inspiration and spiritual wisdom to one's life. Skills are shared in how to listen and maintain connection with guidance. All areas of healing in the intuitive field strongly affect the mental field and filter down to the etheric field.

Level Four: Soul Kinesiology

Soul Kinesiology is a research program that uncovers ways to work with past life patterns and karmic conditions. This process helps the student tot develop a deep attunement in the healing process through the art of listening and sacred dialogue. The goal of LEAP Level Four is to offer ways to uncover the gifts of the soul and release obstacles to uncovering these gifts, creating a path to profound healing and transformation.

The study of energy field healing illuminates the fact that we are truly more than our physical body, mind and emotions. This research guides us to consider the vastness of our energy system and to reach beyond our identification with the body, emotions and mind into the realm of the spirit. The Well Being Institute offers a path to study subtle energies and a way to dialogue with the soul. As we learn how to balance and integrate our energy fields we can increase our energy to its full capacity and live our birthright of happiness.

Energy Field and Soul Kinesiology sessions are greatly enhanced with Vibrational Remedies. LEAP offers education, training and Kinesiology Testing Methods to determine which vibrational remedies will support the healing process. A complete list of remedies and guidance for their use can be found the Energy Field Toolbox section of this book.

Own The Divine Light Series

Book 1: Sacred Kinesiology
Book 2: The Path of Return
Book 3: Trust In Yourself
Book 4: Living Meditations

Additional Books:

- Life Essence Awakening Process ™ Manual
- Sacred Code of Love
- Awakening Your Chakras
- Sacred Path To Peace
- Sacred Energy Healing
- Divine Flowering

Charts & Posters

- Individual Chakra Posters
- Kundalini Chakra Poster
- Set of 7 Colored Chakra Posters
- Chakra & Divine Light Greeting Cards
- Coordinated Bookmarks
- Chakra Postcards
- The Sacred Woman Clothing Line

To order books and other products go to:
DivineLightGifts.com

- Books
- Videos
- eBooks
- Charts & Posters
- Training & Education

- Seminar Information
- Audio Books
- Calendar of Events
- Free Downloads
- & More!

Visit DivineLightGifts.com or call: 1.855.505.3935

CPSIA information can be obtained
at www.ICGtesting.com
Printed in the USA
BVHW012329260321
603509BV00015B/232